Delinquency Careers in Two Birth Cohorts

THE PLENUM SERIES IN CRIME AND JUSTICE

Series Editors:
James Alan Fox, *Northeastern University, Boston, Massachusetts*
Joseph Weis, *University of Washington, Seattle, Washington*

DELINQUENCY CAREERS IN TWO BIRTH COHORTS
Paul E. Tracy, Marvin E. Wolfgang, and Robert M. Figlio

A Continuation Order Plan is available for this series. A continuation order will bring delivery of each new volume immediately upon publication. Volumes are billed only upon actual shipment. For further information please contact the publisher.

Delinquency Careers in Two Birth Cohorts

Paul E. Tracy
College of Criminal Justice
Northeastern University
Boston, Massachusetts

Marvin E. Wolfgang
Sellin Center for Studies in Criminology and Criminal Law
Wharton School
University of Pennsylvania
Philadelphia, Pennsylvania

and

Robert M. Figlio
University of California, Riverside
Riverside, California

Plenum Press • New York and London

Library of Congress Cataloging-in-Publication Data

Tracy, Paul E.
    Delinquency careers in two birth cohorts / Paul E. Tracy, Marvin
E. Wolfgang, and Robert M. Figlio.
        p.   cm. -- (Plenum series in crime and justice)
    Includes bibliographical references and index.
    ISBN 0-306-43631-0
    1. Juvenile delinquency--Pennsylvania--Philadelphia--Longitudinal
studies.   2. Criminal behavior--Pennsylvania--Philadelphia-
-Longitudinal studies.   I. Wolfgang, Marvin E., 1924-   .
II. Figlio, Robert M.   III. Title.   IV. Series.
HV9106.P5T73   1990
364.3'6'0974811--dc20   90-42067
                                                                  CIP

ISBN 0-306-43631-0

© 1990 Plenum Press, New York
A Division of Plenum Publishing Corporation
233 Spring Street, New York, N.Y. 10013

Printed in the United States of America

Preface

Delinquency in a Birth Cohort, published in 1972, was the first criminological birth cohort study in the United States. Nils Christie, in *Unge norske
lovorertredere*, had done the first such study as his dissertation at the
University of Oslo in 1960. Professor Thorsten Sellin was the inspiration
for the U.S. study. He could read Norwegian, and I could a little because
I studied at the University of Oslo in my graduate years.

Our interest in pursuing a birth cohort study in the United States
was fostered by the encouragement of Saleem Shah who awarded us a
grant from the National Institute of Mental Health to begin our birth
cohort studies at the University of Pennsylvania by investigating the
delinquency of the 1945 cohort. We studied this group of 9,945 boys
extensively through official criminal history and school records of their
juvenile years. Subsequently, we followed up the cohort as adults using
both adult arrest histories and an interview of a sample of the cohort.
Our follow-up study was published as *From Boy to Man, From Delinquency to Crime* in 1987.

Our interest in studying the delinquency and criminality of cohorts
continued and was bolstered by the reception given to our previous
study. Through a series of grants from the Office of Juvenile Justice and
Delinquency Prevention, we began in 1977 to replicate our earlier work
with a new Philadelphia cohort, born in 1958, which contained both
males and females. This volume is a comparison of males in the 1958
cohort (Cohort II) with the 1945 birth cohort (Cohort I). The data in
Cohort II pertaining to the 14,000 females have been partially analyzed
in the doctoral dissertations of Carol Facella, Laura Otten, and Elizabeth
Piper.

As we now analyze the 1958 birth cohort and compare it with the
1945 birth cohort, we are convinced that a third birth cohort should be
examined, perhaps one born in 1973 or thereabouts. Our center has
done research with Dr. Dora Nevares on a Puerto Rican birth cohort
born in 1970, with which we make comparisons to the 1945 and 1958
Philadelphia cohorts (Nevares, 1990). The Sellin Criminology Center

v

is conducting a similar birth cohort study in Wuhan, China, for cross-cultural comparisons with the Philadelphia and San Juan findings.

Longitudinal studies from Copenhagen, Stockholm, Tokyo, London, and Racine and others yet unpublished will be continued at least until the end of this century. These studies are producing dramatic, causally inferential results in a discipline little blessed with solid replications. Eastern Europe and Moscow are good candidates for the next round of longitudinal research in delinquency.

Within this volume, we offer a full comparative birth cohort research analysis in the same jurisdiction: Philadelphia. The effect of age of cohorts, of the spacing of offensive behavior over time, and of historical moments in time are referred to in this volume. We have only some answers, some allusions to causation, for most of our work is descriptive. But description lends strength and commonly leads to explanation, especially to inferences that can be drawn from life cycles such as we try to display in this work.

Research with longitudinal data is long, arduous, tedious, and requires tenacious adherence and devotion to the tenets of research management and analysis. We have benefited greatly from the research teams of graduate students who participated in these tasks. Their assistance was instrumental in the completion of our research and they deserve our deep appreciation. As Research Associate at our center, Dr. Neil Weiner has been especially important to all of these tasks and we wish to acknowledge his devoted work with us. We have also benefited from the continued support of the National Institute of Juvenile Justice and Delinquency Prevention. We would like to acknowledge the professional efforts of our initial program monitor, Pamela Swain, who saw us through the difficult early stages of the research, and her successor, Wendy Wilson, who worked with us to bring the study to completion.

We hope that the efforts of this research will encourage further longitudinal analyses that may offer policy implications as well as enhance our knowledge of patterns of delinquency.

Marvin E. Wolfgang

Philadelphia

Contents

1. Introduction 1

2. Cohort Studies in Criminology 5

   The Recognized Need for Cohort Studies 5
   Previous Studies of a Cohort Character 7
   Subsequent Studies of a Cohort Character 9
   Why a New Birth Cohort Study? 11

3. Contemporary Issues in Longitudinal Research 13

   Criminal Careers Historically 13
   The Value of Longitudinal Research on Criminal Careers 17

4. The 1958 Birth Cohort Study 21

   Objectives 21
   Capturing the Cohort 24
   Collection of Police Data 28
   Measuring Delinquency 29
   Scaling the Gravity of Crime 30
   The Seriousness Scoring System 32
   Measuring Socioeconomic Status 33
   Background Data 35

5. The Prevalence of Delinquency 37

   Race and SES 38
   Background Variables 46

6. *The Incidence of Delinquency* 57

Extent of Delinquency 57
Severity of Delinquency 70

7. *The Chronic Juvenile Offender* 81

Chronicity and Frequency of Delinquency 82
Chronicity and Severity of Delinquency 92

8. *Delinquent Recidivism: Static Probabilities* 99

Introduction 99
The First Offense 100
Rank Number of Offense 103

9. *Delinquent Recidivism: Specialization and Escalation* 113

Introduction 113
Offense Transition Probabilities: All Offenders 116
Offense Transition Residuals: All Offenders 127
Offense Transition Residuals: All Offender Recidivists 131
Offense Transition Probabilities by Race 140
Offense Transition Residuals by Race 153
Offense Escalation: All Offenders 159

10. *Age-at-Onset and Delinquency* 175

Introduction 175
Age-at-Onset Percentages 176
Age-at-Onset and Mean Number of Offenses 187
Age-at-Onset and Offense Severity 189
Age-at-Onset and Offense Types 196

11. *Delinquency and Age-at-Offense* 213

Distribution of Offenses by Age 213
Offense Rates by Age 216
Offense Types by Age 220

12.   *Police and Court Dispositions* 245

Disposition Distributions 246
Disposition Contingencies 254

13.   *Summary and Implications* 273

Summary of Results 275
   Prevalence 275
   Incidence 276
   Delinquent Subgroups 279
   Recidivism 280
   Age and Delinquency 286
   Disposition 289
Implications 292

References 299

Index 305

1

Introduction

Delinquency in a Birth Cohort (Wolfgang, Figlio, and Sellin, 1972) was the first large-scale birth cohort study of delinquency undertaken in the United States based upon a generalizable, urban population. The official delinquency careers of all those boys ($n = 9{,}945$) born in 1945, who resided in Philadelphia at least from their tenth to their eighteenth birthdays, were described and analyzed. Compared to the cross-sectional variety of research, it is noteworthy that the 1945 birth cohort study developed baseline, career delinquency rates and parameters using a data source for a study population unlike any other previously researched in this country. Desistance and recidivism probabilities, offense switching, offense severity escalation, and court disposition probabilities and their effects on subsequent delinquency are fundamental delinquency career measures that, prior to the 1945 cohort study, were investigated with less than optimum data and/or limited study populations.

Because the 1945 birth cohort study was unique and proved to be very valuable to the discipline, the present research project was undertaken to replicate its pioneering predecessor. Replications of scientific findings and particular research approaches, methods, and strategies are crucially necessary in science. Although replications are quite common in the natural and physical sciences, they are relatively rare—albeit still very necessary—in the social sciences.

Unfortunately, replications are especially uncommon in criminology/criminal justice. In a discipline closer to its nascency than most, criminology requires replications to determine or to ensure reliability and validity, and also to provide for the thorough theory testing and conceptual refinement that a comparatively new discipline surely needs. However, researchers in criminology seem to have been more interested in trying to break new ground than to confirm an earlier traveled terrain.

When a methodology, like the birth cohort approach, is demonstrated to be important both to theory development and empirical application, and when this method produces a new set of important findings, it should be reiterated in order to determine whether it is possible to buttress consistency and to affirm the observed findings with other data and with different study populations.

Study replications conducted in the same setting maximize the chances of affirming the validity and reliability of research data for the benefit of both the scientific discipline and the social policy which is directly based on that discipline. Thus, another birth cohort using Philadelphia as the site affords the opportunity to examine the effects on delinquency of growing up in a different time and sociocultural setting. The 1945 cohort was born in the final year of World War II, which sets its years of possible delinquency involvement in the period from 1955 through 1962. Born 13 years later, the 1958 cohort, on the other hand, experienced a delinquency risk period from 1968 through 1975.

The social milieu of the two cohorts clearly differs and may represent different "pushes toward" or "pulls away from" delinquency involvement. For the 1958 cohort, the period at risk for delinquency coincides with America's involvement in the Vietnam conflict, the rise in drug abuse, increasing social protest, and the like. This period of rapid and profound social change and pervasive social unrest is in very sharp contrast to the more tranquil period of adolescence experienced by the 1945 cohort.

Although the underlying social environments thus differed considerably, the criminal justice environments of the two cohorts were very much alike. The policies and procedures of law enforcement, especially in the handling of juvenile offenders, were the same for both cohorts. Likewise, juvenile court policy followed the same statutory provisions for the intake and disposition of delinquents in both the 1958 and 1945 cohorts.

The intercohort consistency in both statutory codes and agency policy, which we very carefully investigated, does not preclude the possibility of differences in the informal handling of delinquents in the two cohorts, either by the police or by the juvenile court. However, the uniformity of the criminal justice process applied to the two cohorts at least ensures that differences in either the extent or character of delinquency are probably not artifacts of the system, a situation that very likely would obtain if the replication had been conducted in a different jurisdiction.

Thus, by replicating the 1945 cohort with another birth cohort from the same city, the cohort continuities and differences can be displayed in a setting that had a governmental style and political tone, as well as a law enforcement and judicial background, that were very similar. Whether offense probabilities by age, race, social class, crime type, and

severity are different for the respective cohorts will be readily measurable and recordable within the same geographic boundaries. Another
birth cohort study in a different jurisdiction would be useful, but compared to differences arising in the present same-site replication, any
cohort disparities would be more difficult to attribute to generational
factors owing to the possible influence of different geography, or different demographic composition, or the interaction of the two. Thus, it
would seem that any differences obtained in this replication would more
likely rest upon real differences in the delinquency phenomenon than
upon extraneous factors.

In addition to these general replication issues are a number of obvious research questions that are only addressable by a replication in the
same jurisdiction. Is delinquency in general, and are crimes of violence
in particular, more pervasive in the generational wave of a cohort born
13 years later than the World War II birth cohort of 1945? Or, is the rate
essentially the same but the volume merely swelled by the total size of
the cohort population? Is the juvenile crime committed by the 1958
group more serious on an empirical gravity scale than it was for the 1945
cohort? Is the second generation more specialized in delinquency than
was the older group? Do offense careers have similar desistance rates?
Has there been any measurable change in the way delinquents are handled by the courts? These are but a few of the many relevant issues that
our cohort replication will attempt to address.

The prevention and deterrence of crime, and the adjudication and
punishment of criminals, are significant forms of social intervention,
especially in a democracy. These purposive invasions of the biographies
of people have serious implications not only for policy, but also for the
general citizenry as well. Thus, criminal justice policies and practices
cannot be divorced from the criminological research enterprise; they
must reflect the best available insight based upon the best available
evidence. We believe that birth cohorts in particular, and longitudinal
research in general, offer the most promising approach for the produc-
tion of research data that are capable of both increasing the knowledge
base in criminology and properly informing criminal justice policy initiatives.

The research study reported in this volume concerns a continuing
longitudinal investigation of a cohort of persons who were born in 1958,
and who continuously resided in the city of Philadelphia during the
years for which they were at risk for delinquency—at least from age 10
through age 17. The specific focus of this publication is the replication
effort to compare the juvenile delinquency careers of the males in the
1958 cohort with those of their 1945 predecessors. We have restricted

this particular volume to the males in the two cohorts for several reasons. First, the 1945 birth cohort did not contain females, and thus, the females in the 1958 cohort cannot be used within the comparative focus of this book. Second, there are two excellent analyses of the 1958 females available elsewhere (see Facella, 1983; Otten, 1985). Last, we have addressed the female delinquency and crime of the 1958 females in our follow-up of the 1958 cohort (see Tracy *et al.*, 1989).

In addition to this replication, which compares the males in the two birth cohorts, the 1958 cohort study has also examined the violent juvenile offenders (Piper, 1983), the females (Facella, 1983), and the male versus female differences in the 1958 birth cohort (Otten, 1985). Further, we have just completed the second major component of the project, which follows the entire cohort into the sphere of adult crime through Philadelphia police and court records and FBI files (Tracy *et al.*, 1989). Last, at present we are just concluding a third component of the project, which involves a comprehensive interview with a sample of approximately 1,000 members of the cohort.

The 1958 birth cohort project is a longitudinal study that has been ongoing since 1977 and has continuously occupied the professional efforts of the small research team for 12 years and counting. We have put forth this effort because we are committed to the longitudinal approach to the study of delinquent and criminal careers and to what we believe are unique benefits that accrue, in particular, from the birth cohort approach.

We are aware that this particular view of longitudinal research is not universally held in the discipline. In fact, there is a very vocal minority that has recently been highly critical of longitudinal research on delinquency and crime. We shall briefly address these views in Chapter 3. We are confident, however, that the test of time will serve to validate our efforts, if not silence the critics of longitudinal research in criminology altogether.

2

Cohort Studies in Criminology

The Recognized Need for Cohort Studies

The present longitudinal research concerning the comparative delinquency careers of males in two large birth cohorts must be viewed within an historical criminological context. The discipline has only recently embraced the investigation of criminal careers using the longitudinal method, although the desirability of investigating the criminal behavior of cohorts has been indicated in the literature for a very long time.

For instance, at the end of the nineteenth century, H. von Scheel, director of Germany's National Bureau of Statistics, pointed out the need to follow groups of offenders. He wrote:

> Ideal criminal statistics that would follow carefully the evolution of criminal tendencies in a given population should not work with crude annual contingents but with generations. They should start with the first offenders of a given year and continue to observe these persons, showing their later convictions, instead of counting them as new individuals each time they are convicted. (1890: 191)

A few years later, Otto Kobner recognized the need to study individuals, not just groups of offenders. He noted that "correct statistics of offenders can be developed only by a study of the total life history of individuals" (1893: 670).

Georg von Mayr explicitly raised the issue of birth cohorts when he argued that,

> A deeper insight into the statistics of criminality is made possible by the disclosure of developmental regularities which must be sought through a study of the manner in which criminality develops in the course of a human lifetime. To do this it is necessary to identify the offender and his offense in the population and to keep him under constant statistical control so that it is possible for each birth cohort entering punishable age and until all its members are dead, to study statistically its participation or nonparticipation in criminality and the intensity of such participation in its various forms. . . This is the task of the "criminality table" or the "marriage table," etc. This also has significance for the important problem of recidivism. (1917: 425-426)

Similarly, Trenaman and Emmet have suggested that,

> In order to estimate the incidence of delinquency, one needs to know more than just the annual ratio of offenders to population. One needs to consider the outcropping of crime throughout the life-time of a whole generation. One needs to know the probability of any child born at any given time becoming a delinquent sometime during his life. To estimate such a probability, we must consider the number of children born each year (numbers which may conveniently be referred to as "generations") and count year by year the individuals of each generation who are convicted in the courts for first offenses. When all the members of a particular generation are dead, it will then be possible to express the probability as a ratio of the total number who were convicted at least once to the total number of the generation at birth. (1952: 204-205)

In 1960, at a conference held by the British Home Office on research into the causes of delinquency, D. V. Glass advocated studies of birth cohorts, and Sir Aubrey Lewis said that "one advantage to cohort studies was that they were not to any great extent dependent on retrospective data, as some other types of research are" (British Home Office, 1960: 2).

In their work on the measurement of delinquency, Sellin and Wolfgang noted how students of juvenile delinquency believe that,

> A true index of delinquency or delinquents must be based on an assessment of conduct during the entire time that juveniles are subject to the law. They say that indices based on annual data give no hint of the number of juveniles who become delinquents before they reach adulthood. (1964: 66)

Wolfgang and Sellin were led to conclude that, if the information available in police records would permit the retrospective construction of an age cohort index, and if the records would also permit the construction of measures of the delinquency of each age cohort entering the juvenile age bracket as it grows to adulthood, then

> We could discover at what age different members of the cohort first became delinquent and the extent and nature of their recidivism during their juvenile years. If this were done for each successive age cohort, the relative value of preventative action programs aimed at juveniles could be tested by investigating changes in patterns of delinquent conduct, reduction in recidivism, etc., in successive age cohorts as they progressively come under the influence of such programs. (1964: 67)

Hirschi and Selvin, in discussing the problem of causal order, the criterion for judging the claim that one variable causes another, have suggested that a solution to the problem, at least in principle, is the longitudinal or panel study. "In an ideal version of this design, the investigator would select a sample of infants and continually collect data on them until they become adults" (Hirschi and Selvin, 1967: 53). Similarly, Farrington (1981) has remarked that longitudinal surveys are especially useful in studying the course of development, the natural history, and the prevalence of a phenomenon at different ages, how phenomena emerge, and continuities and discontinuities from earlier to later ages.

Previous Studies of a Cohort Character

In light of the importance attached to cohort studies, one might expect such research to be quite prevalent. However, a review of the literature reveals the opposite—very few cohort studies (examining delinquency) have been attempted. Also, the few studies which have been made contain even fewer genuine birth cohorts. The cohort studies published prior to the appearance of the results of our first cohort (1972) are reviewed below.

The earliest study of the delinquency of a cohort was published by Ferguson in 1952. The study concerned 1,349 Glasgow boys for whom police and court conviction data were collected up to their seventeenth birthdays. The study dealt generally with the well-being of the boys at home, at school, and in their early postschool years, with delinquency considered as one of the yardsticks of well-being. In a subsequent work, Ferguson and Cunnison (1956) followed up 568 of the boys and collected criminality data from their eighteenth birthday up to the age of 22.

In England in the mid-1940s, a national survey of health and development was launched. From a total of 12,268 legitimate single births occurring throughout England, Scotland, and Wales during the week of 3-9 March 1946, a sample of 5,362 births were selected for continuous longitudinal study. Thus far, two studies of delinquency in the sample have appeared. One concerns the boys who had been convicted of at least one indictable offense before their sixteenth birthday, and compares them with the nondelinquents with respect to the presence or absence of symptoms of maladjustment (Mulligan et al., 1963). The other study, which deals with the 2,402 boys in the birth sample who were living in Great Britain in 1963, focuses on the social class origin of the delinquents (Douglass et al., 1966).

In 1960 a study finally appeared which contained the results of a very extensive study of a birth cohort. With the cooperation of the military, Nils Christie was able to locate the names of all males born in 1933 who had registered in Norway for compulsory military service ($n = 20,000$). The national penal register was searched for any criminal records of the men up to 1958. Although much briefer, a Danish birth cohort study was reported a year later (Christiansen, 1961).

The period before 1972 also saw the publication of two near-birth cohort studies. One, dealing only incidentally with delinquency, concerned 487 children in the sixth grade of the public schools of a midwestern city who were followed for a 9-year period (Havighurst *et al.*, 1966). The interest in delinquency centered on social class differences and the development of a prediction instrument based on social maladjustment. The study was not a true birth cohort because 30% of the subjects were born in five earlier or later years than the rest (1940). The other study was much more concerned with investigating delinquency (Conger and Miller, 1966). This research involved a cohort of males (*n* = 2,348) born in 1939 or 1940 in Denver, Colorado, whose history of delinquency up to the age of 18 was studied.

In addition to the cohort studies reported above, other studies utilized the longitudinal approach to investigate the "age" and "period" effects that may be related to delinquency. Leslie Wilkins (1960) was concerned with whether children born in certain years (e.g., during wartime) are more likely to commit offenses than are others. The basic data of this study were obtained from official criminal statistics of persons convicted of indictable offenses in England and Wales from 1946 through 1957 and from the ages of 8 through 20. This focus on generational effects was replicated in Denmark by Christiansen (1964), in Poland by Jasinki (1966), and in New Zealand by Slater *et al.* (1966).

Despite the studies reviewed above, the research literature in criminology up to 1972 was mostly characterized by reports of studies that were not longitudinal in nature and were clearly not of the cohort design. That is, most studies of recidivism have been retrospective and were based on selected groups of offenders—such as juveniles committed to correctional schools, or persons convicted of crimes or committed to penal institutions—whose prior history of delinquency or crime could be analyzed. Prospective studies have been much less common. That is, studies of the conduct of selected groups of offenders during a period of considerable length—usually beginning at the adjudication of a person as a delinquent, his conviction of crime, or his commitment to or release from a correctional institution—have been neglected.

Because most previous research did not arrive at more than partial information about recidivism, Wolfgang, Figlio, and Sellin determined that it would be worthwhile to approach the problem in a different manner: namely, by a study of the history of the delinquency of a birth cohort—a population born in a particular year, whose conflicts with the law could be examined during a segment of the cohort's lifetime, ending with entry into adulthood. An inquiry of this type, they said,

> would permit us to note the age of onset and the progression or cessation of delinquency; it would allow us to relate these phenomena to certain personal or social characteristics of the delinquents and to make appropriate comparisons with that part of the cohort that did not have official contact with the law. (1972: 4)

The decision was made, therefore, to study delinquency and its absence in a cohort consisting of all boys born in 1945 and residing in Philadelphia from a date no later than their tenth birthday until at least their eighteenth. Girls were excluded, partly because of their low delinquency rates and partly because the presence of the boys in the city at the terminal age mentioned could be conclusively established from the record of their registration for military service. The fact that no large-scale study of this particular kind had been done previously in the United States gave an additional stimulus to the project.

Subsequent Studies of a Cohort Character

Since the publication of the 1945 birth cohort study, there has continued to be interest in cohort studies concerned with crime and delinquency. Below we review this cohort-based research. Because our review is necessarily brief, and because it focuses on cohort research rather than all longitudinal studies, the reader is referred to an excellent review of the longitudinal approach in criminology available in Farrington et al. (1986).

Our own Sellin Center for Studies in Criminology and Criminal Law has completed the follow-up of the 1945 cohort into adulthood (Wolfgang et al., 1987). We have completed a follow-up of the chronic recidivists (five or more officially recorded offenses) in the police files up to the age of 30 (Collins, 1977). In addition to our work on the 1945 cohort and the present research with the 1958 birth cohort, for the past 10 years we have been engaged in a longitudinal study of a variety of possible biological, sociological, and psychological correlates of delinquency and crime (see Denno, 1982). The project consists of seven consecutive birth cohorts of children, born in Philadelphia between 1959 and 1965, whose mothers had participated in the Collaborative Perinatal Project (a national biomedical project that was sponsored by NIH).

Several birth cohort studies have been conducted in the Scandinavian countries essentially to investigate biological theories, especially the importance of hereditary factors in relation to criminal behavior. Christiansen (1974) followed up all twin pairs born in Denmark from 1881 to 1910 to investigate the comparative criminality of monozygotic versus dizygotic twins. Similarly, Dalgard and Kringlen (1976) followed up all male twins born in Norway from 1921 to 1930 and tried to contact pairs containing at least one convicted offender. Hutchings and Mednick (1974a, 1974b) have followed all males born in Copenhagen from 1927 to 1941 and adopted by someone outside their family in order to compare the conviction records of the adoptees with those of their biological and adoptive fathers.

In addition to hereditary factors, birth cohort studies are being used to investigate the relationship between convictions and psychophysiological variables. Mednick and Hutchings (1978) have studied 1,944 males born in a large Copenhagen hospital from 1936 to 1938 through the use of interviews and records. Witkin (1976) followed up all males born in Copenhagen between 1944 and 1947 who achieved adult height of at least 180 cm. The purpose of the research was to investigate the relationship between XXY and XYY chromosome abnormalities.

Although not a birth cohort study, the Cambridge Study in Delinquent Development (West, 1969; West and Farrington, 1973, 1977) is a longitudinal survey which followed a group of subjects for over 10 years. The group, which consisted of 411 males in six state primary schools in a working-class area of London, England, was first contacted in 1961-62, when the boys were ages 8-9. The boys were tested in their schools at ages 8, 10, and 14, and they were interviewed outside school at ages 16, 18, and 21. Interviews with parents were conducted about once a year, while teachers filled in questionnaires about the boys at ages 8, 10, 12, and 14. Official criminal records have been obtained, and self-report measures were collected at ages 14, 16, 18, and 21.

The research in the United States has continued this interest in near-birth cohorts (subjects born in different years). One longitudinal study consisted of a 1964 cohort of male high school sophomores ($n = 1,227$) from a medium-sized county in Oregon. The data have been used to measure the relationship between schools and delinquency (Polk, 1975; Polk and Schafer, 1972) and social class and delinquency (Polk *et al.*, 1974).

Lefkowitz *et al.* (1977) have studied aggression among a cohort of 875 children who comprised the third-grade population of Columbia County, New York. Hamparian *et al.* (1978) employed the cohort method to study violent juvenile behavior in Franklin County, Ohio. The cohort consisted of those youths who had been arrested at least once for a violent offense and had been born in 1956, 1957, or 1958. These selection criteria produced a cohort of 811 offenders who had committed 3,373 offenses (of which 985 were violent) before reaching the age of 18.

Since 1976, Shannon (1978, 1980, 1988) has been conducting a longitudinal study of three birth cohorts in Racine, Wisconsin (1942, $n = 633$; 1949, $n = 1,297$; and 1955, $n = 2,149$). The Shannon research is close in design and in birth years of the cohorts to the Philadelphia birth cohort studies, although the size of the Racine cohorts (4,079 total subjects) is considerably smaller than the Philadelphia cohorts, which contain 37,105 persons.

Although still in the data-gathering stage, a prospective longitudinal study is underway in Oregon (Patterson, 1983). Two small birth cohorts ($n = 450$ 9-year-olds; $n = 200$ 6-year-olds) are being studied to investigate antisocial behavior through childhood and adolescence, the identification of high-risk youngsters, and the relationship between family management skills and antisocial delinquent behavior.

Although valuable, none of these studies can be exactly compared to our original 1945 Philadelphia birth cohort. The majority are not actual birth cohorts, but rather, consist of groups of subjects of similar age. More important, none of the studies approaches the size, the generalizability, or the complexity of the 1945 birth cohort.

Why a New Birth Cohort Study?

In a report of recommendations by the Vera Institute of Justice (1976) concerned primarily with violent delinquents, references were made to the need for more cohort studies, one of which should be a Philadelphia replication:

> The most meaningful and widely cited source of data on delinquency is the Philadelphia cohort study. . . The cohort format makes possible an understanding of the pattern of criminal behavior over a delinquent's entire 'career'. When done on the scale of the Philadelphia study, it also permits analysis of the relationship of delinquent behavior—and changes in delinquent behavior—to many demographic, social and other factors. An optimum research strategy would call for more cohort studies. . . *One of the locations studied should be Philadelphia in order to provide a comparison with the earlier. . . study which could yield useful information about changes in delinquent behavior over time.* (VERA, 1976: 3; emphasis added)

This statement concisely explains the underlying rationale of a new birth cohort study. Longitudinal cohort studies that collect data on maturation of the same persons are the best if not the only way to provide probabilities and prevalence statistics. Another birth cohort in Philadelphia, the site of the first study, affords a comparative basis to examine the effects of differential time on a geographically similarly situated set of subjects.

Contemporary Issues in Longitudinal Research

Criminal Careers Historically

Criminology has increasingly embraced the longitudinal approach to the study of delinquency and crime. Most significantly, longitudinal methods, or at least data that are longitudinal in character, have become the principal means for the investigation of criminal careers. Indeed, over the past two decades, criminological research has increasingly focused on a particular category of offender and his associated criminal behavior. This particular focus has concerned what was originally referred to as the "chronic offender" (Wolfgang *et al.*, 1972). The current focus, however, has evolved beyond just the category of the habitual or chronic offender itself, to a broader concern with topics such as "criminal careers" and "career criminals" (see Blumstein *et al.*, 1986).

The research focusing on criminal careers has been quite varied in terms of fundamental research particulars such as subject groups (general population vs. known offenders), methodological approach (longitudinal vs. cross-sectional), and especially the measurement of crime (official archival data vs. self-report surveys).

Despite these design or measurement differences in past studies, the research on criminal careers/career criminals has generally investigated a set of concepts that are represented to have both theoretical/substantive significance to the discipline and current policy importance to criminal justice practitioners. These research concepts range from the onset, duration, and cessation of criminal behavior, to rates of participation in crime (usually referred to as *prevalence*) and measures of frequency (often referred to as *incidence* or *individual offense rates*), and to the sociodemographic correlates of these concepts (race, sex, and social class have been the most usual correlates investigated).

It is indisputable that the "criminal career paradigm" has dominated criminological research over the past 15 to 20 years. It is also quite true that, despite a widely held belief that this highly delineated area of inquiry has been both desirable and significant, there recently have been a number of polemical publications (Blumstein *et al.*, 1988a, 1988b; Gottfredson and Hirschi, 1986, 1987, 1988; Hagan and Palloni, 1988; Tittle, 1988) that have spawned a debate over the yield attained through criminal career research, on the one hand, and the value of or necessity for a longitudinal approach to studying criminal behavior, on the other hand.

It is not our intention to continue this debate here by fueling the flames of the controversy. Certainly, the present context is inappropriate for such a polemical exercise. Rather, our purpose is simply to acknowledge briefly the important issues that concern criminal career research and the absence of consensus surrounding this research agenda. In this way, we can provide an appropriate context for our comparative longitudinal birth cohort study which is summarized herein.

Longitudinal research on criminal careers is not a recent phenomenon in criminology, but dates back at least 50 years to the pioneering investigations of the Gluecks (see, for example, Glueck and Glueck, 1930, 1937, 1943, and 1968). Criminal careers have also been investigated longitudinally through the use of survey methods. The survey of probably longest duration in the United States is the Cambridge-Somerville Youth study, which was begun in 1951 and then continued by McCord *et al.* (1959) and McCord (1978, 1979). The most recent and most representative longitudinal survey is the National Youth Survey (see Elliott *et al.*, 1985), which involves a panel design of some 1,800 youths, aged 11-17 in 1976, who were given follow-up surveys annually until 1981 and then again in 1984.

Historically, an important dimension to longitudinal research on delinquency and crime emerged with the appearance of the work *Delinquency in a Birth Cohort* in 1972. In this pioneering research with the 1945 Philadelphia birth cohort, Wolfgang and associates used a retrospective birth cohort design to investigate the delinquency careers of 9,945 boys who were born in 1945 and who had lived in Philadelphia throughout the course of their juvenile years at risk (ages 10-17). With the benefit of a longitudinal cohort design, Wolfgang, Figlio, and Sellin (1972) were the first to report population-based data concerning the onset, offense patterns, and duration of juvenile careers.

Among the most significant findings of the research was the fact that a very small fraction of the birth cohort, those offenders that had accumulated at least five police contacts before becoming adults, had committed a far greater share of the delinquency in the birth cohort than their proportionate representation in the birth cohort might have suggested. Specifically, the 627 chronic delinquents constituted just 6% of the cohort ($n = 9,945$) and 18% of the delinquent subset ($n = 3,475$), yet these chronic offenders were responsible for a total of 5,305 offenses, or 52% of all the delinquency in the cohort through age 17. With regard to the subset of serious index crimes, Wolfgang et al. found that the chronics had committed 63% of the Uniform Crime Report (UCR) index offenses, including 71% of the homicides, 73% of the rapes, 82% of the robberies, and 69% of the aggravated assaults.

These results of the 1945 birth cohort study concerning the chronic offenders have very probably become the most important and enduring findings of the research. Although criminologists had long suspected that rates of offending were skewed, that a small group of habitual offenders were committing crimes at a high rate, the Philadelphia birth cohort study showed just how small the chronic offender group actually was, and just how skewed their rates of offending actually were.

Since the emergence of the 1945 cohort study, replications of the chronic delinquency phenomenon have continued to be reported. For example, in his work with three Racine birth cohorts, Shannon (1980, 1988) has also found evidence of a chronic offender effect. In the 1942 cohort, 1% of the males had four or more felony contacts, but this group was responsible for 29% of all such felony contacts. In the 1949 cohort, the chronic offenders were 3% of the cohort, but had 50% of the felony contacts. In the last cohort, 1955, the 6% with four or more felony contacts accounted for 70% of this type of police contact. Hamparian et al. (1978) have also reported that in an Ohio cohort of violent delinquents, chronic offending was restricted to 31% of the offenders.

Other studies have confirmed that the disproportionate volume of crime attributable to chronic offenders is not restricted to juveniles, and that despite the familiar inverse trend evident in age-specific arrest rates, the habitual offender or chronic recidivism effect is observable among adult criminals. The Rand inmate surveys have found that a relatively small group of offenders report the commission of a substantial proportion of crime. For example, Peterson et al. (1980) have found that 25% of a group of California inmates could be classified as career criminals and this group of chronics reported committing approximately 60% of the armed robberies, burglaries, and auto thefts, and about one-half of the assaults and drug sales, reported by the full sample of inmates (see also Petersilia et al., 1977). Visher (1986) has reanalyzed Rand's second inmate survey (prison and jail inmates in California, Michigan, and Texas) and has found that one-half of the inmates reported committing less than four robberies per year, while the very high-rate offenders, who constituted just 5% of the inmates, reported committing more than 180 robberies per year.

These results concerning chronic recidivism have demonstrated that skewed rates of illegal behavior are a problem in both the juvenile and adult reference periods separately. But, there is now good evidence to suggest that the problem of chronic offending is longitudinal, and in fact can begin very early in a delinquent's career and can continue unabated into adulthood.

This situation is most clearly evidenced by the follow-up study of the 1945 Philadelphia birth cohort. Wolfgang *et al.* (1987) followed up a representative sample of 974 members of the 1945 birth cohort to age 30 using Philadelphia police and court records. The data indicated that chronic offenders constituted 15% of the cohort, and these chronics, or career criminals, were found to have committed 74% of all the official crime, and further, they accounted for 84% of the personal injury offenses and 82% of the property offenses recorded from the onset of the career up to age 30.

Further evidence of longitudinal chronicity comes from the continuing Cambridge Study in Delinquent Development (Farrington, 1981). Farrington has reported that up to age 24, the chronic offenders constituted just 6% of the sample and 17% of the convicted youths, yet these chronics were responsible for one-half of the convictions. The Farrington results thus provide cross-cultural evidence of chronicity and its prolonged tenure.

The research reviewed above provides sufficient evidence that in any group or cohort of subjects, there is an uneven distribution of offenses. Most people will never commit or be arrested for a crime, some individuals will commit only one or two crimes and then desist, while others will recidivate frequently, and some will recidivate very frequently. In response to this criminological fact, some politicians and researchers alike have attempted to identify the group of habitual or career criminals for the sake of special criminal justice intervention, such as targeted law enforcement and prosecution procedures, to be followed by selective incapacitation strategies and stringent sentencing guidelines. These are just a few of the most popular measures being implemented to combat the career criminal and his excessive and prolonged involvement in criminal behavior.

Barnett *et al.* (1987) have acknowledged that there is indeed a distinct policy-related interest in career criminal research. They have observed that: "It has been argued that, if prosecution resources and institutional and other treatment facilities could be used more selectively for these high-rate offenders, this might prevent a significant number of crimes" (1987: 83). However, Barnett *et al.* have also made the crucial observation that the substantive importance of collecting and analyzing criminal career information goes beyond the mere identification of career criminals for criminal justice policy purposes because:

> Detailed information about criminal careers is fundamental to isolating the different facets of the career—initiation, the pattern of offending during the active period, and termination. It is necessary to separate these different facets in order to test various approaches to the prevention or reduction of crime and to investigate different ways in which possible "causes of crime" affect these different aspects of criminal careers. (1987: 83-84)

The Value of Longitudinal Research on Criminal Careers

This characterization of the research on criminal careers has been strongly rejected by Gottfredson and Hirschi beginning with their paper "The True Value of Lambda Would Appear to Be Zero" (1986), which they have described elsewhere as an effort to "introduce some small degree of tension into an otherwise complacent system that had, we thought, limited thinking about crime to the repetition of pretentious slogans, ignored research contrary to its assumptions, and proposed to lead public policy about crime in the wrong direction" (1988: 37).

The substance of the early Gottfredson-Hirschi position can be evidenced with a few passages from their initial paper. First, with reference to the relationship between criminal career research and federal funding they write, "the criminal career notion so dominates discussion of criminal justice policy and so controls expenditure of federal research funds that it may now be said that criminal justice research in this country is centrally planned" (1986: 213). Second, with respect to the terminology of the academic community they observe that "the language of criminology is now saturated with the vocabulary of this perspective—with terms like lambda, prevalence and incidence, onset and desistance, chronicity and selective incapacitation" (1986: 214). Third, after reviewing the research evidence they assert that "the evidence is clear that the career criminal idea is not sufficiently substantial to command more than a small portion of the time and effort of the criminal justice practitioner or academic community" (1986: 231).

In a second polemical paper, Gottfredson and Hirschi (1987) turn their attention to the adequacy of longitudinal research designs to investigate not only criminal careers, but also crime in general. After reviewing the evidence from a host of studies concerning the two presumed benefits of longitudinal research—methodological and substantive superiority—they offer the following conclusions.

Concerning the hegemony enjoyed by longitudinal perspectives, Hirschi and Gottfredson maintain that "neither the results of current longitudinal research in criminology nor reasonable expectations about proposed longitudinal research in the area justifies the dominance this design has achieved" (1987: 610). Given this arguable absence of either current findings or future potential, Gottfredson and Hirschi thus believe that longitudinal advocates are guilty of blurring "the distinction between theory and method to such an extent that they seem to be making important substantive and logical assertions when in fact they are merely repeating an extremely narrow conception of crime and its causation" (1987: 610).

These two papers have stimulated a controversy that has witnessed a comment by Blumstein *et al.* (1988a), a reply by Gottfredson and Hirschi (1988), a further rejoinder by Blumstein *et al.* (1988b), and two other related commentaries (Hagan and Palloni, 1988; Tittle, 1988). It is doubtful that this controversy will abate quickly, and certainly our intention here is not to dismiss the value of the Gottfredson-Hirschi arguments. Scientific disagreement is healthy, and criminology will surely benefit from the exchange of ideas stimulated by the criminal career controversy.

It is necessary, however, for us to reiterate for the record the following particulars concerning the longitudinal methods that we have successfully employed and will continue to employ productively as we follow our cohorts through their life courses.

We believe, as do a host of others, that there are distinct advantages to the utilization of longitudinal methods in the study of delinquency and crime. As Farrington *et al.* have argued:

> Longitudinal research can show when criminal careers begin, when they end, and how long they last. It can also show the prevalence and incidence of offending, the cumulative prevalence rate, and the seriousness and diversity of offending, at different stages of a criminal career. (1986: 25)

We acknowledge the premise that cross-sectional research is not incapable of examining these important topics. We are convinced, nonetheless, that the longitudinal approach, especially the birth cohort method, is the most viable and productive way to study the multitude of issues that surround delinquency and adult careers in crime and the transition between the two. Again we offer the following observations from informed colleagues concerning longitudinal surveys, observations that we would argue are primarily applicable to birth cohort research.

> The main advantage of such surveys of crime and delinquency lies in their ability to provide detailed information about the natural history and course of development of offending. In particular, longitudinal surveys can show the extent of continuity or discontinuity between offending at different ages, the extent to which one event precedes or follows another in developmental sequences, and how well later events can be predicted by earlier ones. They can also provide information about the time ordering of different events, which can be useful in drawing conclusions about cause and effect, and they can show the effects of different events on the course of development of criminal careers. (Blumstein *et al.*, 1988: 67)

Perhaps a simple example will help to clarify the longitudinal versus cross-sectional issue. Suppose a researcher took a sample of high school students so that ninth through twelfth graders (which would probably span ages 14 to 17) were equally represented. After collecting the official delinquency data on this sample, the researcher might find that the prevalence of delinquency was highest among ninth graders and declined consistently thereafter. The researcher might conclude that delinquency declines with age, and he or she might then search for explanations of this effect.

One possible explanation might be that as the student becomes increasingly socialized by and integrated into the school environment, a social control effect occurs. Of course, an alternative explanation for this "age effect" is that in the earlier grades the sample contains a disproportionate share of the "troublemakers" who are already delinquent by the ninth grade, or who become delinquent in this first year of high school. Since many of these delinquents drop out before reaching the twelfth grade, the prevalence of delinquency naturally declines because they are no longer counted in the school population.

A longitudinal design would not be susceptible to this problem which surrounds the dropouts. A longitudinal design would study a particular cohort (birth or other, such as ninth graders) of youth and would follow these subjects for a period of years. Because the entire cohort of youth would be enumerated and examined regardless of their school status, real prevalence rates would be derivable—rates which would not be artifacts of changing sample composition.

We maintain, contrary to the minority opinion represented in the arguments of Gottfredson and Hirschi, that the investigation of delinquent or criminal "careers" is not only a legitimate enterprise for criminological research, it is one of the more important areas of substantive inquiry that criminologists have been engaged in. Further, we strongly suggest that, because criminology has long been characterized as a discipline of varied theoretical perspectives, and research methods or methodological designs, it is entirely desirable and appropriate, if not axiomatic, that scholars should continue to adopt the particular perspectives and research methods they find most promising and suitable for their inquiries. The discipline itself will be the best judge of whether the particular course chosen has been a fruitful one.

4

The 1958 Birth Cohort Study

Objectives

Delinquency in a Birth Cohort (Wolfgang et al., 1972) remains the only large-scale birth cohort study undertaken in the United States based upon a generalizable population. The delinquency careers of all boys born in 1945 who lived in Philadelphia from their tenth to their eighteenth birthdays were described, and parametric estimates of their offense rates and recidivism and desistance probabilities were computed. It is important to note that this study developed baseline cohort rates from a data source unlike any other previously investigated in this country: first offense, recidivism, and offense switching rates; offense severity escalation, disposition probabilities, and subsequent offensive behavior. All of these statistics and others can be estimated with validity only from longitudinal, preferably cohort, data.

Because the birth cohort study is unique and, as yet, not duplicated, the major objective of the 1958 birth cohort study is a complete replication of the 1945 Philadelphia birth cohort study as reported by Wolfgang, Figlio, and Sellin in 1972. The data collection sources and procedures, research design, and methodology of the 1945 cohort study have all been applied in the present research. In general we have tried to establish essentially the same set of parametric estimates as developed for the 1945 cohort to determine the "cohort effects" on delinquent behavior of growing up in the 1960s and early 1970s compared to those activities expressed by a cohort some 13 years earlier.

Many demographic and school variables, such as race, socioeconomic status (SES), type of school attended, residential mobility, highest grade completed, IQ, and level of school achievement, were related to each other and the state of having a police record. In addition, the probabilities of committing, by age, a first, second, third, and out to the nth offense were generated, as were the probabilities of switching from one type of offense to another, or to the state of "desistance" (the commission of no more officially recorded delinquencies). A multitude of hypotheses may be investigated with these data.

Indeed, in *Delinquency in a Birth Cohort* we uncovered some surprising and some not so unexpected findings. On the one hand, we found that the offensive careers of juvenile males may be modeled as a simple Markov process; that is, the type of the next offense is not related to the past offense types—career specialization is not apparent. On the other hand, it was clear that delinquent behavior, both in relative incidence and severity, is more prevalent and intense among blacks and lower-SES groups than among whites and higher-SES individuals.

The continuous-age data derived from a longitudinal study enabled us to suggest appropriate intervention points in delinquent careers. Thus we were able to state:

> Because 46 percent of the delinquents stop after the first offense, a major and expensive treatment program at this point would appear to be wasteful. We could even suggest that intervention be held in abeyance until the commission of the third offense for an additional 35 percent of the second-time-offenders desist from then on. Thus, we could reduce the number of boys requiring attention in this cohort from 3475 after the first offense to 1862 after the second offense, to 1212 after the third offense, rather than concentrating on all 9945 or some other large subgroup (such as nonwhites or lower SES boys) under a blanket community action program. Beyond the third offense the desistance probabilities level off. (Wolfgang *et al.*, 1972: 254)

We have mentioned above some of the topic areas addressed in the 1945 birth cohort study. All of these areas have been investigated in the present research with regard for the changing orientations and technologies that have been developed since we last worked with cohort materials.

For example, we have tried to determine the differences (if any) which the data will exhibit between the two cohorts in such areas as: (1) overall cohort delinquency rates; (2) demographic and school correlates of delinquency; (3) first and subsequent offense probabilities; (4) age-at-onset of delinquency and offense accumulation; (5) relative seriousness of offenses; (6) offender typologies (one-time, recidivist, and chronic); (7) patterns of delinquent careers; (8) offense-switching probabilities; (9) disposition rates; (10) the effect of various sanctions on the probabilities of subsequent offenses; and (11) propitious intervention points.

In short, our objective was to replicate the 1945 birth cohort study with a cohort of Philadelphia juveniles born 13 years later in order to assess the extent and character of delinquency in the later-age cohort and to determine the amounts of stability and transitivity over time as expressed in the various data sets.

In addition to these replication issues we tried to address a series of policy-related issues that appear to surround the problem of juvenile delinquency. In testimony before the Subcommittee on Juvenile Justice of the U.S. Senate Committee on the Judiciary, the acting administrator of the Office of Juvenile Justice and Delinquency Prevention (OJJDP) identified several major issues that are part of our research effort. According to Laurer (1981) these issues are the following:

1. Are there unique patterns of serious and violent juvenile behavior?
2. How chronic are serious and violent juvenile offenders?
3. Does the early delinquent have a long career?
4. Do juvenile delinquents progress from bad to worse?

The first issue coincides with our focus on the offense-switching probabilities which we examined to determine whether delinquents specialize in the types of delinquency they commit. The second issue pertaining to chronic offenders is one of the prime questions that was addressed in our 1958 cohort study. For example, do the chronic offenders in the present study exhibit the same disproportionate involvement in delinquency, and particularly, violent delinquency, as their counterparts in the 1945 cohort? Because we have available longitudinal data we can readily address the third issue pertaining to age-at-onset and career length. We have investigated whether beginning delinquency at an early age (for various offense types) is associated with a longer career. Last, because we have available a new set of seriousness score weights with which to quantify the severity of delinquent events, we have addressed the question of whether delinquents progress from bad to worse by examining the relative severity of offenses by age and rank order of offense.

Standard data-handling techniques were used in the descriptive analysis of the cohort offense rates, age probabilities, career severities, correlates among the various demographic and school variables, court disposition and subsequent behavior, and so on. These techniques included the generation of frequency distributions, rates, probabilities, correlations, and multiple regressions. We need not detail this aspect of the project here, because these are commonly accepted and universally applied modes of analyses.

We have continued our work with Markov process analysis, an innovative technique first used in criminological research in *Delinquency in a Birth Cohort*, to examine career patterns of offense switching and specialization. We have also used recently developed techniques (e.g., log-linear, logit, and maximum-likelihood factor analysis) for uncovering and explaining relationships within nominal data in addition to the more traditional forms of multiple regression. Through these methods we attempted to find structural patterns in the various background variables which may be related to various configurations of offensive behavior. At the time of the original birth cohort study these statistical methods were just being developed, but now they are integral parts of most multivariate analysis strategies. It should be noted that, although we have reanalyzed the 1945 data and have analyzed the 1958 data with more robust statistical techniques, we have tried to keep the presentation of results as simple as possible. Thus, we present simple descriptive results unless the more advanced techniques reveal findings that are not readily observable otherwise.

Capturing the Cohort

The cohort used in this research is composed of subjects who were born in 1958 and who resided in the city of Philadelphia at least from their tenth until their eighteenth birthday. Like the 1945 birth cohort study, the birth year of the present cohort was primarily dictated by the availability of complete criminal history data. That is, although the Juvenile Aid Division (JAD) records of the Philadelphia Police Department are available for juveniles until their eighteenth year of age, the police investigation report, which details the specifics of the offense, is not kept for the full period of the juvenile career. Because our research protocol makes extensive use of both the traditional rap sheet data, represented by the JAD record, and the offense details given on the investigation report (Philadelphia police form 75-49), the birth year of the cohort had to coincide with the availability of valid and reliable records over the full years of our concern. It was determined that full police records were available back to at least 1968, and because age 10 is the lower bound to our cohort residence criterion, 1958 was chosen as the birth year for the present cohort.

It was a fortunate convenience that the birth year of the cohort as dictated by our police data requirements turned out to be most suitable in terms of our need for a second cohort that could facilitate the investigation of cohort effects. That is, the 1945 birth cohort was born the year the second World War ended. Its delinquency years essentially span the period from 1955 through 1962. In many ways the rates, types, and severity of delinquency exhibited by the 1945 cohort reflect the social milieu of that period.

Thus, a primary requirement for the second cohort study was a birth cohort born sufficiently later than its predecessor so that its span of delinquency years reflects a different social milieu and, thus, perhaps a different push to or pull from delinquency. The present cohort seems to meet this requirement. It was born 13 years after its predecessor, which puts its delinquency-prone years (i.e., from 1968 to 1975) in a potentially very different milieu. This period coincides with America's involvement in the Vietnam War, the rise in drug use, social protest, and the like, and, thus, represents a time of great social change compared to the more tranquil adolescence of the 1945 cohort. Because of this, distinct cohort effects are quite possible, which suggests that their detection and measurement should constitute the primary focus of our analyses.

In addition to birth in the year 1958, the other eligibility requirement for membership in the present cohort is identical to that of the earlier cohort—continued residence in Philadelphia at least from the age of 10 until the eighteenth birthday. The upper bound simply reflects the statutory age limit of delinquency. The lower bound is, of course, arbitrary but does reflect the age at which the sharpest change in delinquency onset occurs. We would argue that the ages of 10 through 17 reflect the period in which the vast majority of youths begin their delinquency careers. Therefore, 8 years is a sufficiently long period at risk with which to establish a valid cohort rate of delinquency.

After selecting the birth cohort, we examined both the Philadelphia school census and the U.S. Bureau of the Census data in order to frame some rough estimates of the size of the cohort. These data indicated that between 40,000 and 45,000 children were born each year in Philadelphia from 1955 to 1965 and that 37,000 register each year for first grade in the city's public, parochial, and private schools. Of these, some 23,000 attend public school. If the proportion who dwelled in Philadelphia during the ages 10 through 17 (i.e., the eligibility requirement) is the same as was found in the 1945 cohort, then about 14,000 girls and 13,500 boys should be eligible for cohort membership. As will be shown below, these estimates are very close to the final figures for the 1958 cohort.

The data from the private and parochial schools were collected by sending staff members to each of the schools to record the appropriate information from the student records. Public school data were collected from the centralized computer files of the school district so as to provide a master set of subjects who were potential candidates for inclusion in the study. Two sets of Philadelphia Board of Education files were accessed. The first, called the history file, represents the ultimate record of a public school student. The second file is a set of annual entries for each

student encompassing his or her entire period of attendance in the public schools. These files have been computerized since 1971.

The results of the effort to construct a master list of subjects yielded
a total of 44,505 entries, of which 35,964 were recorded in the public
school data and 8,541 were contained in the private and parochial school
files. This number is much higher than the eventual number of subjects
who were included in the study because considerable overlap existed
within and between the two sets of school records. That is, some students attended both public and parochial or private schools and appear
on both lists of entries, and other students were duplicated within each
set. In addition, subjects were deleted from the master list because they
did not meet the eligibility requirements—birth in 1958 and residency in
Philadelphia from the ages of 10 through 17. The results of the purging
process are discussed below and are depicted in Table 4.1.

The merged set of public history and annual files contained 35,964
listings. We produced a master list, sorted by last, first, and middle
names, which included race, sex, date of birth, and address. We inspected this list, line by line, to uncover persons who had been duplicated. We discovered 3,873 sets of duplicates caused by name inconsistencies (e.g., deletion of middle initial, shortening of the first name, or
misspelling of either first or last name). We inspected the set of annual
file entries for each student to see if they met the eligibility requirements. This process identified four sets of cases which did not meet the
criteria. We found 992 subjects that were not born in 1958 and 57 cases
that were not residents of Philadelphia. We deleted 5,608 cases that had
entered the public schools (and did not transfer from private or parochial schools) after the age of 10 (in-migrants). We also deleted 5,016 cases
which left the public school files (and did not transfer to private or
parochial schools) before age 18 (out-migrants). Last, we deleted 44
subjects because they had died before reaching the age of eighteen.

The purging process was also applied to the private and parochial
school records. We deleted 141 duplicates, 10 cases not born in 1958, 337
cases that were not residents of Philadelphia, 67 in-migrants, and 29 out-
migrants. In addition to these, we identified 1,531 cases that had been
registered in public school as well as private/parochial schools. These
transfer duplicates were deleted as well.

As a result of the file-cleaning process, the final size of the cohort
was set at 27,160 subjects, all of whom met the birth and residency
requirements of the study. The race and sex breakdowns of the subjects
are displayed in Table 4.2.

TABLE 4.1
File Cleaning Process

	Deletions						
	Total entries	Duplicate entries	Incorrect birth year	Non-resident	Enter after age 10	Left before age 18	Death
Public school records[a]	35,964	3,873	992	57	5,608	5,016	44
Private school records	8,541	141	10	337	67	29	—

Public school records
35,964 entries
− 15,590 deletions
20,374 eligibles

Private school records
8,541 entries
− 584 deletions
7,957 eligibles

28,691 total of public and private cases
− 1,531 between school duplicates
27,160 total cases in the birth cohort

[a]Public school records consist of 32,372 entries from the history file and 35,271 entries from annual files.

TABLE 4.2
*Number and Percentage of 1958 Cohort
Members by Race and Sex*

Sex	White	Nonwhite	Both
Male	6,216	6,944	13,160
	22.9%	25.6%	48.5%
Female	6,637	7,363	14,000
	24.4%	27.1%	51.5%
	12,853	14,307	27,160
	47.3%	52.7%	100.0%

Collection of Police Data

With the names, birth dates, and addresses in hand from our master list, we entered the files of the Philadelphia police, Juvenile Aid Division. These files list all the contacts the Philadelphia police have had with a child until he or she has reached age 18. After that point, any future police encounters are recorded on the regular police forms (i.e., rap sheets—form 75-10) and reported to the FBI.

Collection of police data was accomplished in two stages. In the first stage, a search was made of the Juvenile Aid Division (JAD) files for the names of all subjects on the master list to see if an offense record existed for any person. If none existed, a notation of nondelinquent was made for that subject. If an offense record did exist, a notation of delinquent was made on the master list, and the JAD record was photocopied and placed in a folder for each delinquent. This stage of the data collection produced over 6,000 JAD records that matched cohort subjects.

Because the JAD record does not contain detailed information about an offense but only serves to identify the charges, date of event, and police district complaint number (for the investigation report), a second stage of data collection was necessary. This process entailed securing all the police investigation reports (form 75-49) for each offense listed on the JADs. These forms are the complete police report of a crime and include such information as date, time, and place of occurrence; name, race, sex, address, and age of victim; a description of the event; name, race, sex, address, and age of person arrested; and so on. The forms are filed by district complaint number and are maintained in a separate warehouse. There were almost 21,000 offense reports identified on the JADs which had to be located and copied.

The offense data were coded by means of an instructional system, developed for the study, which identifies 100 separate variables for each offense. In addition to the police data for each criminal event, we have scored the offenses to represent the seriousness of the event according to the method originally developed by Sellin and Wolfgang (1964) and used in *Delinquency in a Birth Cohort*. The exact procedure for severity scoring is detailed in the measurement section presented below.

Measuring Delinquency

As noted previously, the juvenile delinquency measures used in this research are based on official police contacts recorded by the Juvenile Aid Division of the Philadelphia Police Department. From the JAD record (essentially a juvenile rap sheet), we coded delinquency as a dichotomous attribute, nondelinquent versus delinquent, which thus produces a prevalence measure of delinquency. The number of offenses or police contacts which appear on the JAD constitute the cumulative delinquency record up to the age of 18, and thus represent the incidence of delinquency in the cohort. Because the police contact data include offenses for which the offender was either arrested or informally processed and then released to parents, the total number of offenses can be grouped and counted as either arrests or remedials. Our measures of delinquency thus consist of one qualitative variable pertaining to official delinquency status and several quantitative variables concerning the frequency of delinquent events.

It has often been suggested that official police measures such as those used in this research are both limited and biased. In this view, self-reported delinquency data are not just an alternative measure of delinquent behavior but are really preferred measures that tap somewhat different domains of delinquency and crime. Until recently, it was clear that the domains were quite different. Self-reports tended to address more trivial and less serious offensive behaviors, while official data usually reflected more serious violative activity. The findings which emerged from the use of these two kinds of data were usually quite different. Research drawn from official offense data generally indicated that males, nonwhites, and persons of lower social class were more likely to be offenders with records of less serious offenses, while on the other hand, self-report research did not find sex, race, and social class differences of great magnitude, thus leading to the conclusion that official data must be in error.

Recent research, however, has shown that with more sophisticated

self-report inventories and survey administration procedures, the results of self-report research are much more congruent with those of
official data studies. For example, Elliott and Ageton (1980) have reported from the National Youth Survey that self-report and official correlates of and conclusions about delinquent behavior are quite similar.
Similar findings have also been reported by Farrington (1973) and Hindelang, Hirschi, and Weiss (1979). In addition, our own follow-up of the
1945 birth cohort employed a self-report inventory which permitted direct comparisons between official and unofficial measures. Our findings
support many of those reported by Elliott and Ageton. Essentially, we
found that the sociodemographic groups with high arrest rates were also
likely to self-report the highest frequencies and severity of hidden offenses (Tracy, 1987).

At this point it is difficult to conclude that self-report and official
measures are or are not congruent, particularly in terms of the correlates
of delinquency, because of the lack of concurrent official and self-report
data or sufficient sample sizes in prior research. It is obvious that this
knowledge gap strongly suggests the use of multiple measures of illegal
behavior. The use of such data allows a cross-validation check of official
delinquency measures and provides for the analysis of a host of research
issues that would not be possible with only one kind of offense data.

We intend to employ such multiple measures when we follow up
the 1958 birth cohort into adulthood, as we did when we studied the
1945 cohort in the adult years. At present, however, we are limited to
official delinquency measures. We are satisfied, nonetheless, that our
delinquency data are a valid measure of juvenile delinquency, and in the
present context of official delinquency careers, they can be used without
reservation.

Scaling the Gravity of Crime

The Sellin Center has had a long-standing interest in measuring the
severity or gravity of criminal behavior. The work of Sellin and Wolfgang (1964) in the *Measurement of Delinquency* produced a seriousness
scoring scale which typifies the severity of crime in a quantitative fashion and avoids the often misleading nature of legal labels. The scale was
utilized in the original cohort study. Since then, the Center has continued to investigate the perceived severity of crime and has developed
an updated version of the scale. These data come from a national survey
that was conducted as part of the National Crime Panel Surveys (Wolf-

gang *et al.*, 1985). The rationale for the scale and a summary of the system are briefly discussed below.

Although the value of the particular crime index system (i.e., UCR) developed by the FBI may be questioned, we are in full agreement that an index must be based on certain kinds of offensive conduct. However, instead of selecting these kinds of conduct on the basis of the title given them by the criminal code, we believe that the nature of the harm inflicted should govern the selection of an index. Thus, we conclude that a scale of offense gravity should be constructed utilizing events which involve violations of the criminal law that inflict bodily harm on one or more victims and/or cause property loss by theft, damage, or destruction. We further maintain that these effects are more crucial to the establishment of an index of crime than the specific legal labels attached to the events.

The above criterion of selecting events for a crime index differs in two major respects from the one used in the UCR system. First, it does not allow the inclusion of offenses that produce none of the effects described. Thus, the offenses utilized in our scale all share one very important feature—some degree of measurable social harm to the community. Second, our system includes many offenses that are not counted among the index crimes category of the UCR. Simply, we have chosen the criterion of discernable consequences over that of an ordered set of legal categories which may or may not appropriately reflect the seriousness of criminal behavior.

We have also determined that the class of violations we will utilize in our scoring system should be subdivided into three categories in order to indicate the major effect associated with the offense. The first category includes those events which produce bodily harm to one or more victims even though property theft or damage may also be involved. The second class of events consists of those offenses which do not involve injury but have a property theft component even when accompanied by damage. The last category consists of those offenses that involve only damage to property.

In addition, because we believe that an event should not be evaluated solely in terms of the injuries and losses which occur, our system takes account of certain other factors of the event that aggravate the crime. For example, a crime is aggravated if the offender engages in intimidating behavior (especially the use of a weapon). Further, a property crime may be aggravated if the offender damages the premises by forcible entry. Thus, our crime severity scale takes account of both the components (injury, theft, damage) and the aggravating factors (intimidation and premises forcibly entered).

The Seriousness Scoring System

In order to score criminal events, the following items, insofar as they are applicable to a given event, must be collected and recorded:

1. The number of victims who, during the event, receive minor bodily injuries, or are treated and discharged, hospitalized, or killed.
2. The number of victims of acts of forcible sexual intercourse.
3. The presence of physical or verbal intimidation or intimidation by a dangerous weapon.
4. The number of premises forcibly entered.
5. The number of motor vehicles stolen and whether the vehicle was or was not recovered.
6. The total dollar amount of property loss during an event through theft and damage.

Table 4.3 lists the seriousness scoring components and the associated weights used in the scale. The seriousness score for an event is computed as follows. The weight for components 1 through 5 is multiplied by the number of victims who were so affected and the various

TABLE 4.3
Seriousness Scoring Components and Weights

Component	Weight
1. Physical injury	
a. minor harm	1.474
b. treated & discharged	8.525
c. hospitalized	11.980
d. fatal	35.669
2. Forcible sex acts	25.920
3. Intimidation	
a. verbal or physical	4.900
b. by weapon	5.600
4. Premises forcibly entered	1.500
5. Motor vehicles stolen	
a. recovered	4.460
b. unrecovered	8.070
6. Amount of theft/damage =	

$$\log_{10} Y = .26776656 \log_{10} X,$$
(where Y = seriousness weight and X = dollar value of theft/damage)

scores are summed. In addition, the total dollar loss to the victim(s) in terms of both theft and damage is inserted into the formula for component 6. The severity score for monetary loss is then added to that for the other components.

Measuring Socioeconomic Status

The concept of socioeconomic status, or alternatively social status or social class, has been a phenomenon of long-standing interest in sociology. The social stratification literature is crowded by a vast array of research concerning the measurement of this concept in its own right, and by investigations of the social class relationship to a number of criterion variables. However, the topic of social class/status has not been investigated without controversy. Indeed, given the centrality of the concept to sociological and criminological theory, one is struck by the lack of consensus over both its conceptualization and measurement.

In one sense the debate centers on whether social status and social class are actually alternative indicators or are really different dimensions of the concept. In terms of measurement, unanswered questions persist concerning whether single versus multiple measures are more appropriate, and whether aggregate versus individual-level data should be utilized. Like most social science conceptual debates, the questions remain unresolved because strong positions have been adopted on both sides, and consequently, separate traditions have been established.

The situation has perhaps been even more problematic in criminology. Historically, theories of crime and delinquency have posited a strong inverse relationship between social status (or social class) and illegal behavior. Indeed, it was commonly found that lower status was associated with higher official crime or delinquency arrest rates. However, with the advent of the self-report method, findings became available which did not support such a relationship with unofficial crime data.

Because of this inconsistency, proponents of the self-report method have argued that official crime and delinquency data reflect class (and associated race) biases in the official agents of control, rather than a measurable and valid difference in the actual behavior of persons of different social strata. The direct consequence of this was the development of two distinct research camps—one using official archival data and the other employing the self-report method.

Of course, attempts to reconcile the differences between official and self-report measures of delinquency and crime have continued. But the vast majority of interest has fallen on the dependent measures, with only minor concern exhibited for the measurement of social status. A paper by Thornberry and Farnworth (1982) showed the fallacy of this practice. Thornberry and Farnworth have convincingly argued that:

> Much of the empirical confusion stems from the apparent simplicity of the theoretical proposition that social class and crime are inversely related. We suggest that the assumptions underlying this proposition are more complex than often realized, and that the proper assessment of the relationship between class and crime requires more rigorous conceptual definition and measurement than is apparent in past research. (1982: 505).

According to Thornberry and Farnworth, past measures of crime and social class have been of questionable adequacy, and this improper measurement may be responsible for the contradictory findings that are often reported. In terms of social class and status, they suggested that "despite such general diversity in past measurement, individual studies have typically relied on only a single indicator of social class" (1982: 507). Instead, Thornberry and Farnworth used measures of social status which represented several of the central dimensions of the concept, measures that also represented individual and aggregate levels of data. They concluded that, "indeed, when issues of the relationship between social status and crime are examined in a more extensive manner than has been evident in past empirical analyses, the association between status and criminality is seen to be quite robust" (1982: 516).

We have followed this lead and have thus used a complex measure of social status that encompasses a number of separate indicators. The measure of socioeconomic status used in the 1958 birth cohort study was developed as follows.

From the 1970 Bureau of Census files for Philadelphia we selected a total of 15 census tract variables. The selection of items was guided by past research and our own conceptualization of social status. We inspected the univariate distributions and performed logarithmic transforms because the data were skewed or otherwise unevenly distributed. From the pool of 30 variables, the original 15 variables and the 15 transforms, we selected a final set of 10 indicators of social status. These items were the ones of greatest theoretical value and the most normally distributed across census tracts.

Because we felt that no single indicator of social status was as valid as the full set might be, we decided to represent social status as a function of 10 indicators. Although summary scales and additive indices are often utilized, we preferred to employ a multivariate technique of deriving the social status indicator. Thus, we used the principal components factor analysis procedure. From the first principal component extracted in the factor analysis, we computed the factor score, which was then assigned to each census tract. In turn, cohort subjects were given the factor score for their particular census tract.

The factor scores ranged from -3.04 to +1.89, and like all standard scores, had a mean of 0 and a standard deviation of 1. Because the vast majority of our analyses will consider SES as a qualitative variable, we dichotomized the factor scores (below and above the mean) to produce a discrete SES construct with two levels—low SES and high SES.

We are well aware that although we used very reliable census data, and although we created an SES measure using sophisticated statistical procedures, the issue still obtains that we have assigned individuals to an SES group based upon aggregate rather than individual-level data. There is the possibility, therefore, of measurement error in these assign-ments. We would have preferred individual-level data like income, edu-cation, or occupation of the head of each cohort subject's household. These data could not be obtained in an archival study such as this. Thus, we have used an aggregate-based measure instead, and we are mindful of the limitations thereof.

Background Data

In addition to race, sex, and SES of census tract, we have available several other background variables. However, because these data were not collected from individuals, but rather, were derived from school records, the variables are available only for the public school students (with one exception as noted below). For public school students, we have measured: (1) highest grade completed (in years and as a dichotomy—graduated vs. dropout); (2) the national percentile score on the California Achievement Test; (3) the number of residential addresses since age 10; and (4) three dichotomous variables pertaining to whether the student was handicapped, emotionally disturbed, or a school disciplinary prob-lem. For private school students, the scarcity of data available in paper records limited us to only the graduation dichotomy.

5

The Prevalence of Delinquency

One of the most basic questions surrounding the topic of juvenile delinquency concerns the proportion of youths at risk that have had official contact with the police or other official criminal justice agencies. At a minimum, delinquency research must measure the prevalence of the phenomenon by classifying the at-risk population at least in terms of the delinquent versus nondelinquent dichotomy. The accumulation of prevalence data thus provides information on the relative size of the delinquent population across demographic groups and regions and over time. These basic data are necessary for theory development and testing and are indispensable for informed social policy.

Despite the importance of prevalence data, published results in this area are comparatively rare. In a most comprehensive review of the concept and a survey of available evidence, Gordon (1976) was limited to just eight studies which reported population-based prevalence data for urban areas. Admittedly, reliable prevalence estimates are difficult to generate. These estimates depend upon a detailed search of official records and, most important, they require consistent knowledge of the underlying population at risk throughout the years of juvenile court jurisdiction. It is noteworthy that despite the difficulty surrounding prevalence measures, the published estimates are quite consistent.

When juvenile court appearance is used as the criterion measure for delinquency status, the delinquency prevalence for all male youths can be set just slightly above or below 20%. Monahan (1960) used age-at-onset data to project the proportion of juveniles that would ever come before the Philadelphia juvenile court. The prevalence was 22.3% for all males, 16.5% for white males, and 40.8% for nonwhite males (see also Monahan, 1962, 1970). Ball et al. (1964) have reported a prevalence of 20.7% for the Lexington, Kentucky, Standard Metropolitan Statistical Area using the age-specific rate technique. Results for a British cohort (Douglass et al., 1966) show a prevalence of 14.6% up to the age of 17, which Gordon (1976: 217) has recomputed as 18.0% up to age 18.

A more accessible criterion measure is police contacts. Several studies have used this measure with very similar results. Havighurst *et al.* (1966) found that 38.8% of a group of sixth-grade boys (in an anonymous, medium-sized midwestern community) had come into contact with the police as juveniles. Hathaway and Monachesi (1963) reported that 34.6% of the boys in a statewide Minnesota sample had police contacts before age 18. More recently, Shannon (1980) has reported prevalence data for his Racine, Wisconsin, cohorts. His data show that 29.9% of the 1942 cohort, 35.7% of the 1949 cohort, and 31.0% of the 1955 cohort had a police contact for a felony or misdemeanor before age 18.

The consistency of the police contact-based prevalence measures suggests that the chances of young, urban males becoming delinquent are fairly constant at about one out of three. As a necessary first step in our analysis of the 1945 and 1958 birth cohorts, we analyzed the prevalence of delinquency by race, social status, and the few available background variables. Our goals quite simply were to determine if the two cohorts differed in terms of prevalence and whether various factors were associated with being recorded as a delinquent. Our findings are presented below, with the results for the 1945 and 1958 cohorts being displayed together in the same tables.

Race and SES

In the 1945 birth cohort study (Cohort I) it was found that 34.9% of the boys were recorded as being delinquent (had at least one official police contact) before turning age 18 (see Table 5.1). Further, it was reported that 16.2% of the cohort were one-time offenders, while 18.7% were delinquent recidivists. The latter figure can be broken down into 12.4% nonchronic recidivists (from two to four offenses) and 6.3% chronic recidivists (five or more offenses).

One of the most striking findings with regard to the prevalence of delinquents involved the race differences. In Cohort I, 50.2% of nonwhite boys were delinquent compared to 28.6% of the whites. Moreover, nonwhites were not only more delinquent, but also were more likely to be recidivists (32.9% vs. 12.9%) and were more chronically delinquent (14.4% vs. 3.0%) than white subjects.

The data in Table 5.1 for males in the 1958 birth cohort show a very similar prevalence of delinquency to that observed in Cohort I. Overall, delinquency prevalence is slightly smaller than in the 1945 cohort, as 32.8% of the Cohort II males were delinquent compared to 34.9% in the earlier cohort. In terms of the three delinquency status categories,

TABLE 5.1

*Number and Percentage (of Cohort) of Delinquency Status
by Race and Cohort*

	White	Nonwhite	Both
	1958 Cohort		
Cohort subjects	6216	6944	13160
Delinquents	1412	2903	4315
	22.7	41.8	32.8
One-time	733	1071	1804
	11.8	15.4	13.7
Nonchronic recidivists	470	1059	1529
	7.6	15.3	11.6
Chronic recidivists	209	773	982
	3.4	11.1	7.5
	1945 Cohort		
	White	Nonwhite	Both
Cohort subjects	7043	2902	9945
Delinquents	2019	1456	3475
	28.6	50.2	34.9
One-time	1110	503	1613
	15.7	17.3	16.2
Nonchronic recidivists	699	536	1235
	9.9	18.5	12.4
Chronic recidivists	210	417	627
	3.0	14.4	6.3

Cohort II shows slightly fewer one-time offenders (13.7% vs. 16.2%), but an almost identical proportion of recidivists (19.1% vs. 18.7%). However, the recidivists in Cohort II are slightly more likely to be chronic offenders (7.5% vs. 6.3%) than was the case for Cohort I.

The data reported in Table 5.1 also replicate the Cohort I finding concerning the impact of race on delinquency. Thus, in Cohort II nonwhite males have a higher prevalence of delinquents than whites overall (41.8% vs. 22.7%) and in terms of the various offender categories. The differences are most striking for the recidivist category, where 26.4% of the nonwhites, compared to 11.1% of the whites, may be so classified. The discrepancy is maintained when the prevalence of delinquents is divided into nonchronic (two to four offenses) and chronic (five or more offenses). The proportion of nonwhite subjects to white subjects is about

2 times higher for the nonchronic recidivist category (15.3% vs. 7.6%), and about 3 times higher for the chronic recidivist category (11.1% vs. 3.4%).

Despite these race differences, it should be noted that the impact of race on delinquency in Cohort II is clearly less striking than was the case in Cohort I. That is, nonwhite subjects are more likely to be delinquent and more likely to be classified at the higher frequencies of delinquency status, but the gap between the races has narrowed. Generally, the proportionate difference between the races was about 21.6% for the 1945 cohort, but is approximately 19% for the 1958 cohort.

Although interesting, the data reported in Table 5.1 portray the various prevalence measures as a function of the number of cohort subjects in each subgroup as the base or denominator. Because these figures do not show the delinquent group-based breakdown of delinquents into the various levels of prevalence, it is far more instructive to examine the delinquency status types with the number of delinquent subjects as the base of the percentages. These results are displayed in Table 5.2.

TABLE 5.2
Number and Percentage (of Delinquent Base)
of Delinquency Status by Race and Cohort

	1958 Cohort		
	White	Nonwhite	Both
Delinquents	1412	2903	4315
One-time	733	1071	1804
	51.9	36.9	41.8
Nonchronic recidivists	470	1059	1529
	33.3	36.5	35.4
Chronic recidivists	209	773	982
	14.8	26.6	22.7
	1945 Cohort		
	White	Nonwhite	Both
Delinquents	2019	1456	3475
One-time	1110	503	1613
	54.9	34.5	46.4
Nonchronic recidivists	699	536	1235
	34.6	36.8	35.5
Chronic recidivists	210	417	627
	10.4	28.6	18.0

Table 5.2 indicates that the 1945 cohort offenders are more likely to be one-time offenders (46.4%) than recidivists of either the nonchronic (35.5%) or chronic (18.0%) classification. Further, the chances are about 2 to 1 that among the recidivist subset separately, a delinquent will be nonchronic compared to chronic. The data for Cohort II males given in Table 5.2 also show a declining prevalence as the frequency of delinquency increases, but these data also reflect some noteworthy differences. That is, compared to Cohort I, one-time offenders have declined from 46.4% in 1945 to 41.8% in 1958, while the percentage of chronic delinquents has increased from 18.0% to 22.7% for Cohort II males. The proportion of nonchronic recidivists is almost identical for both cohorts (approximately 35%).

The data given in Table 5.2 also indicate a pronounced race effect in the distribution of the delinquency status types. For Cohort I males, white delinquents are much more likely to be one-time offenders (55% vs. 35%) and much less likely to be classified as chronic offenders (10.4% vs. 28.6%) than nonwhite delinquents. When the recidivist category is viewed separately, the data show that over three-quarters of the white recidivists are nonchronic compared to 56.2% of the nonwhites and that nonwhite chronics exceed white chronics by almost 20%.

For the 1958 cohort, race comparisons reveal very similar percentages which show a greater propensity of white delinquents to commit only one offense and a greater likelihood for nonwhite delinquents to be responsible for five or more offenses. Thus, about 52% of white offenders compared to 37% of nonwhite delinquents were one-time violators. On the other hand, about 15% of white delinquents, compared to 27% of nonwhite delinquents, were classified as chronic recidivists.

Despite these race differences, however, it should be noted that the race disparity observed in Cohort I at the level of chronic recidivists has narrowed in Cohort II. That is, when the recidivist delinquents are classified into nonchronic and chronic types, 43.8% (417 of 953) of nonwhite recidivists were chronic compared to 23.1% (210 of 909) of white recidivists in Cohort I; but in Cohort II the nonwhite figure has remained about the same at 42% (773 of 1,832), while the share of white recidivism attributable to chronics has increased to 30.8% (209 of 679).

In Table 5.3 we turn to a breakdown of the delinquency status data by the SES dichotomy. These data show the relationship between SES and type of delinquent for the two birth cohorts using the pool of delinquents as the percentage base. These data show a pronounced SES effect. In Cohort I, higher-status delinquents are more likely to be one-time offenders (57.2%) compared to lower-status delinquents, for whom one-time offending characterizes a much lower percentage (39.0%). On

TABLE 5.3
Number and Percentage (of Delinquent Base)
of Delinquency Status by SES and Cohort

	1958 Cohort		
	Low SES	High SES	Both
Delinquents	2703	1612	4315
One-time	995	809	1804
	36.8	50.2	41.8
Nonchronic recidivists	987	542	1529
	36.5	33.6	35.4
Chronic recidivists	721	261	982
	26.7	16.2	22.7
	1945 Cohort		
	Low SES	High SES	Both
Delinquents	2056	1419	3475
One-time	802	811	1613
	39.0	57.2	46.4
Nonchronic recidivists	770	465	1235
	37.5	32.7	35.5
Chronic recidivists	484	143	627
	23.5	10.1	18.0

the other hand, lower-status delinquents are over twice as likely to be classified in the chronic subset compared to higher-status delinquents (23.5% vs. 10.1%). The SES effect is similarly pronounced for the recidivist subset separately. For higher-status recidivists the chances are over 3:1 that they will be of the nonchronic type. Among the lower-status group, however, the chances are much lower (1.5:1) that the recidivist will be nonchronic.

The data for Cohort II given in Table 5.3 also show an SES effect, but the effect is somewhat smaller than that for Cohort I. Higher-status delinquents are again more likely to be one-time offenders compared to lower-status delinquents (50.2% vs. 36.8%), but the percentage difference is about 13% compared to 18% in the 1945 data. Similarly, lower-status delinquents in Cohort II are more likely than their higher-SES counterparts to be chronic recidivists (26.7% vs. 16.2%), but this difference is lower, at 10%, compared to 13% obtained for Cohort I. When the comparisons are focused on the recidivist subset separately, the data also indicate a smaller SES effect than was the case for Cohort I. The chances are about 2:1 that a higher-SES recidivist will be nonchronic compared to a ratio of 1.3:1 for lower-status recidivists. These ratios are lower than those observed in the Cohort I data and indicate that chronic offending has increased in Cohort II over that for Cohort I, and more so among higher-SES delinquents.

The results reported in Table 5.4 show the relationship between race and the various offender groups within the two levels of social status. These data show that the previous race effect is maintained regardless of social status for both cohorts. For lower-SES subjects in Cohort I, nonwhites have a higher prevalence of delinquency (52.9% vs.

TABLE 5.4
Number and Percentage (of Cohort) of Delinquency Status
by SES, Race, and Cohort

	1958 Cohort			
	Low SES		High SES	
	White	Nonwhite	White	Nonwhite
Cohort subjects	1318	5096	4898	1848
Delinquents	437	2266	975	637
	33.2	44.5	19.9	34.5
One-time	190	805	543	266
	14.4	15.8	11.1	14.4
Nonchronic recidivists	157	830	313	229
	11.9	16.3	6.4	12.4
Chronic recidivists	90	631	119	142
	6.8	12.4	2.4	7.7
	1945 Cohort			
	Low SES		High SES	
	White	Nonwhite	White	Nonwhite
Cohort subjects	2140	2444	4903	458
Delinquents	763	1293	1254	165
	35.6	52.9	25.6	36.0
One-time	368	434	740	71
	17.2	17.8	15.1	15.5
Nonchronic recidivists	289	481	410	55
	13.5	19.7	8.4	12.0
Chronic recidivists	106	378	104	39
	5.0	15.5	2.1	8.5

35.6%), and the delinquency is more likely to be of the recidivist type (35.1% vs. 18.4%), compared to whites. Chronic offending occurs among low-SES nonwhites about 3 times as often as among low-SES whites (15.5% vs. 5.0%). At the higher level of SES, the race effect is also maintained. At this level, nonwhites are more likely to be delinquent (36.0% vs. 25.6%) and recidivistic (20.5% vs. 10.5%) compared to whites. The ratio of nonwhites to whites is 2:1 at the recidivist level and 4:1 at the chronic recidivist level.

The Cohort II results shown in Table 5.4 suggest that the introduction of race does not diminish the SES effect on delinquency. Delinquency involves about 44% of the nonwhites and 33% of the whites who are of low social status, and 34% versus 19% for nonwhites compared to whites who are of higher social status. The proportion of nonwhites compared to whites that are recidivists is 28.6% versus 18.7% for lower SES and 20.1% versus 8.8% at the higher-SES level. Chronic delinquency occurs among low-SES nonwhites (12.4%) about twice as often as among low-SES whites (6.8%), while the ratio of nonwhites to whites is about 3:1 for higher-status subjects (7.7% vs. 2.4%).

The data given for both cohorts in Table 5.4 thus show that race is strongly related to delinquency in each cohort regardless of SES.

Another way of examining the relationship of race and SES to delinquency status is to compute offender rates per 1,000 cohort subjects. These data are given in Table 5.5 for the 1945 and 1958 birth cohorts for one-time delinquents and the recidivist subset.

Table 5.5 shows that overall in Cohort I, lower-SES subjects have a higher rate of recidivism (273.6) than of one-time delinquency (175.0) and a total offender rate of 448.6. On the other hand, higher-SES subjects show a one-time delinquency rate (151.3) that is higher than the recidivism rate (113.4), for a total offender rate of 264.7. In other words, the offender rate among low-SES cohort members is about 1.8 times higher than that of high-SES subjects. In fact, the recidivism rate for low-SES subjects (273.6) exceeds the total delinquency rate (264.7) for the higher-SES group.

The Cohort II data given in Table 5.5 generally indicate slightly lower offender rates than those of Cohort I, but the SES differences found in Cohort I are maintained. Lower-status subjects show a higher rate of recidivism than for one-time delinquency (266.2 vs. 155.1), while higher-status subjects show lower rates which are virtually equal at about 119 per 1,000 subjects for both delinquency levels. The total offender rate for low-SES subjects (421.3) is about 1.7 times higher than the total rate (238.9) for high-SES subjects. This difference is almost the same as that observed for the Cohort I data (1.8). Similarly, the low-SES

TABLE 5.5

Delinquency Status and Delinquency Rates by Race, SES, and Cohort

	1958 Cohort					
	One-time delinquents			Recidivists		
Race and SES	N	Percentage	Rate/1,000	N	Percentage	Rate/1,000
Both races						
Low SES	995	36.8	155.1	1708	63.2	266.2
High SES	809	50.2	119.9	803	49.8	119.0
Total	1804	41.8	137.0	2511	58.2	190.8
White						
Low SES	190	43.5	144.1	247	56.5	187.4
High SES	543	55.7	110.8	467	44.3	88.1
Total	733	51.9	117.9	679	48.1	109.2
Nonwhite						
Low SES	805	35.5	157.9	1461	64.5	286.6
High SES	266	41.8	143.9	371	58.2	200.7
Total	1071	36.9	154.2	1832	63.1	263.8

	1945 Cohort					
	One-time delinquents			Recidivists		
Race and SES	N	Percentage	Rate/1,000	N	Percentage	Rate/1,000
Both races						
Low SES	802	39.1	175.0	1254	60.9	273.6
High SES	811	57.2	151.3	603	42.9	113.4
Total	1613	46.4	162.2	1862	53.6	187.2
White						
Low SES	372	48.5	173.8	395	51.5	184.5
High SES	738	58.9	150.5	514	41.1	104.8
Total	1110	54.9	157.6	909	45.0	129.1
Nonwhite						
Low SES	430	33.4	175.9	859	66.6	351.5
High SES	73	43.7	159.4	94	56.3	205.2
Total	503	34.6	173.3	953	65.5	328.4

rate of recidivism (266.2) alone exceeds the total delinquency rate of high-SES subjects (238.9), as was the case for the 1945 cohort.

Table 5.5 also shows the expected race effect in both cohorts. The nonwhite total offender rates in Cohort I (501.7) and in Cohort II (418.0) are greater than those of their white counterparts (286.7 and 227.1). In both instances the nonwhite rate is about 1.8 times as high as the white rate. The most pronounced difference occurs with respect to the rate of recidivism. In Cohort I the nonwhite rate of recidivism (328.4) is about 2.5 times as high as the white rate (129.1). For Cohort II data, the rate of nonwhite recidivism exceeds that of white recidivism (263.8 vs. 109.2) by almost the same margin (2.4 times). Like the results by SES reported above, the recidivism rate of nonwhites exceeds the total delinquency rate of whites in both cohorts.

Table 5.5 also reports race-SES-specific rates to show the combined influence of these variables. If the effects are additive, as we might expect from the prior results, then a particular rank ordering of rates should be observed. For both cohorts, the results are as expected. In Cohort I, low-SES nonwhites have the highest recidivism rate (351.5), followed by high-SES nonwhites (205.2) and then low-SES whites (184.5), with high-SES whites showing the lowest rate (104.8).

This same ranking is also obtained for Cohort II. Low-SES non-whites have the highest recidivism rate (286.6), followed by high-SES nonwhites (200.7), then low-SES whites (187.4), with high-SES whites showing the lowest rate (88.1). However, from top to bottom the discrepancy between races in recidivism rates is greater in Cohort I (246.7) than in Cohort II (198.5), which attests to the effects of race and SES being a bit less pronounced in the 1958 cohort, as we have seen in prior tables.

Background Variables

In addition to the race and SES comparisons displayed above, we have tried to discern the differences between nondelinquents and delinquents and between the various levels of delinquency status in terms of background characteristics that were collected from school data. For both cohorts, the data mostly pertain to just public school students owing to the greater availability of data in the computerized public school records. However, it should be noted at the outset that the various comparisons shown below do not always involve the full complement of public school cases as data were not always available for all subjects across all measures.

Table 5.6 shows the average number of residential addresses by delinquency status (dichotomous), race, and SES. It is immediately apparent that male delinquents in both cohorts have, on average, moved more times than nondelinquents. In Cohort I, delinquents have a mean of 2.7 addresses, while nondelinquents have averaged 2.0 addresses. In Cohort II the difference is in the expected direction but is less than that for Cohort I. For the 1958 cohort, delinquents show an average of 1.6 addresses, while nondelinquents show a mean of 1.3 addresses.

TABLE 5.6
Mean Number of Residential Addresses by Delinquency Status, Race, SES, and Cohort[a]

| | 1958 Cohort | | | | | |
| | Low SES | | High SES | | Total | |
	N	Mean	N	Mean	N	Mean
Nondelinquents						
White	412	1.65	1840	1.35	2252	1.40
Nonwhite	2640	1.87	1047	1.74	3687	1.84
Total	3052	1.84	2887	1.49	5939	1.37
Delinquents						
White	296	1.95	537	1.46	833	1.63
Nonwhite	2203	2.10	596	1.93	2799	2.06
Total	2499	2.08	1133	1.70	3632	1.67
	1945 Cohort					
	Low SES		High SES		Total	
	N	Mean	N	Mean	N	Mean
Nondelinquents						
White	1376	1.78	3641	1.71	5017	1.73
Nonwhite	1147	3.04	289	2.61	1436	2.95
Total	2523	2.35	3930	1.78	6453	2.00
Delinquents						
White	761	2.32	1252	1.87	2013	2.04
Nonwhite	1291	3.64	165	3.38	1456	3.61
Total	2052	3.15	1417	2.04	3469	2.70

[a]The number of subjects does not equal the total N in either cohort because data were not available for all subjects.

It is interesting to note that nonwhites have moved more often than whites across SES levels and delinquency status. Cohort I nonwhites have, on average, about 1.0 more addresses than whites among delinquents and nondelinquents. In Cohort II the pattern is the same, but for the later cohort, nonwhites have a mean number of addresses which is about 50% higher than whites, regardless of SES. The SES comparisons show differences similar to those observed by race. For the 1958 cohort, low-SES subjects showed more residential mobility than high-SES subjects.

The pattern of results observed when race, SES, and delinquency are considered together is consistent with the univariate results discussed above. Low-SES nonwhite delinquents have the highest mean number of addresses (2.1 for 1958 and 3.64 for 1945), followed by low-

SES nonwhite nondelinquents, and so on. These data characterized the situation for both cohorts.

The average number of years of school completed is shown by delinquency status (dichotomous), race, and SES in Table 5.7. The data for Cohort I are virtually the same as those reported for residential addresses. Nonwhites, low-SES subjects, and delinquents have achieved a lower number of years of education than their white, high-SES, and nondelinquent counterparts.

The data for Cohort II, however, depart somewhat from this pattern. In the 1958 cohort, delinquents show a smaller average number of years of school completed than nondelinquents (mean = 10.76 versus mean = 11.43). Lower-status subjects have completed fewer years of

TABLE 5.7
Mean Highest Grade Completed by Delinquency Status, Race, SES, and Cohort[a]

| | 1958 Cohort | | | | | |
| | Low SES | | High SES | | Total | |
	N	Mean	N	Mean	N	Mean
Nondelinquents						
White	376	11.14	978	11.63	2163	11.54
Nonwhite	2440	11.34	1787	11.43	3418	11.37
Total	2816	11.31	2765	11.56	5581	11.43
Delinquents						
White	276	10.24	509	10.91	785	10.67
Nonwhite	1841	10.78	502	10.82	2343	10.79
Total	2117	10.71	1011	10.86	3128	10.76
	1945 Cohort					
	Low SES		High SES		Total	
	N	Mean	N	Mean	N	Mean
Nondelinquents						
White	1284	11.26	3481	11.67	4765	11.56
Nonwhite	1005	9.92	263	10.48	1268	10.04
Total	2289	10.67	3744	11.59	6033	11.24
Delinquents						
White	649	10.10	1138	10.94	1787	10.63
Nonwhite	1103	8.92	139	9.65	1242	9.00
Total	1752	9.36	1277	10.79	3029	9.96

[a]The number of subjects does not equal the total N in either cohort because data were not available for all subjects.

education than high-SES subjects, but the difference is only slight. Among nondelinquents the difference is about .2 years of school (11.31 vs. 11.56), while for delinquents the difference is about .1 years of school (10.71 vs. 10.86). These very minor discrepancies are considerably lower than those for Cohort I, where the low-SES versus high-SES difference was 1 year and 1.4 years for nondelinquents and delinquents, respectively. More important than this, the race results are quite different from Cohort I. For the earlier cohort, nonwhites consistently showed a lower average number of years of school regardless of SES or delinquency. In Cohort II, however, this is not the case. Whites have a lower mean number of years of school among low-SES nondelinquents and delinquents. At the high-SES level, whites have competed more years of school, but the difference is only very slight (.2 years for nondelinquents and .1 years for delinquents).

The California Achievement Test (CAT) data for the two cohorts are shown in Table 5.8. These data show a distinct relationship to both delinquency and race. Among the nondelinquents in the 1945 cohort, about 46% of the subjects can be classified as very high achievers, the fourth quartile. For delinquents on the other hand, only about 10% fall at this highest level of achievement. These differences persist when race is introduced. The race comparisons show that for whites, 56.5% among the nondelinquents and 17.7% among the delinquents can be classified as highest achievers compared to 10.5% and 4.5% of the nonwhite nondelinquents and delinquents, respectively.

For Cohort II, we again used the national percentiles on the CAT and grouped the data into quartiles. We again found that nondelinquents achieve in school better than delinquents, as 56% of the former compared to 33% of the latter scored at the 50th percentile or better, and 32% of the former scored in the fourth quartile compared to 13% of the latter. These results are also obtained when race is controlled. The race effect itself is quite pronounced regardless of delinquency status. Of the white nondelinquents, 79% scored above the median compared to 39% percent of the nonwhite nondelinquents. Among delinquents, whites score above the median over twice as often as nonwhites (57% vs. 25%). Thus, being a nonwhite delinquent versus a white nondelinquent is a particularly disadvantageous position. For these groups, 7.7% and 54.3%, respectively, can be classified in the top quartile of achievement.

In addition to the delinquency status dichotomy, we have investigated some of the background variable differences across the levels of delinquency status. These data are shown in Tables 5.9 to 5.11.

Table 5.9 shows that in Cohort I there were pronounced differences in residential addresses as one moves from nondelinquency to the delin-

TABLE 5.8

Achievement Level by Delinquency Status, Race, and Cohort[a]

Achievement quartiles	1958 Cohort					
	Nondelinquents		Delinquents		Total	
	N	Percentage	N	Percentage	N	Percentage
White						
First	108	5.5	82	16.2	190	7.7
Second	283	14.5	132	26.0	415	16.9
Third	499	25.6	143	28.2	642	26.2
Fourth	1058	54.3	150	29.6	1208	49.2
Total	1948	100.0	507	100.0	2455	100.0
Nonwhite						
First	878	31.5	683	45.1	1561	36.3
Second	805	28.9	444	29.3	1249	29.0
Third	644	23.1	273	18.1	917	21.3
Fourth	462	16.6	116	7.7	578	13.4
Total	2789	100.0	1516	100.0	4305	100.0

Achievement quartiles	1945 Cohort					
	Nondelinquents		Delinquents		Total	
	N	Percentage	N	Percentage	N	Percentage
White						
First	105	5.4	89	12.9	194	7.3
Second	215	11.0	153	22.2	368	13.9
Third	529	27.1	253	36.7	782	29.6
Fourth	1103	56.5	195	17.7	1298	49.1
Total	1952	100.0	690	100.0	2642	100.0
Nonwhite						
First	217	38.5	277	43.1	494	40.9
Second	151	26.8	209	32.5	360	29.8
Third	137	24.3	128	19.9	265	21.9
Fourth	59	10.5	29	4.5	88	7.3
Total	564	100.0	1516	100.0	1207	100.0

[a]The number of subjects does not equal the total N in either cohort because data were not available for all subjects.

quent recidivists. The mean number of residential addresses increases, while mean IQ, highest grade completed, and model achievement level decrease for nondelinquents versus one-time delinquents versus recidivists. The data for the 1958 cohort (expanded to include nondelinquents and the three types of delinquents) shown in Table 5.9 follow about the

TABLE 5.9
Delinquency Status by School Variables and Cohort[a]

	1958 Cohort			
	Non-delinquents	One-time offenders	Nonchronic recidivists	Chronic recidivists
Mean number residences	1.7	1.9	2.0	2.1
Mean school achieve-ment percentile	35.9	23.8	19.1	14.4
Modal school achieve-ment quartile	4th	1st	1st	1st
Mean highest grade	11.4	11.1	10.7	10.2
	1945 Cohort			
	Non-delinquents	One-time offenders	Recidivists	
Mean number residences	2.0	2.2	3.1	
Mean IQ score	107.9	104.2	98.1	
Modal school achieve-ment quartile	4th	2nd	1st	
Mean highest grade	11.2	10.8	9.2	

[a]The scores are for less than the total N in either cohort due to incomplete data. Also, not all measures were available for both cohorts.

same pattern. The greatest differences are between nondelinquents and delinquents of any type. That is, nondelinquents have been more residentially stable, have a higher average achievement percentile or modal achievement quartile, and have completed more years of school than have delinquents.

When the level of delinquency status is considered, the only measure that shows a significant decreasing trend is mean achievement level. For this measure, one-time offenders have a score of 23.8 compared to 19.1 for nonchronic recidivists and 14.4 for chronic recidivists. The differences among the three levels of delinquency are only slight for mean highest grade completed and show no difference for modal achievement quartile (all scored in the lowest).

Table 5.10 shows the not too surprising finding (given previous results) that the chronic offenders in Cohort I were much more likely to have been classified as discipline problems in school. At the lower level of SES, 25.6% of the nonwhite chronics and 17.5% of the white chronics were disciplinary cases, compared to just 3.9% and 1.9% of their one-

TABLE 5.10

Percentage of High School Disciplinary Status by SES,
Race, Delinquency Status, and Cohort[a]

| | 1958 Cohort | | | |
| | Low SES | | High SES | |
	White	Nonwhite	White	Nonwhite
Nondelinquents	1.5	2.7	0.3	1.9
One-time offenders	1.9	3.6	0.7	4.1
Nonchronic recidivists	4.4	7.6	1.7	9.7
Chronic recidivists	12.5	35.9	9.2	33.8
	1945 Cohort			
	Low SES		High SES	
	White	Nonwhite	White	Nonwhite
One-time offenders	1.9	3.9	0.5	2.7
Chronic recidivists	17.5	25.6	18.3	26.8

[a]The scores are for less than the total N in either cohort due to incomplete data. Also, not all measures were available for all delinquency statuses in 1945 cohort.

time offender counterparts. At the higher level of SES the results are similar.

Table 5.10 also shows an expanded comparison for Cohort II. Here, the results once again point out the special character of chronic delinquents. For nonwhites the chronics exceed their nearest competitor as discipline problems by a factor of 4.7:1 at the low-SES level and by a factor of 3.4:1 at the higher level. The white comparisons show ratios of 2.8:1 and 5.4:1 at the low-SES and high-SES levels respectively.

For the combined race and SES data, the results show a consistent pattern of increasing discipline problems as one moves from nondelinquent, to one-time offenders, to nonchronic recidivists, and finally to chronic delinquents.

Table 5.11 shows a dramatic comparison in the 1945 cohort between one-time and chronic offenders regarding their graduation status. Regardless of race and SES, one-time offenders are no less than 3 times as likely as chronics to have graduated from high school. The sharpest difference occurs among lower-SES nonwhites, where one-time offenders have graduated over 6 times more often than chronic offenders. The Cohort II data reported in Table 5.11 show a strong inverse trend between percentage graduating and the frequency of delinquency. This

TABLE 5.11

Percentage of High School Graduates by SES,
Race, Delinquency Status, and Cohort[a]

	1958 Cohort			
	Low SES		High SES	
	White	Nonwhite	White	Nonwhite
Nondelinquents	53.8	50.3	77.4	58.6
One-time offenders	33.2	36.7	57.6	40.2
Nonchronic recidivists	17.8	21.8	41.5	21.8
Chronic recidivists	3.3	7.5	16.0	4.9
	1945 Cohort			
	Low SES		High SES	
	White	Nonwhite	White	Nonwhite
One-time offenders	50.8	43.3	72.1	50.0
Chronic recidivists	6.8	10.1	15.7	17.6

[a]The scores are for the total N in both cohorts. But not all measures were available for all delinquency statuses in 1945 cohort.

trend is evident for both races and SES levels. For example, 53.8% of the low-SES white nondelinquents graduated high school, but only 3.3% of the chronic delinquents finished school. Similarly, among low-SES nonwhites, 50.3% of nondelinquents graduated compared to 7.5% of chronic offenders. This trend is also evident for high-SES subjects as well.

As a last step in the analysis of the delinquency prevalence measures, we present in Tables 5.12 and 5.13 a multivariate comparison of the effects of the background variables. The two principal factors we have discussed before, race and SES, are included as well as a dummy variable representing graduated versus not graduated from high school. This variable was included in the models for two reasons. First, it represents in a joint way the separate effects of achievement and years of school completed which were used previously. Second, unlike these variables, data are available on graduation status for all of the 1958 cohort subjects. Thus, the estimates discussed below are more reliable than would have been the case with the reduced sample of cases for which the other measures were available.

The models reported below consist of maximum-likelihood estimates of the effects of variables on the joint multinomial likelihood function of the categories of a dependent variable. Like the methods proposed by Goodman and others, maximum-likelihood estimation is a powerful technique for analyzing contingency tables so that the effects, including interaction effects, on the logarithm of the odds ratio can be estimated and tested for significance. Simple tabular analyses lack the ability to estimate the effects or their significance in multiway contingency tables.

Table 5.12 displays the results of estimating various effects for the nondelinquent versus delinquent dichotomy. The data indicate for Cohort I that the main effects of race and SES are significant, as expected, as is the graduation status factor. For the three two-way interactions we see that the race and SES interaction term is significant, thus indicating that lower status has a greater effect on delinquency for nonwhites; and the race and graduation interaction term is also significant, thus indicating that failure to graduate from high school has a stronger effect for nonwhites. The SES and graduation effect is not significant. The effect parameters indicate that the status of not graduating from high school is by far the stronger correlate of delinquency status, followed by SES and race.

TABLE 5.12

Estimated Effects of Background Variables
on Dichotomous Delinquency Status by Cohort

Effect	DF	Estimate	Chi-square	Probability
		1958 Cohort		
Intercept	1	.806995	1152.14	.0001
Race	1	.233137	92.75	.0001
SES	1	−.173888	50.68	.0001
Graduation	1	−.656565	964.99	.0001
Race × SES	1	.001413	0.00	.9520
Race × Graduation	1	−.015896	0.43	.5128
SES × Graduation	1	.017344	0.52	.4689
		1945 Cohort		
Effect	DF	Estimate	Chi-square	Probability
Intercept	1	.472155	228.01	.0001
Race	1	.147747	22.18	.0001
SES	1	−.195032	39.76	.0001
Graduation	1	−.601330	550.38	.0001
Race × SES	1	.087641	7.87	.0050
Race × Graduation	1	−.136138	23.81	.0001
SES × Graduation	1	−.028270	1.13	.2886

The data for Cohort II show similar results for the main effects. Graduation status is the strongest correlate of delinquency status, followed by race and then SES. In fact, the relative magnitude of the effect is stronger than in Cohort I. Unlike Cohort I, none of the two-way interactions is significant for the 1958 cohort. This result signifies that graduation status depends on neither race nor SES for its effect on delinquency and that race is related to delinquency regardless of SES.

Table 5.13 reports the results, among just delinquents, of estimating

TABLE 5.13

Estimated Effects of Background Variables on Trichotomous Offender Group by Cohort

			1958 Cohort		
Effect	DF	Parameter	Estimate	Chi-square	Probability
Intercept	1	1	1.36936	335.22	.0001
	1	2	1.03216	179.30	.0001
Race	1	3	.27751	10.81	.0010
	1	4	.15753	3.24	.0717
SES	1	5	.21794	6.96	.0084
	1	6	.12627	2.18	n.s.
Graduation	1	7	−1.04813	214.23	.0001
	1	8	−.68377	85.16	.0001
Race × SES	1	9	−.00244	0.00	n.s.
	1	10	.00151	0.00	n.s.
Race × Graduation	1	11	.01491	0.03	n.s.
	1	12	−.00653	0.01	n.s.
SES × Graduation	1	13	.04021	0.25	n.s.
	1	14	.03431	0.17	n.s.
			1945 Cohort		
Effect	DF	Parameter	Estimate	Chi-square	Probability
Intercept	1	1	1.17079	292.97	.0001
	1	2	1.13069	163.12	.0001
Race	1	3	.53041	31.77	.0001
	1	4	.43788	20.11	.0001
SES	1	5	−.13184	1.96	n.s.
	1	6	−.01771	0.03	n.s.
Graduation	1	7	−1.15717	226.48	.0001
	1	8	−.66050	69.73	.0001
Race × SES	1	9	.03480	0.25	n.s.
	1	10	−.03120	0.20	n.s.
Race × Graduation	1	11	−.05547	0.38	n.s.
	1	12	−.05111	0.30	n.s.
SES × Graduation	1	13	−.02847	0.10	n.s.
	1	14	−.02170	0.05	n.s.

the effects of race, SES, and graduation status on the likelihood of being a one-time offender, nonchronic recidivist, or chronic recidivist. Because the dependent variable has three levels, two contrasts are possible. In the first, the odds of being a one-time offender are compared to those of being a chronic (the odd-numbered parameter estimates pertain to this contrast). In the other comparison the odds of being nonchronic are contrasted with those of being chronic (the even-numbered estimates refer to this contrast).

For Cohort I only the main effects of race and graduation status are significant, with the latter being more appreciable. The effects indicate that nonwhites have greater odds than whites of being: (1) chronic delinquents rather than one-time offenders, and (2) chronic compared to nonchronic offenders, assuming they are recidivists. The same interpretation pertains to the effect of not graduating from high school compared to graduating.

The model for Cohort II indicates that both of the graduation status effects are significant, while for race only one effect was significant. Thus, high school dropouts are more likely than graduates to be: (1) chronic rather than one-time offenders, and (2) chronic recidivists rather than nonchronic. Nonwhites, however, only show greater odds than whites of being chronic than one-time offenders. Among recidivists, nonwhites have only slightly greater odds than whites of being chronic.

In summary, the prevalence data reported above show similar relationships for both the 1945 and 1958 cohorts. The overall prevalence of delinquency is about the same for both cohorts, 32.8% in the 1958 cohort and 34.9% in the 1945 cohort. It was also found that both race and SES were related to delinquency status for both cohorts, although the effects, especially for race, were somewhat more pronounced in Cohort I.

With respect to background and school variables, it was found that delinquents compared to nondelinquents have lower achievement scores, fewer years of school completed, and more residential moves. These separate effects culminate in pronounced differences between nondelinquents and delinquents with respect to graduation from high school. Further, however, the graduation status effect was also found to be related to the level of delinquent involvement, not just the status of delinquent versus nondelinquent.

6

The Incidence of Delinquency

The data presented in the previous chapter represent the prevalence of delinquency or the delinquency status dimension in the two birth cohorts. These data thus set the size of the delinquent subgroup and show the relationship of various demographic and school variables to delinquency status. These data, however, do not address at all the delinquent events in the two cohorts. Regardless of the number of cohort subjects, and their correlates, that occupy the various statuses of delinquency, we must investigate how many times these offenders exhibited the delinquency trait. Incidence data supply this necessary information.

In our analyses we use incidence to mean two components of delinquency. First, incidence data show the extent or frequency of delinquent events and can be used to compute overall and offense-specific delinquency rates. Second, incidence also pertains to the severity of delinquency; this component reflects the various offense types, indices, and quantitative seriousness scoring that represent the character of the delinquency committed in the two studies. Incidence, therefore, constitutes a very important basis of comparison between the two cohorts and also within each cohort by the primary demographic factors of race and SES.

Extent of Delinquency

Table 6.1 displays the frequency and offense rate (i.e., the total number of offenses divided by the number of subjects multiplied by 1,000) for all offenses committed by the 1945 and 1958 birth cohorts. The data for the total offenses indicate that the Cohort II offense rate (1,158.7) is higher than the rate in Cohort I (1,027.0). These rates thus show that about 130 more offenses per 1,000 subjects were committed in the later cohort compared to the earlier cohort. This difference, however, is slight compared to the differences in rates for specific offenses or offense groups (particularly serious offenses).

Chapter 6

TABLE 6.1
Number, Percentage, and Rate of Delinquent Offenses by Cohort

Offense	1958 Total offenses			1945 Total offenses		
	N	Percentage	Rate	N	Percentage	Rate
Homicide	55	.36	4.2	14	.14	1.4
Rape	101	.66	7.7	44	.43	4.4
Robbery	1290	8.46	98.0	193	1.89	19.4
Aggravated assault	561	3.68	42.6	220	2.15	22.1
Burglary	1673	10.97	127.1	642	6.29	64.6
Larceny	1671	10.96	127.0	1189	11.64	119.6
Auto theft	640	4.20	48.6	426	4.17	42.8
Simple assault	698	4.58	53.0	537	5.26	54.0
Arson	42	.28	3.2	—	—	—
Forgery	3	.02	0.2	5	.05	.5
Fraud	6	.04	0.5	4	.04	.4
Stolen property	69	.45	5.2	30	.29	3.0
Vandalism	813	5.33	61.8	—	—	—
Weapons	457	3.00	34.7	270	2.64	27.1
Prostitution	11	.07	0.8	3	.03	.5
Sex offense	66	.43	5.0	147	1.44	14.8
Drug offense	714	4.68	54.3	1	.01	.1
Gambling	8	.05	0.6	89	.87	8.9
Drunk driving	40	.26	3.0	—	—	—
Liquor laws	211	1.38	16.0	273	2.67	27.5
Drunkenness	166	1.09	12.6	219	2.14	22.0
Disorderliness	1837	12.05	139.6	1734	16.98	174.4
Vagrancy	35	.23	2.7	21	.21	2.1
Suspicious person	97	.64	7.4	1	.01	.1
Traffic	69	.45	5.2	41	.40	4.1
Hospital cases	1	.01	0.1	1	.01	.1
Investigations	42	.28	3.2	9	.09	.9
Disturbance	4	.03	0.3	1	.01	.1
Missing person	204	1.34	15.5	3	.03	.3
All others	3664	24.03	278.4	4097	40.11	412.0
Total offenses	15,248	100.0	1158.7	10,214	100.0	1027.0

The rate of the seven FBI index offenses is higher in the 1958 cohort than for Cohort I. With respect to specific serious offenses, the Cohort II offense rate is 3 times higher for homicide, 1.7 times higher for rape, 5 times higher for robbery, and 1.9 times higher for aggravated assault and burglary than the Cohort I offense rate. These data are in sharp contrast to rates for the relatively minor index crimes of larceny and auto theft for which the two cohorts have very nearly equal rates.

In fact, we show in Table 6.2 that when the offenses are grouped into UCR index and nonindex, and then the index offenses further classified into violent index and property index, all the index rates are higher in the 1958 cohort. The rate of UCR index crimes in Cohort II (455.2) is about 1.6 times higher than the rate in Cohort I (274.3). The discrepancy between the two cohorts rises to a ratio of 3.2:1 when a violent index rate is computed; in Cohort II the rate is 152.5 compared to 47.4 in Cohort I. The comparison for the property index rate shows that the 1958 delinquents committed these offenses at a rate of 302.7 per 1,000 subjects compared to 226.9 in the 1945 cohort. Only for the less serious nonindex offenses is the rate in Cohort I (752.7) higher than in Cohort II (703.4).

With respect to the other specific offense categories (see Table 6.1), the rates for the two cohorts are very similar. In some instances, the Cohort I rates are higher (e.g., sex offenses, liquor violations, simple assaults), while in other instances the Cohort II rates are higher (e.g., weapons and stolen property). In most cases the offense rates are quite close. The two exceptions to this are noteworthy. The rate of disorderly conduct in the 1945 cohort (174.4) is higher than the rate in Cohort II (139.6). The most glaring exception, however, is the drug offense rate. This offense was virtually nonexistent in Cohort I, with only one offense recorded for a rate of .1 per 1,000 subjects. Whereas in Cohort II the rate is 500 times more frequent (54.3 per 1,000), and there were 714 arrests recorded for drug crimes.

The incidence data for the two cohorts not only indicate considerable differences in the total offense rate and the various serious offense rates, but they also show a race effect that varies considerably and importantly between the two cohorts. In Tables 6.3 and 6.4 we see that for

TABLE 6.2
Number, Percentage, and Rate of UCR Offense Groups by Cohort

Offense group	1958 Total offenses			1945 Total offenses		
	N	Percentage	Rate	N	Percentage	Rate
UCR index	5991	39.3	455.2	2728	26.7	274.3
UCR nonindex	9257	60.7	703.4	7486	73.3	752.7
Total	15,248	100.0	1158.7	10,214	100.0	1027.0
UCR violent	2007	37.5	152.5	471	17.3	47.4
UCR property	3984	62.5	302.7	2257	82.7	226.9
Index total	5991	100.0	455.2	2728	100.0	274.3

TABLE 6.3

Number, Percentage, and Rate of Delinquent Offenses by Race and Cohort

| | 1958 Cohort | | | | | |
| | White | | | Nonwhite | | |
Offense	N	Percentage	Rate	N	Percentage	Rate
Homicide	4	.1	.6	51	.5	7.3
Rape	9	.2	1.4	92	.8	13.2
Robbery	80	2.1	12.9	1210	10.7	174.3
Aggravated assault	103	2.6	16.6	458	4.0	66.0
Burglary	412	10.5	66.3	1261	11.1	181.6
Larceny	367	9.4	59.0	1304	11.5	187.8
Auto theft	182	4.7	29.3	458	4.0	66.0
Simple assault	194	4.9	31.2	504	4.4	72.6
Arson	15	.4	2.4	27	.2	3.9
Forgery	—	—	—	3		.4
Fraud	2	.1	.3	4		.6
Stolen property	28	.7	4.5	41	.4	5.9
Vandalism	285	7.3	45.8	528	4.7	76.0
Weapons	62	1.6	10.0	95	3.5	56.9
Prostitution	3	.1	.5	8	.1	1.2
Sex offense	29	.7	4.7	37	.3	5.3
Drug offense	247	6.3	39.7	467	4.1	67.3
Gambling	1		.2	7	.1	1.0
Drunk driving	35	.9	5.6	5	.0	.7
Liquor laws	134	3.4	21.6	77	.7	11.1
Drunkenness	72	1.8	11.6	94	.8	13.5
Disorderliness	748	19.1	120.3	1089	9.6	156.8
Vagrancy	8	.2	1.3	27	.2	3.9
Suspicious person	24	.6	3.9	73	.6	10.5
Traffic	30	.8	4.8	39	.3	5.6
Hospital cases	1		.2	—	—	—
Investigations	9	.2	1.4	33	.3	4.8
Disturbance	1		.2	3		.4
Missing person	70	1.8	11.3	134	1.2	19.3
All others	753	19.3	121.1	2911	25.7	419.2
Total offenses	3908	100.0	628.7	11340	100.0	1633.1
	1945 Cohort					
	White			Nonwhite		
Offense	N	Percentage	Rate	N	Percentage	Rate
Homicide	—	—	—	14	.24	4.8
Rape	6	.13	.9	38	66	13.1
Robbery	20	.45	2.8	173	3.01	59.6
Aggravated assault	39	.87	5.5	181	3.14	62.4

TABLE 6.3 (continued)

| | 1945 Cohort | | | | | |
| | White | | | Nonwhite | | |
Offense	N	Percentage	Rate	N	Percentage	Rate
Burglary	248	5.56	35.2	394	6.84	135.8
Larceny	387	8.68	54.9	802	13.93	276.4
Auto theft	239	5.36	33.9	187	3.25	64.4
Simple assault	172	3.86	24.4	365	6.34	125.8
Arson	—	—	—	—	—	—
Forgery	1	.02	.1	4	.07	1.4
Fraud	3	.07	.4	1	.02	.3
Stolen property	7	.16	1.0	23	.40	7.9
Vandalism	—	—	—	—	—	—
Weapons	58	1.30	8.2	212	3.68	73.1
Prostitution	2	.04	.3	1	.02	.3
Sex offense	63	1.41	8.9	84	1.46	28.9
Drug offense	1	.02	.1	—	—	—
Gambling	40	.90	5.7	49	.85	16.9
Drunk driving	—	—	—	—	—	—
Liquor laws	165	3.70	23.4	108	1.88	37.2
Drunkenness	102	2.29	14.5	117	2.03	40.3
Disorderliness	883	19.81	125.4	851	14.78	293.2
Vagrancy	6	.13	.9	15	.26	5.2
Suspicious person	1	.02	.1	—	—	—
Traffic	29	.65	4.1	12	.21	4.1
Hospital cases	1	.02	.1	—	—	—
Investigations	9	.20	1.3	—	—	—
Disturbance	—	—	—	1	.02	.3
Missing person	2	.04	.3	1	.02	.3
All others	1974	44.28	280.3	2123	36.88	731.6
Total offenses	4458	100.0	633.0	5756	100.0	1983.5

Cohort I the overall nonwhite offense rate of 1,983.5 is 3 times that of the white rate (633.0). The disproportionate involvement of nonwhites expands to a factor of 4.6 times for the UCR index offense rate (NW = 615.8 vs. W = 133.6) and swells to a factor of 14.9 times for the UCR violent offense rate (NW = 139.6 vs. W = 9.4). For the property index rate, the comparison somewhat returns to the size of the overall discrepancy with the nonwhite rate (476.2) being 3.8 times higher than the white rate (124.2).

The Cohort II data reported in Tables 6.3 and 6.4 also show a race effect, but one that is much smaller across these rates. For total offenses

TABLE 6.4

Number, Percentage, and Rate of UCR Offense Groups by Race and Cohort

| | 1958 Cohort | | | | | |
| | White Total offenses | | | Nonwhite Total offenses | | |
Offense group	N	Percentage	Rate	N	Percentage	Rate
UCR index	1157	29.6	186.1	4834	42.6	696.2
UCR nonindex	2751	70.4	442.6	6506	57.4	936.9
Total	3908	100.0	628.7	11,340	100.0	1633.1
UCR violent	196	16.9	31.5	1811	37.5	260.8
UCR property	961	83.1	154.6	3023	62.5	435.3
Index total	1157	100.0	186.1	4834	100.0	696.2
	1945 Cohort					
	White Total offenses			Nonwhite Total offenses		
Offense group	N	Percentage	Rate	N	Percentage	Rate
UCR index	941	21.1	133.6	1787	31.1	615.8
UCR nonindex	3517	78.9	499.4	3969	68.9	1367.7
Total	4458	100.0	633.0	5756	100.0	1983.5
UCR violent	66	7.0	9.4	405	22.7	139.6
UCR property	875	93.0	124.2	1382	77.3	476.2
Index total	941	100.0	133.6	1787	100.0	615.8

the nonwhite rate (1,633.1) is about 2.6 times higher than the white rate (628.7), which indicates that nonwhites in 1958 committed offenses at a lower rate than their nonwhite counterparts in 1945, and, most important of all, that whites in 1958 committed overall offenses at a rate that is very nearly equal to their white counterparts in 1945 (628.7 vs. 633.0).

Similarly, the UCR index offense rate comparison shows a smaller difference (3.7) than was the case for Cohort I (4.6). The most dramatic instance of the closing of the racial disparity occurs for violent offenses. The Cohort II nonwhite violent offense rate (260.8) is only 5.8 times higher than the rate for whites (44.4), compared to the factor of 14.9 that was observed for the 1945 cohort. The reason for this narrowing of the races is quite evident. Although the Cohort II rates are higher than those in Cohort I, whites have shown the sharper increase between the two studies. That is, for violent offenses the nonwhite rate increased by 86%

(260.8 vs. 139.9), but the white rate increased more substantially, about 3.3 times (31.5 vs. 9.4).

Inspection of the serious offense specific rates (Table 6.3) provides additional evidence that the white rates have risen sharply. For whites, the rates in the 1958 versus the 1945 cohorts are .6 versus zero for homicide, 1.4 versus .9 for rape, 12.9 versus 2.8 for robbery, and 16.6 versus 5.5 for aggravated assault. The corresponding data for nonwhites (homicide, 7.3 vs. 4.8; rape, 13.2 vs. 13.1; robbery, 174.3 vs. 59.6; aggravated assault, 66.0 vs. 62.4) do not show the same sharp increase in rates between the cohorts.

Thus, the difference between nonwhites and whites in their rate of violent crimes for the 1945 versus the 1958 cohort is 48:1 versus 12:1 for homicide, 14.5:1 versus 9:1 for rape, 21:1 versus 13.5:1 for robbery, and 11.3:1 versus 3.9:1 for aggravated assault. It is clear that Cohort II juveniles are more violent than their Cohort I counterparts. But it is also very clear that whites in Cohort II show the more dramatic increase.

Another way of looking at the incidence of delinquent events in the cohorts is to group offenses according to classification schemes and to show the mean level of delinquency for these categories. Table 6.5 thus reports the offense data in terms of both the UCR classification scheme and in terms of the severity index developed by Sellin and Wolfgang (1964) that we discussed in Chapter 3. The Sellin-Wolfgang measurement scheme ignores the legal labels attached to criminal events and classifies the offense according to the presence of injury, theft, damage, or some combination of these effects. An event that does not involve any of these components is scored as a nonindex event.

The data in Table 6.5 for Cohort I show that UCR index offenses represent about 27% (2,728/10,214) of all offenses recorded for the cohort. Index offenses were committed with an average of 2.01 offenses per index offender compared to a mean of 2.93 for total offenses. These index offenses may be partitioned into approximately 10% violent, 7% robberies, 24% burglaries, and 60% thefts. By comparison, the Sellin-Wolfgang system finds that almost 37% of the delinquencies can be classified as index owing to the presence of at least one of the scoring components. Further, the Sellin-Wolfgang system also finds a much higher proportion of violent (i.e., injury) offenses than does the UCR scheme (23% vs. 10%).

For offenders in Cohort II, the data given in Table 6.5 clearly indicate that the delinquencies of this group are of a more serious nature than those of the earlier cohort. Compared to the 1945 cohort, the UCR index offenses in Cohort II make up a larger share (39% vs. 27%) of the total offenses, involve a larger share (55% vs. 39%) of the delinquents,

TABLE 6.5
*Number of Offenders and Offenses and Mean Number of Offenses
for Select Crimes by Cohort*

	1958 Cohort			1945 Cohort		
	Offender	Offenses	Mean	Offender	Offenses	Mean
All offenses	4315	15,248	3.53	3475	10,214	2.93
Homicide, rape, and ag-gravated assault	564	717	1.27	231	278	1.20
Robbery	791	1290	1.63	155	193	1.24
Burglary	990	1673	1.69	446	642	1.43
Larceny and vehicle theft	1374	2311	1.68	991	1615	1.62
UCR index	2354	5991	2.55	1357	2728	2.01
UCR nonindex	3671	9357	2.52	3159	7486	2.36
S-W injury	881	1220	1.38	664	878	1.32
S-W theft	1445	2525	1.75	1009	1649	1.63
S-W damage	1053	1492	1.42	437	485	1.10
S-W combination	997	1623	1.63	530	801	1.51
S-W nonindex	3468	8389	2.42	2919	6401	2.19

and were committed with a greater mean (2.55 vs. 2.01). In addition, the Cohort II index offenses contain proportionately fewer theft offenses (38% vs. 60%) and proportionately more violent and robbery offenses (33% vs. 17%). With respect to the Sellin-Wolfgang classifications, over 45% of the Cohort II events were classified as involving injury, theft, damage, or combinations of these, compared to 37% in Cohort I. Moreover, all of the offense classifications given in the table were committed a greater average number of times in Cohort II than in Cohort I. Thus, regardless of which offense grouping one chooses for comparison, the data show the more recent cohort to be more delinquent and more seriously so than the earlier group.

Following the offense rate differences by race reported previously for the 1945 cohort, it is not unexpected that nonwhite offenses would be more likely to be classified as index offenses than those of whites (31% vs. 21%) and 3 times the proportion of violent/robbery index events (22% vs. 7%). The data in Table 6.6 for the 1958 cohort show a race effect as well. UCR index crimes constitute a greater share of offenses for nonwhites (42%) compared to whites (30%). Yet, the discrepancy for violent/robbery offenses for Cohort II is smaller than was the case for Cohort I. In the later cohort, nonwhite index events are about twice as likely to involve violence compared to the factor of 3 obtained

TABLE 6.6
Number of Offenders and Offenses and Mean Number of Offenses
for Select Crimes by Race and Cohort

| | 1958 Cohort | | | | | |
| | White | | | Nonwhite | | |
	Offender	Offenses	Mean	Offender	Offenses	Mean
All offenses	1412	3908	2.77	2903	11,340	3.91
Homicide, rape, and aggravated assault	104	116	1.12	460	601	1.31
Robbery	67	80	1.19	724	1210	1.67
Burglary	242	412	1.70	748	1261	1.69
Larceny and vehicle theft	351	549	1.56	1023	1762	1.72
UCR index	551	1157	2.10	1803	4834	2.68
UCR nonindex	1236	2751	2.23	2435	6506	2.67
S-W injury	193	239	1.24	688	981	1.43
S-W theft	311	463	1.49	1134	2061	1.82
S-W damage	322	448	1.39	731	1044	1.43
S-W combination	222	341	1.54	775	1282	1.65
S-W nonindex	1143	2417	2.11	2325	5972	2.57

| | 1945 Cohort | | | | | |
| | White | | | Nonwhite | | |
	Offender	Offenses	Mean	Offender	Offenses	Mean
All offenses	2019	4458	2.20	1456	5756	3.95
Homicide, rape, and aggravated assault	42	46	1.09	189	232	1.22
Robbery	18	20	1.11	137	173	1.26
Burglary	173	247	1.42	273	395	1.44
Larceny and vehicle theft	444	628	1.41	547	987	1.80
UCR index	580	941	1.62	777	1787	2.29
UCR nonindex	1850	3517	1.90	1309	3969	3.03
S-W injury	230	262	1.13	434	616	1.41
S-W theft	459	668	1.45	550	981	1.78
S-W damage	223	244	1.09	214	241	1.12
S-W combination	180	229	1.27	350	572	1.63
S-W nonindex	1697	3055	1.80	1222	3346	2.74

with the 1945 data. Further, inspection of the mean number of offenses shows that the nonwhite/white differences in the 1958 cohort are less substantial than the results for the 1945 cohort.

Table 6.7 reports the serious offense (i.e., assaults, property, and robberies) data by race, SES, and the one-time versus recidivist dicho-

TABLE 6.7

Number, Percentage, and Rate of Assault, Property, and Robbery Offenses by SES, Race, and Cohort

1958 Cohort

	Assaults			Property			Robbery		
	N	Percentage	Rate	N	Percentage	Rate	N	Percentage	Rate
NW both SES									
One-time	100	23.8	14.4	249	59.3	35.8	71	16.9	10.2
Recidivists	1005	20.4	144.7	2774	56.4	399.5	1139	23.2	164.0
All	1105	20.7	159.1	3023	56.6	435.3	1210	22.7	174.2
W both SES									
One-time	38	21.6	6.1	133	75.6	21.4	5	2.8	0.8
Recidivists	272	23.2	43.8	828	70.5	133.2	75	6.4	12.1
All	310	22.9	49.9	961	71.1	154.6	80	5.9	12.9
Low SES both races									
One-time	87	23.6	13.6	220	59.8	34.3	61	16.6	9.5
Recidivists	918	20.2	143.1	2606	57.3	406.3	1025	22.5	159.8
All	1005	20.4	156.7	2826	57.5	440.6	1086	22.1	169.3
High SES both races									
One-time	51	22.4	7.6	162	71.1	24.0	15	6.6	2.2
Recidivists	359	23.3	53.2	996	64.5	147.6	189	12.2	28.0
All	410	23.1	60.8	1158	65.4	171.7	204	11.5	30.2
Low SES NW									
One-time	75	23.2	14.7	190	58.8	37.3	58	17.9	11.4
Recidivists	816	20.1	160.1	2263	55.7	444.1	985	24.3	193.3
All	891	20.3	174.8	2453	55.9	481.4	1043	23.8	204.7

	Assaults			Property			Robbery		
	N	Percentage	Rate	N	Percentage	Rate	N	Percentage	Rate
Low SES W									
One-time	12	26.7	9.1	30	66.7	22.8	3	6.7	2.3
Recidivists	102	21.0	77.4	343	70.7	260.2	40	8.3	30.3
All	114	21.5	86.5	373	70.4	283.0	43	8.1	32.6
High SES NW									
One-time	25	25.8	13.5	59	60.8	31.9	13	13.4	7.0
Recidivists	189	22.1	102.3	511	59.8	276.5	154	18.0	83.3
All	214	22.5	115.8	570	59.9	308.4	167	17.5	90.0
High SES W									
One-time	26	19.9	5.3	103	78.6	21.0	2	1.5	0.4
Recidivists	170	24.6	34.7	485	70.3	99.0	35	5.1	7.1
All	196	23.8	40.0	588	71.6	120.0	37	4.5	7.5

1945 Cohort

	Assaults			Property			Robbery		
	N	Percentage	Rate	N	Percentage	Rate	N	Percentage	Rate
NW both SES									
One-time	40	27.9	13.8	97	67.8	33.4	6	4.2	2.1
Recidivists	558	27.8	192.3	1286	63.9	443.4	167	8.3	57.6
All	598	27.8	206.1	1383	64.2	476.8	173	8.0	59.7
W both SES									
One-time	49	26.2	7.0	134	71.7	19.0	4	2.1	0.6
Recidivists	168	18.2	23.9	740	80.1	105.1	16	1.7	2.3
All	217	19.5	30.9	874	78.7	124.1	20	1.8	2.9
Low SES both races									
One-time	59	29.2	12.9	138	68.3	30.1	5	2.5	1.1
Recidivists	594	25.7	129.6	1559	67.5	340.1	157	6.8	34.2
All	653	26.0	142.4	1697	67.5	370.2	162	6.5	35.3
High SES both races									
One-time	30	23.4	5.6	93	72.7	17.3	5	3.9	0.9

(continued)

TABLE 6.7 (continued)

1945 Cohort

	Assaults			Property			Robbery		
	N	Percentage	Rate	N	Percentage	Rate	N	Percentage	Rate
Recidivists	132	21.1	24.6	467	74.7	87.1	26	4.2	4.8
All	162	21.5	30.2	560	74.4	104.5	31	4.1	5.7
Low SES NW									
One-time	35	28.7	14.3	84	68.9	34.3	3	2.5	1.2
Recidivists	509	27.7	208.3	1180	64.2	482.8	150	8.2	61.4
All	544	27.7	222.6	1264	64.5	517.2	153	7.8	62.6
Low SES W									
One-time	24	30.0	11.2	54	67.5	25.2	2	2.5	0.9
Recidivists	85	18.1	39.7	379	80.5	177.1	7	1.5	3.3
All	109	19.8	50.9	433	78.6	202.3	9	1.6	4.2
High SES NW									
One-time	5	23.8	10.9	13	61.9	28.4	3	14.3	6.6
Recidivists	49	28.5	107.0	106	61.6	231.4	17	9.9	37.1
All	54	27.9	117.9	119	61.7	259.8	20	10.4	43.7
High SES W									
One-time	25	23.4	5.1	80	74.8	16.3	2	1.9	0.4
Recidivists	83	18.3	16.9	361	79.7	73.6	9	1.9	1.8
All	108	19.3	22.0	441	78.8	89.9	11	1.9	2.2

tomy. The assault category includes homicide, rape, aggravated assault, and simple assault. The property offense category includes burglary, larceny, and auto theft. Robbery has been retained as a separate category because it can be a violent offense against the person and/or just a property-type offense.

The race comparisons are displayed in the first panel of Table 6.7. These data indicate that Cohort II nonwhites had rates of offense 3.2 times higher for assaults, 2.8 times higher for property crimes, and 13.5 times higher for robbery than those of Cohort II whites. In Cohort I, the rate comparisons for nonwhites versus whites were greater, showing factors of 6.7 for assaults, 3.8 for property crimes, and 20.6 for robberies.

When we consider delinquency status, we find that nonwhites predominate over whites by the following factors in the 1958 cohort: *one-time*—assaults, 2.4, property, 1.7, and robbery, 12.8; *recidivist*—assaults, 3.3, property, 2.9, and robbery, 13.5. For the 1945 cohort we found that nonwhites predominated over whites by the following factors: *one-time*—assaults, 1.9, property, 1.8, and robbery, 3.5; *recidivist*—assaults, 8.0, property, 4.2, and robbery, 25.0. These data thus show that 1958 nonwhite rates are higher than corresponding white rates by much larger margins among recidivists than among one-time offenders. Further, these margins among recidivists are not nearly so high as the corresponding scores in the 1945 cohort. Again, therefore, our data indicate that whites, especially recidivists, have closed the gap between themselves and their nonwhite counterparts that existed in Cohort I.

The SES comparisons are shown in the second panel of the table. Table 6.7 shows for Cohort I that the ratio of the low-SES rate to the high-SES rate is 4.7 for assaults, 3.5 for property offenses, and 6.0 for robbery. The one-time versus recidivist effect observed above for race holds for SES as well. The Cohort II data shown in Table 6.7 repeat the race finding we have just observed above. That is, SES is related to delinquency in the 1958 study, but the difference between the low and high levels of SES is smaller in magnitude than what was observed in the 1945 cohort. The total rate of serious delinquency is 3 times higher for low SES compared to high SES, or a reduction of 25% from the difference in Cohort I. For specific serious offense rates, the ratios of 4.7 and 3.5 for assaults and property offenses in Cohort I are reduced to a factor of 2.5 in Cohort II. The rates for robbery, however, are different by SES by about the same factor. Low-SES subjects in the 1958 cohort have a robbery rate (169.3) that is about 5.6 times higher than the rate for high-SES subjects (30.2). The difference in Cohort I was a factor of 6.

The results for the race-SES combinations shown in panels three and four of Table 6.7 demonstrate that the main effects of race and SES are not spurious and appear to be additive. The effect of race is stronger than that for SES regardless of cohort. Again, however, the race effect in Cohort I is stronger than that in Cohort II. For serious offenses taken together, Cohort I low-SES nonwhites show a rate that is 3 times higher than low-SES whites, while the Cohort II difference is less, about 2 times. Similarly, the high-SES comparisons show that in Cohort I the total serious offense rate for nonwhites (421.4) is over 3.5 times that for whites (114.2), but in Cohort II the nonwhite rate (514.5) is about 3 times higher than the white rate (167.5). The rates across the specific offense categories show the same nonwhite overinvolvement by a discrepancy which has narrowed substantially.

The last point to be raised here about the data is the difference between one-time offenders and recidivists. Although Table 6.7 does not report a separate panel for these categories overall, the data we analyzed do indicate that, without regard to race or SES, one-time offenders in the 1945 cohort have an exceedingly low rate for serious offenses. Their rate (33.2) is almost 9 times lower than that for recidivists (295.1). The 330 serious offenses committed by one-time offenders is but one-ninth of the total serious crime of recidivists (2,935). For Cohort II the data show that this disparity has widened. The serious offense rate for recidivists (462.9) is 10 times that of the one-time offenders (45.3). This comparison produces further ratios of 9:1 for assaults, 9.4:1 for property offenses, and 15:1 for robbery. The corresponding ratios for Cohort I were 8:1 for assaults, 8.7:1 for property offenses, and 9:1 for robbery. It is clear from these data that juveniles who commit only one offense are very rarely involved in the more serious kinds of offenses.

Severity of Delinquency

Because grouping offenses into categories only partially reflects the actual seriousness of the events, we have scored the events by weighting the components according to the system developed by Sellin and Wolfgang (see Table 4.3). By summing the weights across all the components we can arrive at a quantitative measure of offense severity. Table 6.8 reports the distribution of offenses by certain ranges of severity.

It should be noted here at the outset of our severity discussion that we have avoided direct comparisons between the two cohorts in terms of weighted rates because the Cohort II seriousness weights are higher than those used in the earlier cohort. Thus, it would be inappropriate to compare Cohort I to Cohort II, either overall or for the race and SES categories. It is appropriate, however, to compare within each cohort

TABLE 6.8

Offense Severity Scores by Race and Cohort

Offense severity	1958 Cohort White N	White Percentage	Nonwhite N	Nonwhite Percentage	1945 Cohort White N	White Percentage	Nonwhite N	Nonwhite Percentage
<100	696	17.8	2605	22.9	2985	66.9	3094	53.7
100–199	1286	32.9	2269	20.0	470	10.5	1046	18.2
200–299	329	8.4	851	7.5	566	12.7	771	13.4
300–399	178	4.6	476	4.2	221	4.9	384	6.7
400–499	136	3.5	396	3.5	133	2.9	234	4.1
500–599	91	2.3	259	2.3	25	.6	34	.6
600–699	112	2.9	477	4.2	14	.5	47	.8
700–799	115	2.9	509	4.5	15	.5	52	.9
800–899	142	3.6	529	4.7	3	.07	22	.4
900–999	138	3.5	454	4.0	1	.02	7	.1
1000–1999	628	16.1	2203	19.4	20	.5	46	.8
2000–2999	39	1.0	145	1.3	2	.04	18	.3
3000–3999	10	.26	73	.64	2	.04	1	.02
4000+	8	.20	94	.83	1	.02	—	—
Total	3908	100.0	11,340	100.0	4458	100.0	5756	100.0
Mean score		581.2		461.9		92.9		130.8
Weighted rate per 1,000 subjects		2903.8		9490.9		587.9		2594.4
Weighted rate per 1,000 delinquents		12,783.5		22,702.3		2052.8		5163.8

the various race and SES effects. Thus, we must limit ourselves to comparisons concerning the relative size of the race, SES, and offender dichotomy differences for each cohort.

Before proceeding with these comparisons it is useful to present a few scores that clearly indicate the effect of the two different scoring schemes used in the two cohorts. The best example that we can use concerns the differences between the distribution of seriousness scores. That is, the Cohort I data are more highly skewed to the lower end of the continuum compared to Cohort II. For example, 87% of Cohort I offenses fall into seriousness score categories below 300 which reflects the fact that the delinquents have committed primarily nonindex events. However, for Cohort II data, about 56% of the offenses fall below the 300 level. At the other end of the seriousness range, less than 1% of Cohort I offenses fall at or beyond the 1,000 level, compared to 20% for offenses in the 1958 birth cohort. Thus, we will restrict our analyses below to within-cohort comparisons only.

For Cohort I, the fact that offenses committed by whites are less serious than offenses committed by nonwhites is reflected in the fact that the proportion of whites in the categories represented under severity score 100 is larger (66.9% vs. 53.7%) than that of nonwhites. On the other hand, the proportion of nonwhites in each of the 13 score categories of 100 and above exceeds that of whites (save for one white delinquent with a score of 4,400).

The seriousness of Cohort II offenses exhibits a much more even distribution by race. For example, 22.9% of nonwhite events, compared to 17.8% of white events, fall below 100, while 20% of the former, compared to 33% of the latter, fall between 100 and 199. At or beyond 1,000, we find 17.6% of the white offenses compared to 22.1% of nonwhite offenses. Clearly, the race difference in offense severity is much less substantial than was the case in Cohort I.

Table 6.8 also reports the weighted offense rates derived from the offense severity scores. The weighted rate is computed by summing the seriousness scores across offenses, then dividing by the population of interest, and then multiplying by 1,000. We have computed weighted rates for the subject population and the delinquent subgroup for each race. These data attest once again to the closing of the race gap in delinquency between the two cohorts. In Cohort I, the nonwhite weighted rate per 1,000 subjects (2,594.4) is about 4.4 times as great as the weighted rate for white subjects (587.9). The weighted rates for the delinquent population show the nonwhite rate (5,163.8) to be about 2.5 times higher than the white rate (2,052.8). In the 1958 cohort, the subject-based weighted rates show a nonwhite (9,490.9) to white

(2,903.8) ratio of just over 3, while the delinquent-based rates show a difference between nonwhites (22,702.3) and whites (12,783.5) that is on the order of 1.7 times as great for the former. Thus, the race disparity has fallen from 4.4 to 3.3 for subject rates, and from 2.5 to 1.7 for delinquent subgroup rates in the second cohort.

Table 6.9 presents weighted rates by race, SES, and the one-time offender versus recidivist dichotomy. Consistent with previous findings, SES is related to weighted offense rates. Ignoring race and the offender dichotomy for the moment, we see for the 1945 cohort that the rate for low-SES subjects is 1,886.2 compared to a rate of 536.6 for high-SES subjects, or a difference of 3.5 times. For Cohort II we observe that

TABLE 6.9

Number, Mean Severity, and Weighted Rate of Offenses by SES,
Race, Delinquency Status, and Cohort

		1958 Cohort							
	One-time			Recidivists			Total		
	N	Mean	Rate	N	Mean	Rate	N	Mean	Rate
Low SES									
White	190	346.3	499.2	1241	506.7	4771.0	1431	485.4	5270.2
Nonwhite	805	470.6	743.4	8420	600.2	9914.0	9225	588.7	10657.4
All	995	446.8	693.2	9661	588.0	8857.1	1043	574.9	9550.3
High SES									
White	543	363.1	402.5	1934	472.2	1864.6	2477	448.3	2267.1
Nonwhite	266	466.8	671.9	1849	559.9	5602.5	2115	548.2	6374.4
All	809	397.2	476.3	3783	515.1	2888.6	4592	494.3	3364.9
				1945 Cohort					
	One-time			Recidivists			Total		
	N	Mean	Rate	N	Mean	Rate	N	Mean	Rate
Low SES									
White	372	90.4	157.1	1569	105.8	775.6	1941	102.8	932.7
Nonwhite	430	106.0	186.5	4760	130.1	2534.6	5190	128.1	2721.1
All	802	98.7	172.8	6329	124.1	1713.4	7131	121.3	1886.2
High SES									
White	738	60.4	90.9	1779	95.5	346.3	2517	85.2	437.3
Nonwhite	73	88.5	141.0	493	135.4	1457.5	566	129.4	1598.5
All	811	62.9	95.2	2272	104.1	441.3	3083	93.3	536.5

the low-SES rate (9,550.3) differs less from the high-SES rate (3,364.9), a factor of 2.8 compared to 3.5 for Cohort I.

As expected, the differences between one-time delinquents and recidivists in the weighted offense rates are pronounced regardless of SES and race. In the 1945 cohort the recidivist's rate is greater than that of the one-timer by a factor of 10 at the low-SES level and by a factor of almost 5 at the high-SES level. In the 1958 cohort the ratio of the recidivist's weighted rate to that of the one-time offender has increased. At the low-SES level the ratio is almost 13, while at the high-SES level the ratio is 6.

When we examine the race data across SES levels, we do not uncover any unexpected findings. Regardless of SES and offender status, the nonwhite rates in each cohort are higher than those of the white counterparts. As we have seen before, however, the race disparity is stronger in Cohort I than in Cohort II.

Table 6.10 presents the same tabular array as above for injury offenses. These data show pronounced differences by race, SES, and the offender dichotomy that are uniformly strong for both cohorts.

Nonwhites have significantly higher weighted injury offense rates. In Cohort I the nonwhite rate is 4 times higher among low-SES subjects and 5.5 times higher among high-SES subjects than the white rates. For the 1958 cohort the nonwhite-to-white ratio at the lower level of SES is 3:1, and at the higher level of SES the ratio is 4.2:1. The data by SES show a distinct low-SES effect regardless of race. Overall, low-SES subjects have an injury offense rate that is 4 times higher in Cohort I and 3.2 times higher in Cohort II than do high-SES subjects. It is also not surprising that recidivists show weighted injury offense rates that are considerably higher than their one-time delinquent counterparts. This result is obtained for both race and SES categories. For example, the recidivist rate (494.4) is 14 times higher than the one-timer rate (33.6) in Cohort I, and the former (1,226.7) is 11.5 times as great as the latter (106.0) in Cohort II at the lower-SES level. The results are similar at the high-SES level for both cohorts as well.

Because injury offenses can involve a range of different levels of injury, we have reported in Table 6.11 the four levels of injury to the victim by race for the two cohorts. It is quite evident from these data that the Cohort II injury offenses involve more serious amounts of harm than do the Cohort I offenses, regardless of the difference in scoring weights alluded to earlier. Minor harm accounts for 58% of the 1958 injury offenses but 71% of the 1945 injury offenses. Seven percent more treated and discharged cases occurred in Cohort II (28%) compared to Cohort I (21%). At the two highest levels of injury, there are almost twice as

TABLE 6.10

Number, Mean Severity, and Weighted Rate of Injury Offenses by SES, Race, Delinquency Status, and Cohort

	1958 Cohort								
	One-time			Recidivists			Total		
	N	Mean	Rate	N	Mean	Rate	N	Mean	Rate
Low SES									
White	10	650.0	49.3	96	642.4	467.9	106	643.1	517.2
Nonwhite	79	778.5	120.7	1137	637.8	1423.0	1216	646.9	1543.7
All	89	764.1	106.0	1233	638.1	1226.7	1322	646.6	1322.7
High SES									
White	30	505.0	30.9	144	628.6	184.8	174	607.3	215.7
Nonwhite	26	537.3	75.6	225	693.2	843.9	251	677.0	919.5
All	56	520.0	43.2	369	667.9	365.4	425	648.5	408.6

	1945 Cohort								
	One-time			Recidivists			Total		
	N	Mean	Rate	N	Mean	Rate	N	Mean	Rate
Low SES									
White	29	234.5	31.8	155	233.9	169.4	184	233.9	201.2
Nonwhite	41	209.8	35.2	787	241.9	779.0	828	240.3	814.2
All	70	220.0	33.6	942	240.6	494.4	1012	239.2	528.0
High SES									
White	39	184.6	14.7	233	151.5	72.0	272	156.3	86.7
Nonwhite	8	100.0	17.5	96	222.9	467.3	104	213.5	484.7
All	47	170.2	14.9	329	172.3	105.8	376	172.1	120.7

many hospitalizations and nearly 3 times as many deaths in the proportions of these events in Cohort II compared to Cohort I.

The offense-level data show a pronounced race effect for both cohorts. There is very little difference between the races (especially in Cohort II) in terms of the relative proportions of the various levels, but the weighted rates are quite different. In Cohort II the ratio of the nonwhite rate to the white rate is 10 times higher for deaths, 6 times higher for hospitalizations, almost 4 times higher for treated and discharged, and 4.5 times higher for minor harm. The rate comparisons for Cohort I are very similar. The ratio difference for nonwhites over whites is 6.5 times for hospitalization, 6.2 times for treated and discharged, and 4.4

TABLE 6.11
Number, Percentage, and Weighted Rate of Injury Offense Types by SES, Race, Delinquency Status, and Cohort

1958 Cohort

	White			Nonwhite			Total		
	N	Percentage	Rate	N	Percentage	Rate	N	Percentage	Rate
Death	4	1.4	23.0	46	3.1	244.6	50	2.9	139.9
Hospitalized	21	7.5	54.9	164	11.2	334.8	185	10.6	202.6
Treated and discharged	91	32.5	155.9	400	27.3	591.2	491	28.1	385.6
Minor harm	164	58.6	45.8	857	58.4	206.9	1021	58.4	130.9
Total	280	100.0	279.6	1467	100.0	1377.5	1747	100.0	859.0
(Unknown)	(43)			(188)			(231)		
Grand total	323			1655			1978		
Mean severity		620.8			652.1			647.1	

1945 Cohort

	White			Nonwhite			Total		
	N	Percentage	Rate	N	Percentage	Rate	N	Percentage	Rate
Death	0	—	—	14	3.1	125.4	14	1.0	36.6
Hospitalized	22	4.8	21.9	59	11.2	142.3	81	5.8	57.0
Treated and discharged	84	18.4	47.7	217	27.3	299.1	301	21.6	121.1
Minor harm	350	76.8	49.7	645	58.4	222.3	995	71.5	100.0
Total	456	100.0	119.3	935	100.0	789.1	1391	100.0	314.7
(Unknown)	(11)			(64)			(75)		
Grand total	467			999			1466		
Mean severity		184.2			244.9			225.0	

TABLE 6.12
Dollar Loss in Theft Offenses by Race and Cohort

Offense severity	1958 Cohort White N	White Percentage	Nonwhite N	Nonwhite Percentage	1945 Cohort White N	White Percentage	Nonwhite N	Nonwhite Percentage
<10	96	16.9	646	25.2	236	31.2	599	49.5
10–25	97	17.2	553	21.5	126	16.7	185	15.3
26–49	58	10.3	266	10.4	51	6.8	87	7.2
50–99	94	16.6	372	14.5	60	7.9	87	7.2
100–250	120	21.2	425	16.5	85	11.2	91	7.5
251–499	38	6.7	145	5.6	25	3.3	27	2.2
500–999	26	4.6	82	3.2	59	7.8	39	3.2
1000–1999	13	2.3	42	1.6	46	6.1	46	3.8
2000–2999	11	1.9	16	.62	35	4.6	28	2.3
3000–3999	1	.18	7	.27	25	3.3	14	1.2
4000–4999	2	.35	4	.16	4	.53	5	.41
5000+	9	1.6	11	.42	4	.53	3	.25
Total	565	100.0	2569	100.0	756	100.0	1211	100.0
(Unknown)	(80)		(391)		(131)		(303)	
Grand total	645		2960		887		1514	
Median loss	50		32		33		10	
Weighted rate per 1,000 subjects	351.8		610.1		214.7		834.6	

TABLE 6.13
Dollar Loss in Damage Offenses by Race and Cohort

Offense severity	1958 Cohort				1945 Cohort			
	White		Nonwhite		White		Nonwhite	
	N	Percentage	N	Percentage	N	Percentage	N	Percentage
<10	12	1.8	46	25.2	151	31.2	280	47.2
10–25	290	43.4	795	21.5	102	16.7	173	29.2
26–49	24	3.6	79	10.4	21	6.8	37	6.2
50–99	201	30.0	355	14.5	30	7.9	38	6.4
100–250	63	9.4	152	16.5	43	11.2	46	7.8
251–499	31	4.6	54	5.6	4	3.3	6	1.0
500–999	26	3.9	35	3.2	6	7.8	5	.84
1000–1999	9	1.4	11	1.6	4	6.1	5	.84
2000–2999	3	.45	12	.62	—	—	1	.17
3000–3999	—	—	2	.27	—	—	—	—
4000–4999	1	.15	—	.16	—	—	—	—
5000+	9	1.4	11	.42	4	.53	2	.34
Total	699	100.0	1552	100.0	365	100.0	593	100.0
(Unknown)	(124)		(426)		(91)		(120)	
Grand total	823		1978		456		713	
Median loss	50		25		15		11	
Weighted rate per 1,000 subjects	523.0		464.9		103.6		408.7	

times for minor harm. The homicide rate for nonwhites (125.4) compares to a rate of 0.0 for whites. Thus, for both cohorts race is related to the level of injury incurred by the victim in injury offenses.

Theft and damage offenses represent the two other major types of index offenses. For these events the seriousness score is primarily a function of the dollar value of theft or damage. Thus we have broken down the theft and damage events by the amount of loss and race. These data are found in Table 6.12 for theft offenses and Table 6.13 for damage offenses.

In Cohort I about 40% of the theft offenses involved amounts less than $10. This figure has fallen to about 23% in Cohort II. Similarly, the overall median dollar loss is twice as high in Cohort II ($40) as in Cohort I ($17). By race the data are similar across cohorts. In Cohort II a smaller percentage of white events than nonwhite events involve amounts less than $10 (17% vs. 25%). Although nonwhites have committed over 4 times as many thefts, the white events involve a larger amount stolen than do nonwhite thefts (the median dollar value is $50 for whites and $32 for nonwhites). In Cohort I nonwhites have committed 1.6 times as many thefts, but whites have a median dollar loss ($34) which is 3 times greater than the nonwhite median ($11). Like Cohort II, nonwhite thefts in Cohort I are more concentrated in the less than $10 range than is the case for whites (49% vs. 31%).

The damage offense data given in Table 6.13 show similar results to those for theft. Nonwhites have committed more damage offenses than whites. In Cohort I the weighted rate for nonwhites (408.7) is about 4 times greater than the white rate (103.6), while in Cohort II the weighted rate for whites is 1.1 times greater than that for nonwhites. The difference in median dollar loss between whites ($50) and nonwhites ($25) shows that whites commit more serious damage offenses. As for the cohorts themselves, damage offenses are twice as frequent and involve twice as much dollar loss in Cohort II compared to Cohort I.

The incidence and seriousness data reported above show distinct differences between the cohorts and within the cohorts for various factors. First, the data show that the Cohort II offense rate for total offenses, index offenses, and violent index offenses is higher than the rate in Cohort I. The two cohorts were only similar for relatively minor offenses. Second, in terms of the race and SES effects, both cohorts show differences between low and high SES and between nonwhites and whites. However, the data also show that the effects are generally stronger in Cohort I than in Cohort II.

The Chronic Juvenile Offender

One of the most significant findings to emerge from criminological re-search over the past decade concerns the increasing evidence that a few chronic, or habitual, offenders commit a disproportionate share of crime, particularly serious crime. To be sure, criminology has always taken an interest in recidivists and repeated criminality, but until the recent past, the body of research evidence lagged far behind the the-oretical formulations. As we noted in Chapter 3, empirical evidence has been accumulating which documents the disproportionately small size of the chronic delinquent population and their overinvolvement in crime.

For example, a study of arrest data in the District of Columbia, conducted by INSLAW (1977, 1979), showed that only 7% of the defen-dants were arrested at least four times, 4% were arrested at least five times, and these two groups were responsible for 24% and 16% of the total arrests, respectively. Similarly, the results of Shannon's (1980, 1988) cohort research reveal that a small number of persons was respon-sible for a disproportionately large share of the police contacts. In his two cohorts, 7% of the subjects committed about 50% of the offenses. Hamparian et al. (1978) have also reported that chronic offending in a cohort of offenders arrested at least once for a violent offense was re-stricted to 31% of the offenders. Farrington (1981) has reported findings which show that the magnitude of chronicity in cohorts is cross-culturally replicated. In his continuing Cambridge Study in Delinquent Development, Farrington has found that up to age 24, the chronic offenders constitute just 6% of the sample and 17% of the convicted youths, yet they were responsible for one-half of the convictions.

The apparent consistency of the findings concerning chronic offenders has suggested to some the need for a selective focus or appli-cation of criminal justice resources on the arrest, prosecution, and incar-ceration of the high-rate offenders (see, for example, Moore et al., 1983). It is not altogether clear that, just because chronic or high-rate offenders exist or because they are responsible for such a disproportionate share of delinquency or crime, the appropriate response is to arrest, prosecute, and punish these offenders selectively. There are a number of problematic issues concerning the so-called selective incapacitation approach and/or the just-desserts model of punishment. We raise this selective focus issue mainly to point out the extent to which the problem of chronic offending commands the attention of the discipline and the criminal justice community.

We acknowledge that the relative size of the chronic offender population and its share of delinquency or crime are very important questions for both research and policy. However, we maintain that several other issues must be addressed in addition to the question of the skewness of rates of offending. These issues concern two major topics.

First, what is the relationship between a record of chronic delinquency and the probability of ever committing an adult crime? This assessment necessarily entails focusing on the transition from the status of delinquent to that of adult criminal with emphasis on the predictive effects of such delinquency-related facts as age-at-onset, offense rates, the timing of offenses in the juvenile years (i.e., early, late, or continuous), offense specialization, and offense severity and severity escalation.

Second, this issue raises a more fundamental question, because if chronic adult offenders are drawn disproportionately from the ranks of juvenile offenders, then it is necessary to learn whether the chronic juveniles so recruited are different (in respects other than just their chronic rates of delinquency) from their delinquent counterparts who do not commit adult crime or do so infrequently.

We mention these issues, on the one hand, to point out the context of our analyses below. We are devoting a separate chapter to chronic delinquents because these individuals are an important research focus. The chronic offender was associated with a crucial set of findings in Cohort I. As we discuss below, the same is true in the 1958 cohort. However, we also point out these related chronic offender issues, not because we can address them here, but instead, because we wish to lay the foundation for our subsequent work with the 1958 birth cohort as we follow it through the important transition of juvenile delinquency to adult crime in our later work with this cohort.

Chronicity and Frequency of Delinquency

Thus far, we have examined data relative to the prevalence and the incidence of delinquency in the two birth cohorts. Although useful in many respects, the prevalence and incidence data reported above do not allow a precise comparison of the delinquent behavior across the categories of delinquency status. That is, comparing just the proportions of delinquents ignores the important factor of the quantity of the delinquent behavior. Similarly, relying solely on the incidence and seriousness of the offenses obscures the issue of how many delinquents are responsible for the violations of the groups. In order to remedy this problem, we report in this chapter the offense data as a function of the various delinquency status types—one-time, nonchronic recidivists, and chronic recidivists.

Table 7.1 shows that of the 3,475 delinquents in the 1945 birth cohort, 46.4% were arrested only once before their eighteenth birthdays and slightly more than half, 53.6%, could be classified as recidivists. Moreover, the recidivists can be further broken down into nonchronic and chronic offenders. The nonchronic recidivists numbered 1,235 and constituted 35.6% of the delinquents and 12.4% of the entire cohort. On the other hand, the chronic recidivists, who had been arrested at least five times, numbered 627, accounting for 18% of the delinquents and 6% of the entire cohort.

In terms of offenses, however, the chronic offenders committed a far greater share than their distribution in the cohort would suggest. Although accounting for only 6% of the cohort subjects and 18% of the delinquents, the chronic offenders were responsible for a total of 5,305, or 52%, of all police contacts in the cohort. Further, the chronic offenders constituted about one-third of the recidivist subset but committed over 60% of the offenses attributable to the recidivists.

Table 7.1 shows that the concentration of chronic delinquents increased slightly in the 1958 cohort compared to the earlier study. Chronic delinquency in the second cohort involves 7.5% of the cohort subjects compared to 6.3% in the earlier study. Similarly, the proportion of chronic offenders has increased among delinquents (23%) and among the recidivist subset (39%) compared to 18% and 33%, respectively, in the 1945 study.

The chronic offender share of the delinquent behavior of the 1958 cohort is quite pronounced. The 982 chronic recidivists were responsible for 9,240 offenses, or 61% of the total offenses, and these 9,240 offenses represent 69% of the offenses (13,444) committed by the recidivist subset. These percentages represent an increase of 10% over the figures obtained for the 1945 data.

In order to illustrate the race effects reported previously for prevalence and incidence, we have displayed the offender and offense data by race in Table 7.2. The findings for Cohort I indicate that the chronic offender effect is contingent on race, and this is a very important find-

TABLE 7.1

Number and Percentage of Offenders and Offenses by Delinquency Status and Cohort[a]

	1958 Cohort				1945 Cohort			
	Offenders		Offenses		Offenders		Offenses	
	Number	Percentage	Number	Percentage	Number	Percentage	Number	Percentage
Delinquents	4315		15,248		3475		10,214	
One-time	1804	41.8	1804	11.8	1613	46.4	1613	15.8
Two to four time recid.	1529	35.4	4204	27.6	1235	35.6	3296	32.3
Five or more time recid.	982	22.8	9240	60.6	627	18.0	5305	51.9
Recidivists	2511		13,444		1862		8601	
Two to four time recid.	1529	60.9	4204	31.3	1235	66.3	3296	38.3
Five or more time recid.	982	39.1	9240	68.7	627	33.7	5305	61.7

[a]Percentages are column percents of the total number of delinquents and then the total number of recidivists.

TABLE 7.2

Number and Percentage of Offenders and Offenses by Delinquency Status, Race, and Cohort

1958 Cohort

	White				Nonwhite			
	Offenders		Offenses		Offenders		Offenses	
	Number	Percentage	Number	Percentage	Number	Percentage	Number	Percentage
Delinquents	1412		3908		2903		11,340	
One-time	733	51.9	733	18.8	1071	36.9	1071	9.4
Two or four time recid.	470	33.3	1260	32.2	1059	36.5	2944	26.0
Five or more time recid.	209	14.8	1915	49.0	773	26.6	7325	64.6
Recidivists	679		3175		1832		10,269	
Two or four time recid.	470	69.2	1260	39.7	1059	57.8	2944	28.7
Five or more time recid.	209	30.8	1915	60.3	773	42.8	7325	71.3

(continued)

TABLE 7.2 (continued)

1945 Cohort

	White				Nonwhite			
	Offenders		Offenses		Offenders		Offenses	
	Number	Percentage	Number	Percentage	Number	Percentage	Number	Percentage
Delinquents	2019		4458		1456		5756	
One-time	1110	54.9	1110	24.9	503	34.5	503	8.7
Two to four time recid.	699	34.6	1817	40.7	536	36.8	1479	25.7
Five or more time recid.	210	10.4	1531	34.3	417	28.6	3774	65.6
Recidivists	909		3348		953		5253	
Two to four time recid.	699	76.9	1817	54.3	536	56.2	1479	28.1
Five or more time recid.	210	23.1	1531	45.7	417	43.8	3774	71.8

[a]Percentages are column percents of the total number of delinquents and then the total number of recidivists.

ing. That is, although the recidivists account for the majority of offenses for both races (75% for whites and 91% for nonwhites), the white chronic offenders account for only 34% of the offenses by white delinquents as a whole, and 45% of the offenses of the white recidivist subset, compared to 65% and 72% for nonwhite chronic delinquents. Thus, the chronic offender effect in Cohort I is mostly a function of the nonwhite males who fall in the five-or-more offenses group.

The data given in Table 7.2 for the 1958 cohort indicate roughly the same disproportionate share of delinquent behavior for chronic delinquents among recidivists as in Cohort I for whites (81%) and nonwhites (90%). But the Cohort II data also indicate that the chronic offender effect is maintained for both races, although it is more dramatic for nonwhites. Thus, among whites, the chronic offenders account for about 49% of all offenses and 60% of recidivist offenses; for nonwhites, the chronic delinquents were responsible for a more appreciable share of overall delinquency (65%) and the vast majority of recidivist delinquency (71%).

Once again, therefore, the current cohort does not exhibit the same degree of race differences that characterized the earlier study. To be sure, there are race effects, but white offenders have drawn closer to their nonwhite counterparts. In fact, the data clearly point out that in Cohort II, the chronic offender effect holds for whites and nonwhites, while in Cohort I, it holds only for nonwhites.

Similar to the case of race, the SES comparison for chronic delinquents holds only for one level of SES (low) in the 1945 cohort but appears for both levels in the 1958 cohort. For Cohort I, Table 7.3 shows that the chronic delinquent constitutes the usual small percentage of the total delinquent group (23% for low SES and 10% for high SES). However, only for the low-SES level does the chronic offender account for a disproportionate share of the total offenses (60%); at the higher level of SES only 35% of the offenses can be assigned to this category of offender.

On the other hand, Cohort II data given in Table 7.3 reveal that the chronic delinquent holds a minority position among offenders (26% for low SES and 16% for high SES) and yet commits a disproportionate share of the offenses of his particular SES group (65% for low SES and 51% for high SES). Using recidivists as the base further shows that chronic recidivism is appreciable. For the low-SES level of Cohort I, the chronics committed 66.7% of the offenses, and at both levels of SES in Cohort II (71% low and 62% high) chronic recidivism is high. This is not the case at the high-SES level in Cohort I, where chronics commit less than half of the recidivist offenses.

TABLE 7.3

Number and Percentage of Offenders and Offenses by Delinquency Status, SES, and Cohort[a]

	1958 Cohort							
	Low SES				High SES			
	Offenders		Offenses		Offenders		Offenses	
	Number	Percentage	Number	Percentage	Number	Percentage	Number	Percentage
Delinquents	2703		10656		1612		4592	
One-time	995	36.8	995	9.3	809	50.2	809	17.6
Two to four time recid.	987	36.5	2760	25.9	542	33.6	1444	31.5
Five or more time recid.	721	26.7	6901	64.8	261	16.2	2339	50.9
Recidivists	1708		9661		803		3783	
Two to four time recid.	987	57.8	2760	28.5	542	67.5	1444	38.2
Five or more time recid.	721	42.2	6901	71.5	261	32.5	2339	61.9

1945 Cohort

	Low SES				High SES			
	Offenders		Offenses		Offenders		Offenses	
	Number	Percentage	Number	Percentage	Number	Percentage	Number	Percentage
Delinquents	2056		7131		1419		3083	
One-time	802	39.0	802	11.3	811	57.1	811	26.3
Two to four time recid.	770	37.5	2109	29.6	465	32.7	1187	38.5
Five or more time recid.	484	23.5	4220	60.1	143	10.0	1085	35.2
Recidivists	1254		6329		608		2272	
Two to four time recid.	770	61.4	2109	33.3	465	76.5	1187	52.2
Five or more time recid.	484	38.6	4220	66.7	143	23.5	1085	47.8

[a]Percentages are column percents of the total number of delinquents and then the total number of recidivists.

The relationship between delinquency status types and delinquent behavior, especially the role of chronic offenders, is most evident when the offenses are grouped by type of event. These data are given in Table 7.4. The results for Cohort I show that the chronic offender involvement in serious delinquency is quite high. For example, the chronics committed 63% of the index offenses and even higher shares among the serious index offenses (e.g., 71% of homicides, 73% of rapes, 82% of robberies, 70% of aggravated assaults, and 58% of injury offenses). The data for Cohort II indicate that chronic offenders are again responsible for the majority of serious crime (68% of the index offenses, 60% of the murders, 75% of the rapes, 73% of the robberies, 65% of the aggravated assaults, and 66% of the Sellin-Wolfgang injury offenses).

More important than these overall differences, the data displayed in Table 7.5 indicate that this chronic offender effect in Cohort II pertains to both whites and nonwhites, unlike Cohort I, in which the chronic offender effect was restricted mostly to nonwhites. The white chronics in Cohort I are far less delinquent than their nonwhite counterparts, even among the serious crime categories. White chronics show a disproportionate share of only robbery offenses (93%) compared to the consis-

TABLE 7.4
Number and Percentage of Select Offenses by Delinquency Status and Cohort[a]

	1958 Cohort			1945 Cohort		
	One-time	Non-chronic	Chronic	One-time	Non-chronic	Chronic
All	1804	4204	9240	1613	3296	5305
	11.8	27.6	60.6	15.8	32.3	51.9
Index	520	1373	4098	264	738	1726
	8.7	22.9	68.4	9.7	27.1	63.3
Nonindex	866	1865	3094	1349	2558	3579
	14.9	32.0	53.1	18.0	34.2	47.8
Homicide	6	16	33	1	3	10
	10.9	29.1	60.0	7.1	21.4	71.4
Rape	6	19	76	4	8	32
	5.9	18.8	75.2	9.1	18.2	72.7
Robbery	76	270	944	10	48	260
	5.9	20.9	73.2	3.1	15.1	81.8
Aggravated assault	50	146	365	18	50	152
	8.9	26.0	65.1	8.2	22.7	69.1
Injury	158	480	1255	124	320	611
	8.3	25.4	66.3	11.7	30.3	57.9

[a]Percentages are row percents of the row total of specific offenses.

TABLE 7.5

Number and Percentage of Select Offenses by Delinquency Status, Race, and Cohort[a]

	1958 Cohort					
	White			Nonwhite		
	One-time	Non-chronic	Chronic	One-time	Non-chronic	Chronic
All	733	1260	1915	1071	2944	7325
	18.8	32.2	49.0	9.4	26.0	64.6
Index	153	300	704	367	1073	3394
	13.2	25.9	60.8	7.6	22.4	70.2
Nonindex	454	742	845	412	1123	2249
	22.0	36.4	41.4	10.9	29.7	59.4
Homicide	—	2	2	6	14	31
	—	50.0	50.0	11.8	27.5	60.8
Rape	1	3	5	5	16	71
	11.1	33.3	55.6	5.4	17.4	77.2
Robbery	5	25	50	71	245	894
	6.3	31.3	62.5	5.9	20.2	73.9
Aggravated assault	14	34	55	36	112	310
	13.6	33.0	53.4	7.9	24.5	67.7
Injury	43	107	159	115	373	1096
	13.9	34.6	51.5	7.3	23.5	69.2
	1945 Cohort					
	White			Nonwhite		
	One-time	Non-chronic	Chronic	One-time	Non-chronic	Chronic
All	1110	1817	1531	503	1479	3774
	24.9	40.8	34.3	8.7	25.7	65.6
Index	145	346	450	119	392	1276
	15.4	36.8	47.8	6.7	21.9	71.4
Nonindex	965	1471	1081	384	1087	2498
	27.4	41.8	30.7	9.7	27.4	62.9
Homicide	—	—	—	1	3	10
	—	—	—	7.1	21.4	71.4
Rape	1	2	3	3	6	29
	16.7	33.3	50.0	7.9	15.8	76.3
Robbery	4	6	135	6	42	125
	2.8	4.1	93.1	3.5	24.3	72.3
Aggravated assault	6	15	19	12	35	133
	15.0	37.5	47.5	6.7	19.4	73.9
Injury	68	130	92	56	190	519
	23.5	44.8	31.7	7.3	24.8	67.8

[a]Percentages are row percents of the row total of specific offenses.

tently high involvement of nonwhite chronics across all categories. For Cohort II, a race effect still exists, but now it is one of degree rather than kind. That is, the chronic offender is responsible for the greatest share of all serious offenses for both whites and nonwhites. This effect, however, is more substantial for nonwhites.

The results obtained above using simple percentage differences have been confirmed recently by Fox and Tracy (1988). They reanalyzed the chronic offender data in the two cohorts primarily to explicate a statistical measure that captures the skewness present in offense distributions. This measure, which they called coefficient "alpha," is much more robust than simple percentages and allows one to compare skewness numerically, either across cohorts or within cohort by various subject groups. The alpha results revealed that there was more pronounced skewness in the share of delinquency attributable to the chronic recidivists in Cohort II than in Cohort I. More important, Fox and Tracy also found that the effect of chronic delinquency increased more dramatically for whites than nonwhites in the second cohort.

Chronicity and Severity of Delinquency

Despite having been charged with more serious offenses, the chronic offenders in Cohort I committed delinquent events with a distribution of seriousness scores that closely resembles that of the nonchronic recidivists. Table 7.6 shows, for example, that 54.2% of the offenses by chronics, compared to 63% of the offenses by nonchronic recidivists, fall below 100 on the seriousness scale, and 85.9% of the former versus 88% of the latter fall below a score of 300. Similarly, about .95% of the offenses by chronics, compared to 1% of the offenses by nonchronics, fall at or beyond a severity score of 1,000.

For Cohort II males, however, the chronic offender is not only more likely to be charged with serious offenses but his events actually are more serious in nature. That is, Table 7.6 indicates that only 47.2% of the offenses of chronic recidivists fall below a severity score of 300 compared to 50.6% for nonchronic recidivists. At or beyond the 1,000-point level, we find 24% of the chronics' offenses, compared to 17% for nonchronics.

When the seriousness score data are examined by offender group and race, the previous findings are maintained without exception (see Table 7.7). For Cohort I, there are virtually no differences in the seriousness score distributions between chronic and nonchronic recidivists for both races. However, for the data in the 1958 birth cohort, the chronic

TABLE 7.6

Number and Percentage of Offense Severity Scores by Delinquency Status and Cohort[a]

Severity score	1958 Cohort			1945 Cohort		
	One-time	Non-chronic	Chronic	One-time	Non-chronic	Chronic
1–50	320	693	1284	1064	1925	2595
	17.7	16.5	13.9	65.9	58.4	48.9
51–99	124	303	577	65	147	283
	6.9	7.2	6.2	4.0	4.6	5.3
100–199	568	1194	1793	186	440	890
	31.5	28.4	19.4	11.5	13.4	16.8
200–299	150	317	713	165	381	791
	8.3	7.5	7.7	10.2	11.6	14.9
300–399	84	207	363	58	179	368
	4.7	4.9	3.9	3.6	5.4	6.9
400–499	62	130	340	45	125	197
	3.4	3.1	3.7	2.8	3.8	3.7
500–999	233	643	1950	23	66	131
	12.9	13.1	21.1	1.4	2.0	2.5
1000–1999	225	632	1974	6	25	35
	12.5	15.0	21.4	.37	.76	.66
2000–2999	20	40	124	1	6	13
	1.1	.95	1.3	.06	.18	.25
3000–3999	9	15	59	—	1	2
	.50	.36	.64	—	.03	.04
4000+	9	30	63	—	1	—
	.50	.71	.68	—	.03	—
Total	1804	4204	9240	1613	3296	5305

[a]Percentages are column percents of the total offenses in each group.

offender effect exists for both races. The chronic offenders are responsible for offenses which are less likely to fall at the lower end of the seriousness scale and more likely to be classified at the highest points of the severity continuum.

In Table 7.8 we turn to the average offense severity rather than the severity score levels and thus present the mean offense seriousness score by race and SES for the three offender groups. Generally, it may be said that as the delinquency status group moves from one-time to chronic (thus indicating an increase in offense frequency), there is a companion increase in the average severity of the events. This is true for both cohorts for most race and SES categories.

TABLE 7.7
Number and Percentage of Offense Severity Scores by Delinquency Status,
Race, and Cohort[a]

Severity score	1958 Cohort					
	White			Nonwhite		
	One-time	Non-chronic	Chronic	One-time	Non-chronic	Chronic
1–50	85	130	194	235	563	1090
	10.9	10.3	10.1	21.9	19.1	14.9
51–99	59	89	139	65	214	438
	7.6	7.1	7.3	6.1	7.3	5.9
100–199	320	479	487	248	715	1306
	43.7	28.0	25.4	23.2	24.3	17.8
200–299	61	91	177	89	226	536
	8.3	7.2	9.2	8.3	7.7	7.3
300–399	29	77	72	55	130	291
	3.9	6.1	3.8	5.5	4.4	3.9
400–499	23	35	78	39	95	262
	3.1	2.8	4.1	3.6	3.2	3.6
500–999	71	176	351	162	467	1599
	9.2	13.9	18.3	15.1	15.9	21.8
1000–1999	72	162	394	153	470	1580
	9.8	12.9	20.6	14.3	15.9	21.6
2000–2999	8	16	15	12	24	109
	1.1	1.3	.78	1.1	.82	1.5
3000–3999	3	3	4	6	12	55
	.41	.24	.21	.56	.41	.75
4000+	2	2	4	7	28	59
	.27	.16	.21	.65	.95	.81
Total	733	1260	1915	1071	2944	7325

TABLE 7.7 (continued)

Severity score	1945 Cohort					
	White			Nonwhite		
	One-time	Non-chronic	Chronic	One-time	Non-chronic	Chronic
1–50	779	1143	829	285	782	1766
	70.1	63.3	54.1	56.7	52.9	47.1
51–99	53	89	92	12	58	191
	4.8	4.9	6.0	2.4	3.9	5.1
100–199	95	202	173	91	238	717
	8.6	11.1	11.3	18.1	16.1	19.0
200–299	106	201	259	59	180	532
	9.6	11.1	16.9	11.7	12.2	14.1
300–399	33	82	106	25	97	262
	2.9	4.5	6.9	4.9	6.6	6.9
400–499	28	57	48	17	68	149
	2.5	3.1	3.1	3.4	4.6	3.9
500–999	12	31	15	11	35	116
	1.1	1.7	.09	2.2	2.4	3.1
1000–1999	4	8	8	2	17	27
	.36	.44	.52	.40	1.2	.72
2000–2999	—	2	—	1	4	13
	—	.11	—	.20	.27	.34
3000–3999	—	1	1	—	—	1
	—	.06	.07	—	—	.03
4000+	—	1	—	—	—	—
	—	.06	—	—	—	—
Total	1110	1817	1531	503	1479	3774

[a]Percentages are column percents of the total offenses in each group.

TABLE 7.8
Mean Severity Score by Race, SES Delinquency Status,
and Cohort

	1958 Cohort		
	One-time	Nonchronic	Chronic
Low SES			
White	346.3	463.3	530.5
Nonwhite	470.6	516.4	631.8
High SES			
White	363.1	408.7	519.0
Nonwhite	466.8	444.3	618.9
	1945 Cohort		
	One-time	Nonchronic	Chronic
Low SES			
White	90.4	96.4	115.3
Nonwhite	106.0	123.1	136.4
High SES			
White	60.4	93.5	96.7
Nonwhite	88.5	124.8	124.7

There are, however, two exceptions to this trend that can be noted. First, for Cohort I at the higher-SES level for nonwhites, the nonchronic recidivists (mean = 124.8) and the chronics (mean = 124.7) have virtually identical average seriousness scores. Second, in Cohort II at the higher-SES level for nonwhites, the one-time offenders (mean = 466.8) have a higher mean seriousness score than nonchronic recidivists (mean = 444.3). Because there are so few high-SES nonwhites compared to the other groups, the relationship between offender group and offense severity holds overall and, most important, at the lower level of SES, where the majority of delinquency occurs.

The data presented in this chapter with respect to the relationship between delinquency status group and the incidence and severity of delinquency show a pronounced chronic offender effect. In both cohorts, the chronic recidivists are responsible for a disproportionate share of offenses, generally, and for the very serious offenses, in particular. In Cohort I the chronic offender effect is conditional and holds for nonwhites and low-SES subjects. In the 1958 birth cohort, the chronic offender effect on delinquency is unconditional and thus holds for both races and SES levels.

The major difference between the two cohorts occurs for seriousness scores by offender group. In Cohort I the offense severity scores do not show a strong difference across offender types. The majority of delinquent acts cluster at the lower end of the severity continuum. This result is observed regardless of race or SES. In Cohort II, however, the offenses by chronics are not only more frequent but are more serious as well. This result holds for both the race and SES comparisons.

It is clear, therefore, that the effect of chronic recidivism that was first uncovered in Cohort I is again a significant finding in Cohort II. Moreover, in Cohort II the chronic offender syndrome not only exists overall, but also affects all comparison groups, not just the usually disadvantaged (i.e., nonwhites and low SES) offenders as was the case in Cohort I. In fact, the data indicate that it is whites, not nonwhites, who experienced the sharper chronic offender effect.

Given these results, and the continued importance of delinquent recidivism in the discipline, we will continue our focus on the comparative recidivism in the two cohorts in Chapters 8 and 9. First, in Chapter 8 we examine the static dimension of recidivism in which offense ranks are studied without regard to the type of prior delinquency. Subsequently, in Chapter 9 we focus on the dynamic aspects (i.e., specialization and escalation) of repeat delinquency.

Delinquent Recidivism
STATIC PROBABILITIES

Introduction

In the next two chapters we shall address a variety of issues surrounding the phenomenon of repeat delinquency. Specifically, in this chapter we shall discuss data pertaining to the probability of recidivism generally and for select offense types without taking into account knowledge of the number or type of prior offenses. We will also investigate the severity and timing of offenses by rank number of offense. We have labelled these analyses as static because we examine the offense by rank number without taking into account information concerning the offender's prior delinquency. In the next chapter we explicitly explore the extent to which a prior offense type influences the type and severity of the next offense committed. These are dynamic aspects of delinquency and concern the topics of offense specialization or switching and offense severity escalation. Before we present these data, it is useful to review the parameters of the recidivism issue.

We reported in the initial section of this volume that the majority of delinquents committed at least two offenses. The percentage of recidivists in Cohort I (53.6%) was less than in Cohort II, for which 58.2% of the offenders were arrested more than once. Thus, more than half of the delinquents in the two birth cohorts engaged in repeat delinquency. More important, in Chapter 7, we presented data which indicated the special nature of chronic delinquency. We found that in the 1945 cohort, 18% of the delinquents had been arrested five or more times. In the 1958 cohort, the phenomenon of chronic delinquency was found to be characteristic of 23% of the offenders. Although these chronic delinquents thus represent less than one-quarter of the delinquents in both cohorts, they nonetheless accounted for a substantial share of the delinquent acts. In Cohort II the chronics account for 61% of the total delinquency in the cohort, while in Cohort I the chronic offenders committed 52% of the offenses.

In addition to these general aspects of the chronic recidivist phenomenon, we also noted that, while the problem of chronic offending was race specific in Cohort I, it affected both races in Cohort II. In the 1945 birth cohort 28.6% of nonwhite delinquents were chronic compared to just 10.4% of white delinquents. In the 1958 cohort a race differential still exists, for 26.6% of nonwhites compared to 14.8% of whites are chronic delinquents. However, in the second cohort just under 12 percentage points separate the races, while over 18 percentage points separated the races in Cohort I.

Regardless of these slight differences it is clear that chronic recidivists represent a special category of delinquent offender across the cohorts. They represent a minority of the delinquent group, yet they account for a disproportionate share of the delinquent acts. Therefore, the analyses in the following two chapters are meant to illuminate further the careers of chronic recidivists.

The First Offense

Table 8.1 displays a series of data concerning the first offense of the delinquent career. These data indicate the great similarity between the cohorts concerning the type and timing of the initial offense, but they also show a clear dissimilarity in offense seriousness. In both cohorts, nonindex offenses dominate the first-offenses probabilities: 65% of the first offenses in Cohort I and 61% of the offenses in Cohort II were nonindex. A first offense in Cohort I was slightly more likely to involve injury than in Cohort II (7.6% vs. 6.6%). The first offenses for both cohorts happen to be theft events in almost the same proportion (13.9% vs. 13.2%). Compared to Cohort I the first offenses in the second cohort are more likely to involve damage (11.7% vs. 7.2%) and some combination of the index components (7.0% vs. 5.7%).

In terms of age at first offense the two cohorts are very similar. The nonindex and injury offenses occur at virtually the same ages, nonindex, 14.5 years in Cohort II and 14.6 years in Cohort I, injury, 14.3 in Cohort II and in Cohort I. The first theft offense is committed about 7 months earlier in Cohort I than in Cohort II (14.1 years vs. 14.8 years). The combination offenses differ by nearly the same amount (6 months), but with Cohort II offenses occurring earlier. Damage offenses occur as a first offense about 2 months later in Cohort II than in Cohort I (13.0 vs. 12.8). None of these differences are dramatic, however.

TABLE 8.1

Probability, Severity, and Time of First Offense by Offense Type and Cohort

Type of offense	Probability of subjects	Probability of delinquents	Mean severity	Mean time mos.	Mean time yrs.
		1958 Cohort			
Nonindex	.2012	.6137	146.9	174.6	14.5
Injury	.0217	.0663	1207.33	171.9	14.3
Theft	.0434	.1323	801.22	177.3	14.8
Damage	.0386	.1177	460.62	156.5	13.0
Combination	.0229	.0700	1235.08	172.2	14.3
		1945 Cohort			
Nonindex	.2288	.6547	23.7	175.9	14.6
Injury	.0265	.0760	331.03	171.4	14.3
Theft	.0487	.1393	183.02	169.4	14.1
Damage	.0253	.0725	157.02	153.3	12.8
Combination	.0201	.0576	291.28	164.3	13.7

The seriousness scores for first offenses are different for the two cohorts. In Cohort I the trend in mean seriousness is injury (331.0), combination (291.2), theft (183.0), damage (157.0), and last, nonindex (23.7). For the 1958 cohort, combination offenses (1,235.08) have a higher mean seriousness than injury offenses (1,207.33), while the remaining offenses follow the same pattern as Cohort I—theft (801.22), damage (460.62), and then nonindex (146.9). In addition to this slight difference in patterns, the Cohort II data show the much greater range in first offense seriousness scores across offense types. There is a difference of 1,088.80 severity points in Cohort II compared to a range of 307.3 points in Cohort I.

In sum, the initial points of the delinquency careers are quite similar for the two cohorts in terms of the type of offenses that are committed and the age at which the first offense by each type is committed. The two cohorts are different, however, in the dispersion of seriousness and the type of offenses committed; the Cohort II scores are higher and show greater variation.

In Table 8.2 we present the probabilities of a first offense by type for one-time offenders and recidivists, and we also display the first-offense

TABLE 8.2
Probability of First Offense by Offense Type,
Offender Type, and Cohort

Type of offense	1958 Cohort		
	One-time ($n = 1804$)	Desisted ($n = 1804$)	Recidivists ($n = 2511$)
Nonindex	.6325	.4309	.6002
Injury	.0626	.3951	.0689
Theft	.1430	.4518	.1247
Damage	.0976	.3465	.1322
Combination	.0643	.3841	.0741
Type of offense	1945 Cohort		
	One-time ($n = 1613$)	Desisted ($n = 1613$)	Recidivists ($n = 1862$)
Nonindex	.7204	.5108	.5977
Injury	.0700	.4280	.0810
Theft	.1110	.3698	.1638
Damage	.0589	.3770	.0843
Combination	.0397	.3200	.0730

specific desistance probabilities. Although generally similar, the two cohorts show noteworthy differences. In both cohorts one-time offenders are most likely to commit a nonindex type of offense. This probability was higher in Cohort I (.7204) than in Cohort II (.6325). In Cohort I, one-time offenders are more likely to commit a theft index offense (.1110) than injury (.0700), damage (.0589), or combination (.0397). In Cohort II, one-time offenders are also more likely to have theft (.1430) as their only offense. This offense type is followed by damage (.0976), combination (.0643), and then injury (.0626).

The cohorts also differ slightly with respect to the chances that a one-time offender desists across the offense types. About half of the nonindex first offenders desisted in Cohort I (51%), while 43% did so in Cohort II. For index offenses, injury offenders desist next (.4280), followed by first offenders that committed damage (.3770), then theft (.3698), and then combination (.3200). In Cohort II the rankings for first-offense desisters differ, with theft offenders showing the highest probability of stopping (.4518), followed by injury (.3951), combination (.3841), and damage (.3465). Collectively, these data show that at least one-third of the offenders desist after having committed an index first offense and that up to one-half of the nonindex first offenders desist.

Turning to the type of first offenses committed by recidivists, we see that they are not greatly different from the offenses of one-time offenders. In Cohort I, the probability of a first offense being a nonindex offense was lower for recidivists (.5977) than for one-time offenders (.7204). However, for index offenses recidivists show slightly higher probabilities compared to one-timers. The recidivist versus one-timer probabilities are .0810 versus .0700 for injury, .0843 versus .0589 for damage, .0730 versus .0397 for combination, and .1638 versus .1110 for theft, the offense type for which there is the greatest difference. In Cohort II the differences are also slight, which is surprising given the higher rate of recidivism in this cohort. Recidivists compared to one-time delinquents are just about as likely to commit nonindex offenses (.6002 vs. .6325), injury offenses (.0689 vs. .0626), theft offenses (.1247 vs. .1430), combination offenses (.0741 vs. .0643), and damage offenses (.1322 vs. .0976).

None of these first-offense probabilities is sufficiently different to warrant a conclusion that recidivists initiate their delinquent careers significantly differently than do offenders who commit just one delinquent act before desisting. The reason for repeat delinquency thus does not appear to be associated with the type of offense that initiates the career. A particular start point does not carry with it a substantial likelihood of recidivism.

Rank Number of Offense

Table 8.3 presents the static probabilities (the probability of committing another offense, regardless of type of prior offense, from the first to the fifteenth offense by type of offense). The static probability may be defined as:

$$P \text{ (static)} = N_k / N_{k-1}$$

where N_k is the number of boys who commit the kth (rank number) offense and N_{k-1} is the number of boys who committed the prior offense, and thus, represents the population at risk of committing an additional offense.

In first looking at the probabilities of committing any type of offense, it appears that the likelihood of committing a second offense is the smallest of the array. In the 1945 cohort the probability of a second offense is .5358, while the likelihood of a second offense in the 1958 cohort is higher, .5819. This difference in the recidivism probability points to a difference in the relative probabilities of desistance in the two cohorts. In Cohort I, 46.4% of the offenders desisted after the first of-

TABLE 8.3

Probability, of Committing kth Offense by Offense Type and Cohort

				1958 Cohort			
Offense number	All types	Non-index	Injury	Theft	Damage	Combi-nation	Desist
1	1.0000	.6137	.0663	.1323	.1177	.0700	.4181
2	.5819	.5998	.0737	.1466	.0972	.0828	.2808
3	.7192	.5709	.0786	.1539	.0908	.1058	.2780
4	.7220	.5222	.0874	.1925	.0828	.1150	.2469
5	.7531	.5275	.0916	.1965	.0754	.1090	.2159
6	.7841	.5000	.0883	.1948	.0896	.1273	.2519
7	.7481	.4849	.0889	.2030	.0856	.1376	.1997
8	.8003	.4277	.1006	.2138	.1069	.1509	.1551
9	.8449	.4218	.1017	.2184	.0943	.1638	.1861
10	.8139	.4726	.0945	.2073	.0732	.1524	.1707
11	.8293	.4632	.0919	.1801	.1140	.1507	.1691
12	.8309	.4690	.0752	.1947	.0973	.1637	.1770
13	.8230	.3817	.1183	.2258	.1022	.1720	.1989
14	.8011	.5168	.1141	.1678	.0738	.1275	.1678
15	.8322	.4113	.1048	.2419	.0645	.1774	.1290
				1945 Cohort			
Offense number	All types	Non-index	Injury	Theft	Damage	Combi-nation	Desist
1	1.0000	.6547	.0760	.1393	.0725	.0576	.4641
2	.5358	.3430	.0455	.0794	.0222	.0458	.3492
3	.6509	.4044	.0483	.1246	.0236	.0499	.2838
4	.7161	.4439	.0736	.1238	.0248	.0503	.2778
5	.7223	.4320	.0657	.1313	.0264	.0668	.2584
6	.7416	.4705	.0526	.1435	.0128	.0622	.2085
7	.7913	.4409	.0925	.1398	.0387	.0796	.2337
8	.7663	.4511	.0815	.1440	.0163	.0734	.2021
9	.7978	.4787	.0887	.1241	.0177	.0887	.1733
10	.8266	.4489	.1111	.1956	.0089	.0622	.2096
11	.7903	.4624	.0645	.1559	.0054	.1022	.1974
12	.8027	.4830	.0816	.0884	.0544	.0952	.2712
13	.7288	.4068	.0593	.1441	.0254	.0932	.1162
14	.8837	.5233	.1163	.0814	.0349	.1279	.3026
15	.6973	.4474	.1263	.1316	.0000	.0921	.2453

fense, while 41.9% ceased their delinquency career after the first offense in Cohort II. Beyond the first offense, 35% of the Cohort I offenders and 28% of the Cohort II offenders desisted after the second offense, and 28% and 27%, respectively, desisted after the third. Beyond the third offense the likelihood of committing any further offense is higher in Cohort II and generally ranges from .74 to .83 compared to Cohort I in which the range usually falls between .71 and .79.

By offense type the probabilities show no cohort effect, although the likelihood of additional offenses is higher in Cohort II than in Cohort I. The probability of nonindex offenses across rank number of offenses ranges between .42 and .52 in Cohort II and between .41 and .48 in Cohort I. Nonindex offenses are followed in order with the Cohort II versus Cohort I range of probabilities of theft (.15 to .20 vs. .12 to .13), combination (.10 to .15 vs. .05 to .11), injury (.07 to .11 vs. .06 to .08), and damage (.07 to .09 vs. about .02).

Two major conclusions emerge from the static offense probabilities. First, the likelihood of committing various index offenses by type is quite low when compared to the probability of a nonindex commission. Second, the probability of committing an offense of any kind or by each type is almost constant across offense ranks after the third offense. These conclusions pertain to both cohorts, with the only difference being that the magnitude of the recidivism probabilities is higher in Cohort II than Cohort I.

The mean seriousness score for all offenses and the five Sellin-Wolfgang offense types are given in Table 8.4 for the first to the fifteenth offense in Cohort I. The scores do not indicate that offense severity is positively related to the number of offenses a delinquent commits. For offenses of any type the mean seriousness scores show a small upward trend as the offense rank number increases. The increment in offense severity by offense number for nonindex and theft offenses is almost nonexistent, while the seriousness scores for damage and combination offenses appear to be only slightly positively related to the rank number. On the other hand, the mean seriousness scores for injury offenses exhibit a strong upward trend for the first 10 offense ranks. After the tenth offense, the data are somewhat choppy, but the end points show once again the strong upward trend.

By comparison, the data reported in Table 8.4 for Cohort II offenses generally exhibit an upward trend in offense severity as rank number of offense increases. For the all-offense and nonindex offense categories, the scores for the higher offense rank numbers are about 1.5 times as high as those of the lower rank numbers. The range of seriousness scores is somewhat less for theft, damage, and combination offenses,

TABLE 8.4

Mean Severity Score, First to Fifteenth Offense by Offense Type and Cohort

Offense number	All types	Non-index	Injury	Theft	Damage	Combi-nation
			1958 Cohort			
1	416.43	146.19	1207.33	801.22	460.62	1235.08
2	469.07	153.96	1248.18	884.28	483.92	1305.68
3	522.38	156.64	1343.41	901.71	517.61	1338.75
4	583.39	194.99	1345.83	886.72	498.37	1320.92
5	581.89	192.12	1374.16	901.69	507.89	1276.71
6	636.96	239.43	1426.71	884.49	490.27	1375.14
7	681.80	221.31	1610.58	974.06	541.91	1360.13
8	702.04	243.28	1390.22	924.77	578.20	1315.29
9	797.48	285.06	1755.30	1020.19	526.83	1381.23
10	758.74	278.06	1536.74	998.18	617.49	1508.63
11	731.89	258.10	1347.60	982.70	580.77	1627.02
12	785.64	265.75	1371.54	1084.45	637.86	1570.27
13	846.07	340.42	1823.44	1007.01	687.13	1179.17
14	746.40	320.39	1791.18	1059.67	721.76	1140.13
15	818.04	446.77	1091.54	1031.18	747.50	1252.12

Offense number	All types	Non-index	Injury	Theft	Damage	Combi-nation
			1945 Cohort			
1	94.33	23.71	330.95	183.04	157.39	291.18
2	108.32	26.44	346.07	185.37	164.96	324.68
3	111.86	30.39	371.48	192.85	160.86	295.01
4	126.38	33.57	438.67	189.02	164.97	316.25
5	131.12	35.60	417.11	187.88	157.91	345.88
6	113.10	27.28	414.61	192.21	250.00	296.54
7	146.83	32.76	453.53	175.46	170.78	360.43
8	147.47	37.86	560.47	176.02	200.00	294.74
9	141.74	37.21	478.72	217.46	193.00	252.92
10	150.24	30.91	494.72	176.25	200.00	307.14
11	120.46	33.43	300.00	194.97	74.00	289.68
12	150.14	44.44	392.25	200.46	184.25	498.14
13	139.98	47.10	329.57	222.00	166.67	290.55
14	180.58	59.73	606.70	205.00	116.00	289.64
15	166.09	45.26	900.00	173.50	0.00	532.71

but the upward trend is nonetheless quite distinct. For injury offenses, the data are inconsistent across the various ranks, showing great swings upward and downward in the average seriousness of offenses.

In Table 8.5 the mean time in months between the kth and kth+1 offense is seen to be related to offense number. In Cohort I the time between the first and second offense on average is a little over 18 months for nonindex and injury offenses and about 16.5 months for theft, damage, and combination offenses. In Cohort II the time between the first and second offenses is highest at 18.5 months for theft and lowest for damage at 15.4 months. Nonindex (17.6), injury (16.7), and combination (15.8) offenses fall between these points. From the second to the third offense the time drops to between 8.5 and 10.5 months in Cohort II and about 8 to 12 months in Cohort I. The third to the fourth offense has a mean time of approximately 8 months in Cohort I and about 7.5 months in Cohort II. This pattern continues across offense ranks out to the fifteenth offense, with Cohort II offenses showing a shorter time between offenses.

The data given in Table 8.6 confirm that the age spread over the 15 offenses is not very substantial. On average, the Cohort I offenders and the Cohort II delinquents were the same age at the commission of the first offense (14.4 years) and almost the same age at the commission of the fifteenth offense, 16.0 years in Cohort I and 15.9 years in Cohort II. The data by offense type show some variation in the age of the first versus the fifteenth offense, but the dispersion is rather narrow.

Generally speaking, the offense histories are compressed over a rather short period, regardless of the type of offense. This finding is reflected both in the average age at commission of each offense and in the mean time between offenses. Surprisingly, this finding is invariant to the particular cohort under investigation.

Up to now we have investigated the static offense probabilities with reference to the index versus nonindex classification scheme of the crime severity system developed by Sellin and Wolfgang. Before concluding this chapter, it is worthwhile to examine the static probabilities for the UCR index classification system which, unlike the Sellin-Wolfgang scheme, utilizes legal categories. Although we have presented data above for all offenders, regardless of race, in the following few tables we will present both overall results and results by race in order to highlight important differences that were not relevant above, and which would have only complicated the tabular presentations.

Table 8.7 presents static offense data for UCR index offense types. The likelihood that a Cohort I delinquent will engage in a UCR property offense (i.e., burglary, theft, and auto theft) is approximately equal to

TABLE 8.5
Mean Time (in Months) between First and Fifteenth Offense by Offense Type and Cohort

Offense number	1958 Cohort				
	Nonindex	Injury	Theft	Damage	Combination
1–2	17.62	16.71	18.56	15.48	15.80
2–3	10.53	8.79	9.76	8.61	10.48
3–4	7.55	6.98	8.67	7.62	7.08
4–5	5.94	5.16	6.10	6.00	6.47
5–6	5.24	5.40	4.64	4.85	5.29
6–7	4.73	6.18	5.35	4.31	4.88
7–8	4.17	5.54	3.40	4.13	4.61
8–9	4.55	3.70	3.70	3.13	4.24
9–10	3.67	4.00	3.00	1.63	4.44
10–11	4.17	3.15	3.84	3.18	3.11
11–12	3.68	5.74	3.34	2.44	3.50
12–13	3.29	5.02	3.52	1.97	2.95
13–14	2.79	2.69	4.29	3.35	3.78
14–15	3.36	3.34	3.91	1.82	2.59

Offense number	1945 Cohort				
	Nonindex	Injury	Theft	Damage	Combination
1–2	18.57	18.13	16.60	16.81	16.96
2–3	10.62	11.83	10.39	7.31	8.79
3–4	8.06	8.29	7.94	8.36	6.47
4–5	7.10	7.26	6.27	5.20	6.51
5–6	5.38	8.30	6.30	6.30	6.28
6–7	5.22	5.81	5.48	6.59	5.95
7–8	5.23	5.84	4.38	7.12	5.93
8–9	4.59	5.04	2.39	6.36	5.04
9–10	4.09	4.38	6.26	6.10	4.51
10–11	3.96	4.77	4.22	0.20	3.21
11–12	3.35	5.42	5.47	4.85	9.28
12–13	4.17	5.56	5.35	8.63	5.08
13–14	3.15	4.15	1.93	7.37	2.38
14–15	2.98	12.30	4.32	0.00	5.29

that of delinquency overall (.3479 vs. .3494). However, the probability of committing this type of offense more than once is much lower than recidivist delinquency generally. Cohort I delinquents show probabilities of repeat UCR property offenses that range from .38 to .65. Although the probability of committing this group of offenses three or more times up to ten or more times increases steadily, the trend is not great and shows only small differences by rank number of offense.

TABLE 8.6
Mean Age (in years) at First and Fifteenth Offense
by Offense Type and Cohort

| Offense type | 1958 Cohort | | 1945 Cohort | |
	First offense	Fifteenth offense	First offense	Fifteenth offense
Nonindex	14.5	15.8	14.6	16.0
Injury	14.3	16.6	14.3	17.4
Theft	14.8	15.9	14.1	15.8
Damage	13.0	15.1	12.8	16.1 (14th)
Combination	14.3	16.2	13.7	16.1
Any offense	14.4	15.9	14.4	16.0

The Cohort II delinquents show a greater probability of engaging in a UCR property offense than the Cohort I offenders (.43 vs. .34). Similarly, the likelihood of committing serious property offenses more than once is much greater in the 1958 cohort than in the 1945 cohort. The Cohort I probabilities are higher at only the 4+ and 10+ categories. Further, the Cohort II probabilities show the stronger relationship to

TABLE 8.7
Probability of Committing One or More Offenses by Offense Type and Cohort

| Offense total | 1958 Cohort | | | 1945 Cohort | | |
	Any offense[a]	UCR violent[b]	UCR property[b]	Any offense[a]	UCR violent[b]	UCR property[b]
1 +	.3279	.2607	.4352	.3494	.1038	.3479
2 +	.5819	.3529	.4286	.5358	.2077	.3895
3 +	.7192	.4887	.5466	.6509	.3066	.4968
4 +	.7220	.4742	.5727	.7161	.2608	.5854
5 +	.7531	.6304	.6627	.7223	.5000	.5255
6 +	.7841	.5862	.6707	.7416	.3333	.6527
7 +	.7740	.5882	.6786	.7913	.3333	.6595
8 +	.8003	.5000	.7763	.7663	.3333	.6451
9 +	.8449	.7000	.8475	.8014	—	.5000
10 +	.8139	.8571	.7200	.8266	—	.8000

[a]Initial probability based on cohort subjects.
[b]Initial probability based on delinquents.

rank number of offense, as the values increase from .43 at one offense or more to .77, .84, and .72 at the last three ranks.

The two cohorts differ more substantially with respect to the four violent offenses (i.e., homicide, rape, robbery, and aggravated assault). The likelihood that a delinquent will ever commit this type of crime is 2.5 times higher in Cohort II (.26) than in Cohort I (.10). After the first violent offense, the Cohort II probabilities increase from .35 to .63 at the level of five or more, then decline to .50 at eight or more, then rise again to .85 at the point of ten or more violent offenses. The Cohort I scores are much lower and, except for a probability of .50 achieved at the five-or-more offenses level, never exceed a value of .33.

Table 8.8 presents static offense data by race and the UCR index offense classifications. Examination of the overall offense data by race shows that nonwhites have higher probabilities. In Cohort I, about one-half of nonwhites had at least one offense compared to 28% of whites. Nonwhites also had consistently higher probabilities of recidivating. Thus, for example, 65% of the nonwhite delinquents went on to at least a second offense, and almost 75% of these committed at least a third offense. The percentages for whites are lower: 45% for at least two offenses and 55% for at least three offenses.

The Cohort II data also show a race effect but one which is smaller than in Cohort I. The initial probabilities do show a greater likelihood of delinquency for nonwhites than for whites (.41 vs. .22), yet the gap of .19 is less than that achieved in Cohort I (.22). Similarly, there is a difference of about .20 in the recidivism probabilities between non-whites and whites in Cohort I, yet in Cohort II the difference for at least two offenses has narrowed to .15 (.6311 vs. .4809), and the gap is even smaller for at least three offenses, where a difference of only .10 (.7478 vs. .6421) exists. Throughout the rest of the offense ranks the Cohort II difference between nonwhites and whites remains smaller than that in Cohort I, the former being no larger than .07, while the latter ranges as high as .17.

The greatest difference between the cohorts concerns the race effect for both violent and property offenses. In Cohort I, nonwhites showed much greater probabilities than whites of ever committing a violent crime (.20 vs. .02) or committing at least two (.23 vs. .05). The values after this point were too unreliable given cell sizes to afford valid comparison. Similarly, nonwhites showed a greater initial probability of UCR property offenses than whites (.45 vs. .27) and generally higher recidivism probabilities.

Compared to these consistent race differences, the Cohort II data show no race effect for UCR property offenses, but even more dramatic

TABLE 8.8

Probability of Committing One or More Offenses by Offense Type, Race, and Cohort

	1958 Cohort					
	White			Nonwhite		
Offense total	Any offense[a]	UCR violent[b]	UCR property[b]	Any offense[a]	UCR violent[b]	UCR property[b]
1 +	.2272	.1112	.3797	.4181	.3334	.4823
2 +	.4809	.1465	.3828	.6311	.3864	.4443
3 +	.6421	.3478	.5191	.7478	.4973	.5547
4 +	.6927	.3750	.6105	.7314	.4785	.5623
5 +	.6921	.3333	.6896	.7715	.6404	.6546
6 +	.7751	1.0000	.6250	.7865	.5789	.6850
7 +	.7654	1.0000	.6800	.7763	.5758	.6782
8 +	.7581	1.0000	.7647	.8114	.4734	.7797
9 +	.8191	1.0000	.8462	.8512	.6667	.8478
10 +	.7792		.8182	.8221	1.0000	.6923

	1945 Cohort					
	White			Nonwhite		
Offense total	Any offense[a]	UCR violent[b]	UCR property[b]	Any offense[a]	UCR violent[b]	UCR property[b]
1 +	.2866	.0292	.2724	.5017	.2074	.4526
2 +	.4502	.0508	.3018	.6545	.2384	.4628
3 +	.5566	.6666	.4216	.7408	.2916	.5377
4 +	.6581	.5000	.5000	.7577	.2380	.6219
5 +	.6306	.5000	.6000	.7794	.4000	.5000
6 +	.6571	—	.5238	.7841	.5000	.7058
7 +	.7391	—	.4545	.8134	.5000	.7222
8 +	.6372	—	.8000	.8157	.5000	.6153
9 +	.7384	—	.7500	.8156	—	.4375
10 +	.7291	—	.6666	.8531	—	.8571

[a]Initial probability based on cohort subjects.
[b]Initial probability based on delinquents.

race differences in terms of violent offense probabilities. For property offenses, the initial difference between nonwhites and whites (.48 vs. .37) gradually diminishes, and then the probability of recidivism is about the same out to the point of 10 or more UCR property crimes. However, for violent offenses, the differences are distinct and persistent. The nonwhite versus white probabilities are .33 versus .11 at one or more offenses, .38 versus .14 at two or more, .49 versus .34 at three or more, .47

versus .37 at four or more, and .64 versus .33 at five or more. The remaining values are not comparable due to the small sample size for whites. Clearly, however, up to the level of six-or-more violent offenses the data do suggest a much stronger involvement in violent offense recidivism for nonwhites than whites.

Our analyses of the static offense data produced results which generally show the two cohorts to be similar along most dimensions examined. First, the two cohorts were very similar concerning the type, probability, and age of the initial offenses committed. There was a tendency for the Cohort II first offenses to vary in severity.

Second, we also found cohort similarities when we compared one-time offenders with recidivists. Although recidivists have slightly different first-offense probabilities compared to one-time delinquents, none of the differences is substantial enough to explain why the former continue their delinquency careers while the latter desist.

Third, when we examined the static offense probabilities for the first through the fifteenth offense, we found that for all rank numbers, a nonindex offense is the most likely outcome, followed by desistance, theft, injury, combination, and damage. The main difference between the cohorts was in the magnitude of the recidivism probabilities, for which those in Cohort II were higher than those in Cohort I.

Fourth, the Cohort II offenses, unlike Cohort I, showed an upward trend in offense severity as rank number of offense increased. This was especially evident for all offenses and nonindex offenses. The differences were less substantial for theft, damage, and combination offenses, and there was no clear trend for injury offenses.

Fifth, when we analyzed the static offense probabilities for offenses classified according to the UCR index offense scheme, we found some noteworthy differences. The two cohorts differ with respect to the chances of repeat UCR property crimes, and they differ substantially with respect to repeat violent index crimes. In all instances, the recidivism probabilities in the 1958 cohort exceed those of the 1945 cohort. More important, we found that although nonwhites in Cohort I were more recidivistic than whites for both property and violent index offenses, there are almost no race differences for property recidivism, but the nonwhite predominance in violent crime was replicated in Cohort II.

9

Delinquent Recidivism
SPECIALIZATION AND ESCALATION

Introduction

In the previous chapter we discussed the probability of committing an offense, by type of offense, for each rank number of offense from the first offense of the career out to the fifteenth offense. We referred to this probability of committing a first, second, third, and so on out to the kth offense as a "static" probability, because in its computation the likelihood of each offense type was considered without regard to the type of prior offense or offenses. That is, we treated the current offense for statistical purposes as though it were independent of the previous offense type. Consequently, we were unable to make any probabilistic statements about the sequences of types of offenses. One very important finding, however, was clear: the probability of committing an offense, when classified by type, changed very little over offense number. The variation in the probability distributions was surprisingly small.

This result was altogether unexpected. One would imagine that, if more serious offenses (like UCR index offenses) are more likely to appear among the later offenses in a delinquent career as the occasional offender desists, leaving only the committed recidivists as active delinquents, then the probability distributions of index offenses would shift noticeably as the number of offenses increases, thus reflecting a propensity toward the commission of more serious offenses. In short, one might legitimately expect that the chances of committing an index offense would increase more or less directly with offense number.

We found no such increase in the probability of offenses by rank number, particularly for index offenses. Thus, we may suggest that the process which generates these offense-specific probability distributions operates essentially in the same manner at each offense number. This suggestion is an important one, for if it is correct, we are implying that the probability of being involved in a particular type of offensive behavior is independent of the number of offenses that a juvenile may have committed. In other words, the data seem to indicate that an offender is no more likely at, say the eleventh offense, to be involved in a violent act than he was at the fifth.

In this chapter we extend our analytical task beyond the static probabilities to a consideration of the probabilities associated with offense sequences or patterns—the "dynamic" or transition probabilities. Our primary concern here is with the development of inferential statements about switching from one type of offense to another or continuing with the same offense type as offense rank advances. In other words, examination of the transition probabilities allows us to address the question of whether delinquents specialize in the types of offenses that they commit, or whether delinquents reflect versatility in their delinquent acts. In addition, this chapter will address the issue of whether offense repeats are related to offense severity, or what may be termed *escalation*. The question of offense escalation parallels that of offense specialization and concerns not whether offense-type repeats have a higher chance of occurrence, but rather, whether offense repeats show a pattern of increased severity as the juvenile career progresses.

The topic of offense specialization, or versatility in offending, as it has come to be called, occupies a central place in criminological research. As Bursik (1980) has noted, concern over specialization dates back to the pioneering work of Clifford Shaw in the 1930s, which was concerned with the dynamic social processes surrounding delinquency. Farrington *et al*. (1988) have recently noted that, from a theoretical standpoint, research on offense specialization or versatility is an important way of shedding light on the number of dimensions underlying delinquency. From the standpoint of policy, Cohen (1986) has observed that, because crime control policies focus on particular categories of offenders, knowledge of offense specialization may be useful in focusing crime control efforts on offenders who are most likely to continue to exhibit particular offense types that are of policy concern, for example, predatory offenders.

Despite the acknowledged importance of offense specialization research, there are comparatively few studies that report results for substantively meaningful samples of juvenile offenders. There are several reasons for the comparative lack of offense specialization studies.

First, a substantial amount of contemporary research with juveniles utilizes self-report data on offending. Although the self-report technique is generally believed to provide more complete data on an offender's delinquency career owing to the absence of the possible selection effects present in official data, it is quite clear that retrospective self-reports from respondents do not permit the precise sequencing of the illegal acts reported, especially when the subject reports many offenses per year per offense type. Second, even when official data are employed, and even when these data represent the complete delinquency history of the subjects, the usually small sample sizes and the absence of sufficient numbers of high-rate offenders preclude the generalization of results to offender groups for whom specialization is a meaningful construct.

In light of the particular approach to offense specialization (i.e., offense transition matrices) that we employed in Cohort I and will continue to employ in this study, we will concern ourselves below with only a brief review of offense specialization research, and in particular, we will only address those studies that employ some form of transition analysis for juvenile offenders. We should point out, however, that specialization has been researched in ways other than offense transitions in samples other than juveniles. The reader is referred to a very comprehensive review of the subject in Cohen (1986).

Following the publication of the results of our 1945 birth cohort, Bursik (1980) reported an offense specialization analysis of 469 five-time offenders (134 whites and 335 nonwhites) from a sample of 750 adjudicated delinquents in Cook County, Illinois. Bursik used four categories of offenses—personal injury, personal property, impersonal property, and other—and examined the four offense transitions associated with the commission of five offenses. He found evidence of offense specialization for both whites and nonwhites. The decided contribution of Bursik's study was that, unlike the Wolfgang, Figlio, and Sellin (1972) Markov model analyses, Bursik went beyond the analysis of just transition probabilities and focused as well on the differences between the observed and expected values that underlie the transitions. We shall address Bursik's "residual analysis" later in the chapter.

Rojek and Erickson (1982) studied specialization among 868 multiple offenders out of a sample of 1,180 delinquents referred to the Pima County, Arizona, juvenile court. Reflective of their interest in status offending, they used an offense type scheme that included two status offenses—runaway and other—as well as categories for person, property, and other offenses. Like Wolfgang *et al.* (1972) they analyzed offense transition probabilities, and like Bursik they computed cell residuals. Rojek and Erickson found evidence of specialization for property offenses and the status offense of running away, but not for the three other offense types.

Smith and Smith (1984) used a sample of 767 male juveniles who were incarcerated in New Jersey correctional facilities between October 1977 and December 1978. The authors portrayed their sample as "hardcore" delinquents who had been arrested an average of 11.7 times for a total of 9,000 offenses, of which 70% were for index crimes. Using the same harm-based classification scheme as Wolfgang *et al.* (1972), Smith and Smith found some evidence of specialization, especially among those delinquents that began their careers with the commission of robbery.

Recently, Farrington *et al.* (1988) have contributed an important addition to the juvenile offense specialization literature. The first noteworthy aspect of the study concerns the fact that a substantial number of delinquents (n = 69,271) comprise the sample drawn from Utah and Maricopa County, Arizona. This number of delinquents permitted the analysis of some 28,000 two-time offenders, 7,708 five-time offenders, and 2,500 nine-time offenders. The second important feature of the study is that Farrington *et al.* have added a new statistical measure to offense transition analysis, called the "forward specialization coefficient." Farrington *et al.* reported a small but significant degree of specialization in the midst of a great deal of versatility in delinquent offending. It should be noted that, unlike other studies which used 4 or 5 offense-type categories, Farrington *et al.* used 21 offense categories. Thus, the results of this research are not necessarily inconsistent with those reviewed above.

Given this body of prior research, especially the improved analytical/statistical stance offered by the investigation of Bursik (1980), it is our intent in this chapter to examine the extent of juvenile offense specialization evident in the delinquency careers of our two cohorts as follows. First, we shall continue our prior work with Markov models of offense transition probabilities. Second, however, we shall also apply the adjusted standardized residual analyses first reported by Bursik. Third, we shall analyze three groups of offenders: all offenders regardless of the number of career offenses, and two sets of recidivists (five-time offenders and nine-time offenders). These sets of offenders will allow us to determine if specialization requires a certain minimum amount of recidivism before it either develops or can be detected.

Offense Transition Probabilities: All Offenders

The first aspect of our analysis concerns the offense transition probabilities. Essentially, two problems form the substance of this concern: (1) the determination of the transition probability, $P_{ij}(k)$, of committing the *k*th offense (where *k* is the number of the offense in a series of offenses) by the type j of the *k*th offense, given the type i, of the *k*-1st offense; and (2) the comparison of the transition matrices which are generated by the determination of the P_{ij}s mentioned in (1). The specific questions we pose are: (1) does the type of the offense that a cohort member committed at the *k*-1 offense number have any bearing on the probability that he will commit a certain type of offense at the *k*th offense number; and (2) does the same process operate at each offense number (1st, 2nd, 3rd, etc.) so that similar transition matrices will be generated when the offenses are classified by type? In short, are the transition configurations such that a homogenous or number independent Markov chain can be said to exist? A comprehensive discussion of Markov models and their application in criminology is available in Figlio (1981), therefore we shall not elaborate here.

In the transition matrices discussed below we present the transition probabilities of committing each of the five types of offenses that comprise the Sellin-Wolfgang measurement scheme (nonindex, injury, theft, damage, or combination), given the type of prior offense. We may now define as "states" the categories of offenses heretofore denoted as "types." Thus, for each offense number *k*, an offender must move to one of the six possible states of nonindex, injury, theft, damage, combination, or desistance.

It should be noted at the outset that the Sellin-Wolfgang classification scheme permits only a conservative test of offense specialization. That is, because one of the six states is the combination category, and because this category can consist of several crime blends (i.e., injury/theft, injury/damage, injury/theft/damage, or theft/damage), an offender could commit an injury/combination/injury offense sequence and appear to be a nonspecialist owing to the intervening combination offense (even though this combination offense involved injury). At present we are limited to the particular scoring system used for the 1945 cohort. However, in our subsequent work with the 1958 cohort we shall employ a variety of classification schemes. The point here is that whatever degree of offense specialization that we find represents only the minimum that may be actually present in the data.

The usual entries in an offense transition matrix consist of the probabilities of being in the state j at offense number *k* (columns), having been in state i at offense number *k*-1 (rows). Because our interest here principally concerns specialization, or the chances of repeating an offense type, we have reported only the probabilities along the main diagonal (which signify that states i and j are the same for each *k* and *k*-1 offense) and the desistance probabilities for the transitions from the first to second, second to third, third to fourth, and so on out to the eighth to the ninth. There are eight matrices, where the first transition is the movement from the first offense or state to the second offense or state, and the eighth transition is that movement from the eighth to the ninth state. By comparing adjacent matrices we may ascertain whether any pattern of progression exists between pairs.

The matrices shown in Table 9.1 contain the "same" offense and desistance transition probabilities for all male offenders in the two cohorts. Simply, these data do not appear to support the hypothesis that offense specialization exists. The data for Cohort I indicate that the transition probabilities for any particular offense type appear neither high enough nor sufficiently different in terms of the type of prior offense. For the full K-1/K table it may be said that the typical offender is most likely to commit a nonindex offense type at his next delinquent act, regardless of what he did in the past (after the first transition). If he does not commit a nonindex type next, he is most likely to desist from further delinquency. If he does commit an index offense next, it would most likely be the theft of property and would least likely be damage to property. With the exception of a very slight tendency to repeat the same type of offense, the above pattern obtains regardless of the type of the previous offense and transition number.

The matrices given in Table 9.1 for male offenders in Cohort II suggest the same findings as above. At the transition from the first to the second offense, a delinquent will most likely desist (.4309) from further delinquency; if he does not desist he will most likely repeat a nonindex offense (.3584). The chances of repeating the index offense types range from a low of .0559 for injury to a high of .1051 for theft. From the second to the eighth transition, an offender will be more likely to commit a nonindex offense than enter any of the five other states. When an index offense is committed at the kth offense, it will most likely involve theft and least likely injury. Once again, there is a slight tendency for an offender to repeat the same type of offense, but these probabilities are not very high and attain a maximum value of only .2941 for the theft-to-theft repeat at the eighth transition.

In addition to the relationships between the immediately prior and subsequent offenses, we may also try to assess the effect of knowing the types of the two prior offenses. That is, we can investigate the benefit of knowing the k-2 and k-1 types instead of having only the k-1 offense type to predict the type of the kth offense. In Markovian terminology, we should like to determine if the model is first or second order. We are prevented from achieving a complete evaluation because the sample sizes are too small in many of the transitions to permit reliable testing. A

TABLE 9.1

Offense Transition Probabilities: First Nine Offenses, by Transition Number for All Offenders by Cohort

K-1/K	1958 Cohort			1945 Cohort		
			First transition			
	N	Same	Desist	N	Same	Desist
Nonindex	2648	.3584	.4309	2275	.3349	.5107
Injury	286	.0559	.3951	264	.0795	.4280
Theft	571	.1051	.4518	484	.1508	.3698
Damage	508	.0846	.3465	252	.0476	.3769
Combination	302	.0795	.3841	200	.0450	.3200
	4315			3475		
K-1/K			Second transition			
	N	Same	Desist	N	Same	Desist
Nonindex	1506	.4323	.2908	1192	.4077	.3926
Injury	185	.0811	.3135	158	.0633	.3607
Theft	368	.1576	.2962	276	.1993	.2826
Damage	244	.1230	.1885	77	.0260	.2077
Combination	208	.1058	.2596	159	.1384	.1949
	2511			1862		
K-1/K			Third transition			
	N	Same	Desist	N	Same	Desist
Nonindex	1031	.3977	.2890	753	.4502	.3200
Injury	142	.1268	.2465	90	.1444	.2666
Theft	278	.1942	.3058	232	.1638	.2155
Damage	164	.1037	.2134	44	.0227	.3409
Combination	191	.1728	.2565	93	.1075	.1935
	1806			1212		
K-1/K			Fourth transition			
	N	Same	Desist	N	Same	Desist
Nonindex	681	.4332	.2467	538	.4368	.3122
Injury	114	.1667	.3158	89	.0674	.2921
Theft	251	.1912	.2550	150	.2200	.2066
Damage	108	.0926	.1574	30	.0333	.1333
Combination	150	.1600	.2467	61	.1148	.1967
	1304			868		

(continued)

TABLE 9.1 (continued)

K-1/K	Fifth transition					
	N	Same	Desist	N	Same	Desist
Nonindex	518	.4556	.1950	375	.4747	.2800
Injury	90	.1333	.2556	57	.0877	.3333
Theft	193	.2435	.2642	114	.1842	.2280
Damage	74	.1081	.1351	23	.0000	.0869
Combination	107	.2336	.2523	58	.1552	.1724
	982			627		

K-1/K	Sixth transition					
	N	Same	Desist	N	Same	Desist
Nonindex	385	.4286	.1766	295	.2500	.2271
Injury	68	.1471	.3529	33	.1212	.3333
Theft	150	.2067	.2467	81	.2556	.1000
Damage	69	.0725	.2029	8	.2500	.1250
Combination	98	.1531	.3163	39	.2051	.2307
	770			456		

K-1/K	Seventh transition					
	N	Same	Desist	N	Same	Desist
Nonindex	289	.3910	.1869	205	.5073	.2292
Injury	53	.0755	.3585	43	.1395	.3023
Theft	121	.2727	.1488	65	.3231	.1692
Damage	51	.1569	.2353	18	.0556	.1666
Combination	82	.2073	.1951	37	.0541	.3243
	596			368		

K-1/K	Eighth transition					
	N	Same	Desist	N	Same	Desist
Nonindex	204	.4020	.1667	166	.5060	.1807
Injury	48	.1250	.1667	30	.0333	.3333
Theft	102	.2941	.1373	53	.2075	.1320
Damage	51	.1176	.1961	6	.0000	.0000
Combination	72	.2361	.1111	27	.1852	.3703
	477			282		

large number of P_{ijk} cells must be filled in order to permit testing the probabilities in a three-offense sequence. An insufficient number of delinquents in the two cohorts went on to the various offense types beyond the third offense. Thus, the data reported in Table 9.2 consist of only the first three offenses committed by the cohort offenders.

Table 9.2 indicates for both cohorts that the model is probably first order rather than second order. That is, our knowing the type of the k-2 offense does not materially aid us in predicting the kth offense any better in conjunction with the k-1 than the use of only the k-1. Thus, knowing the types of offenses that an offender committed first and second does not greatly help us predict the type of the third offense any better than knowledge of only the second offense.

Thus, returning to the eight transitions that represent a first-order Markov chain, we performed chi-square tests of the matrices taken two at a time (i.e., 1st vs. 2nd, 2nd vs. 3rd, and so on). These tests indicated that each of the data matrices was generated by one transition probability matrix. The separate matrices for the first to the eighth transition are thus sample estimates of this parent or generating matrix. Consequently, we may typify the parent matrix as the average of the separate matrices. This average, or summary matrix, displays the probability of ever moving from one offense state to another regardless of the particular offense number or transition. Table 9.3 displays these data for the two cohorts. Unlike Table 9.1, we have included the transition probabilities for all the states, not just for the same and desistance values.

For the 1945 cohort it is clear from looking at the cells that the most likely transition is to a nonindex offense regardless of the type of the prior offense. Damage offenders show the highest transition probability (.5013) to a nonindex offense, followed by nonindex offenders, with a probability of .4473. Injury, theft, and combination offenders show a probability of about .40 of moving to a nonindex offense state. If a nonindex offense state is not entered, then the next most likely transition is to the desistance state. Injury offenders are the most likely to desist, with a probability of .3314. Nonindex offenders are close behind with a desistance probability of .3068. The remaining chances of desistance are .2478 for combination offenders, .2126 for theft offenders, and .1770 for damage offenders.

The most likely index offense transitions are to the theft state, with values ranging from .0854 as the probability of committing a theft offense having just committed an injury, to .2130 from theft to theft. Injury and combination transitions follow, sharing the range of roughly .05 to .14, with damage being the least likely path with probabilities ranging from .01 to .05.

TABLE 9.2
*Probabilities of Offense Repeats by Type of Prior Two Offenses
for All Offenders by Cohort[a]*

			1958 Cohort				
k-2	k-1	N	N	I	T	D	C
N	N	646	.6347	.0851	.1223	.0604	.0975
N	I	65	.6000	.1231	.1231	.0769	.0769
N	T	139	.4892	.1079	.2446	.0791	.0791
N	D	114	.4649	.0614	.2281	.1491	.0965
N	C	84	.6548	.0833	.1071	.0833	.0714
k-2	k-1	N	N	I	T	D	C
I	N	76	.5263	.1579	.1053	.0789	.1316
I	I	10	.6000	.0000	.2000	.2000	.0000
I	T	15	.7333	.0667	.1333	.0667	.0000
I	D	15	.6000	.0667	.0667	.2000	.0667
I	C	11	.4545	.0000	.2727	.0000	.2727
k-2	k-1	N	N	I	T	D	C
T	N	135	.5556	.0296	.2148	.0889	.1111
T	I	17	.6471	.0588	.0588	.1176	.1176
T	T	45	.5111	.0444	.1111	.1556	.1178
T	D	22	.4545	.1818	.1818	.0909	.0909
T	C	18	.3333	.1111	.3333	.1111	.1111
k-2	k-1	N	N	I	T	D	C
D	N	136	.6250	.0368	.1029	.1029	.1324
D	I	19	.4737	.1579	.1579	.1053	.1053
D	T	31	.3871	.0323	.2903	.1613	.1290
D	D	35	.4571	.0286	.1714	.1714	.1714
D	C	23	.4348	.0870	.1304	.1304	.2174
k-2	k-1	N	N	I	T	D	C
C	N	75	.5467	.0800	.1200	.1467	.1067
C	I	16	.5000	.1875	.2500	.0000	.0626
C	T	29	.4828	.0345	.2759	.1379	.0690
C	D	12	.7500	.0000	.0833	.1667	.0000
C	C	18	.3333	.0556	.2222	.0556	.3333

TABLE 9.2 (continued)

k-2	k-1	N	1945 Cohort				
			N	I	T	D	C
N	N	452	.4199	.0367	.0827	.0197	.0341
N	I	52	.3488	.0698	.1512	.0233	.0116
N	T	95	.3810	.0544	.1156	.0204	.0748
N	D	29	.5676	.0270	.0811	.0541	.0541
N	C	61	.3827	.0864	.1728	.0247	.0864
k-2	**k-1**	**N**	**N**	**I**	**T**	**D**	**C**
I	N	58	.3535	.0505	.0808	.0404	.0606
I	I	13	.4762	.0952	.0000	.0000	.4760
I	T	12	.4000	.0667	.1333	.0000	.2000
I	D	5	.7143	.0000	.0000	.0000	.0000
I	C	9	.2222	.0000	.5556	.1111	.1111
k-2	**k-1**	**N**	**N**	**I**	**T**	**D**	**C**
T	N	101	.3544	.0696	.1456	.0316	.0380
T	I	19	.4281	.0385	.1538	.0385	.0769
T	T	56	.3151	.0274	.3699	.0137	.0411
T	D	12	.4667	.2000	.1333	.0000	.0000
T	C	28	.4242	.0303	.2121	.0000	.1818
k-2	**k-1**	**N**	**N**	**I**	**T**	**D**	**C**
D	N	61	.3800	.0600	.1200	.0200	.0300
D	I	8	.6000	.0000	.2000	.0000	.0000
D	T	24	.4615	.0769	.2692	.0000	.1154
D	D	9	.7778	.0000	.2222	.0000	.0000
D	C	11	.5833	.0833	.0833	.0000	.1667
k-2	**k-1**	**N**	**N**	**I**	**T**	**D**	**C**
C	N	52	.5068	.0411	.1096	.0274	.0274
C	I	9	.2667	.0667	.1333	.0667	.0667
C	T	13	.4667	.0000	.1333	.1333	.1333
C	D	6	.0000	.1111	.4444	.0000	.1111
C	C	19	.3333	.0000	.1557	.0417	.2500

*a*N, nonindex; I, index; T, theft; D, damage; C, combination.

TABLE 9.3

Summary Transition Matrix: First Nine Offenses for All Offenders by Cohort

K-1/K	1958 Cohort					
	N	I	T	D	C	Desist
Nonindex	.4123	.0679	.1280	.0623	.0816	.2478
Injury	.3376	.1139	.1063	.0600	.0816	.3006
Theft	.3276	.0503	.2082	.0700	.0807	.2632
Damage	.3581	.0588	.1586	.1074	.1078	.2094
Combination	.3238	.0662	.1295	.0591	.1685	.2527
Desist	.0000	.0000	.0000	.0000	.0000	.0000
K-1/K	1945 Cohort					
	N	I	T	D	C	Desist
Nonindex	.4473	.0685	.1054	.0228	.0492	.3068
Injury	.4090	.0920	.0854	.0222	.0600	.3314
Theft	.4051	.0530	.2130	.0235	.0928	.2126
Damage	.5013	.0882	.1463	.0529	.0343	.1770
Combination	.3922	.0703	.1378	.0169	.1350	.2478
Desist	.0000	.0000	.0000	.0000	.0000	.0000

The summary matrix for the 1958 offenders reports results similar to that for the 1945 cohort. It is clear from inspecting the cell probabilities that the most likely transition is to a nonindex offense. Prior nonindex offenders show the greatest chances of committing a subsequent nonindex offense (.4123). Among index offenders, those who committed prior damage offenses show the greatest probability of moving to the nonindex state (.3581), while combination offenders show the lowest probability (.3238). Theft and injury offenders are intermediate with probabilities of .3276 and .3376, respectively.

After a nonindex offense commission the next most likely transition is to the state of desistance. Injury offenders are the most likely to desist (.3006). They are followed by theft offenders (.2632), combination offenders (.2527), nonindex offenders (.2478), and last by damage offenders (.2094).

The most likely transition to index offense commission is for theft offenses. The probabilities range from a low of .1063 from injury to theft, to a high of .2082 from theft to theft. Combination transitions are next, with probabilities ranging from .0816 to .1685. Injury and damage transitions are least likely, with probabilities ranging from about .06 to .11.

The primary concern in the analysis of offense transition data is the extent to which specialization is observed in the offense histories of the delinquents. By specialization we mean that the probability of like-offense repeats (e.g., injury to injury or theft to theft) is higher than other transition pairs. The data reported in Table 9.3 show that, for all offense categories in Cohort II and for all index offense categories in Cohort I, like offenses are more likely to follow one another. The values along the main diagonal of the summary matrix for Cohort II show that nonindex offense pairs are the most likely to follow one another (.4123), followed by thefts (.2082), combination (.1685), injury (.1139), and then damage pairs (.1074). For the 1945 cohort the diagonal values for index offenses show the same sequence. Theft offenses are the most likely to follow one another (.2130), then combination (.1350), injury (.0920), and last, damage pairs (.0529).

As a general statement, it is possible to suggest that these data offer some evidence that offense specialization exists. The strength of the evidence is difficult to assess just from the observed probabilities. Customarily one would suggest that strong support for a hypothesis of offense specialization would be gained if the probability of moving to the same type of offense is of the magnitude of .50. A more reasonable approach would be to apply a standard based on the expected values of the present data. One way to determine such values is to investigate the probability of committing an additional offense of the same type committed before, regardless of the number of different kinds of offenses which may have occurred between the first occurrence and the repeat. In other words, what are the chances of *ever* repeating an offense type regardless of the number or type of intervening offenses? These data are given in Table 9.4.

Table 9.4 shows that for Cohort I the probability that another nonindex offense will be committed sometime in the delinquent career is high compared to the other offense probabilities, the chances ranging between .4590 and .7738. The probability that an additional injury offense will be committed ranges from .2138 to .3309. The theft probabilities lie between .3349 and .4722. The two combination repeats have probabilities of .2773 and .4081. The damage offense type was repeated only once with a probability of .0961.

For Cohort II, which is clearly characterized by more extensive recidivism than Cohort I, the nonindex offense data in Table 9.4 show values of .5078 for one repeat to .7500 for nine repeats. Most important, the index offense types were committed with much greater frequency. The injury offenses show up to six repeats and probabilities ranging from .2222 to .5000. The theft offenses were committed up to nine times,

TABLE 9.4
Probability of Ever Committing the Same Type of Offense Disregarding Type of Intervening Offenses for All Offenders by Cohort

kth repeat	1958 Cohort				
	Nonindex	Injury	Theft	Damage	Combination
1st	.5078	.2599	.3453	.2403	.3170
2nd	.5967	.3231	.4770	.3794	.4019
3rd	.6034	.3243	.5210	.3958	.5039
4th	.6904	.3750	.5806	.5000	.5625
5th	.6888	.2222	.6806	.5789	.6389
6th	.6811	.5000	.6735	.6364	.3913
7th	.6780	.0000	.6970	.5714	.7777
8th	.7194	.0000	.6957	.7500	.7143
9th	.7500	.0000	.4375	.6667	.6000

kth repeat	1945 Cohort				
	Nonindex	Injury	Theft	Damage	Combination
1st	.4590	.2138	.3349	.0961	.2773
2nd	.5701	.3309	.4615	.0000	.4081
3rd	.6164	.2978	.4615	.0000	.0000
4th	.6390	.0000	.4722	.0000	.0000
5th	.6578	.0000	.4705	.0000	.0000
6th	.6717	.0000	.4375	.0000	.0000
7th	.6315	.0000	.0000	.0000	.0000
8th	.7738	.0000	.0000	.0000	.0000
9th	.6153	.0000	.0000	.0000	.0000

with probabilities as low as .3453 for one repeat and as high as .6970 for seven repeat thefts. Quite unlike Cohort I, where repeat damage and combination offenses were very scarce, the Cohort II data show that for both offense types at least nine repetitions are available. The range for damage repeats is from .24 to .75, while the combination probabilities lie between .31 and .77. These data confirm earlier data which showed that recidivism, particularly index recidivism, is more extensive in the 1958 cohort.

The data given in Table 9.4 thus set the ceiling of repeat offense probabilities. Given these expected values, the summary transition matrix probabilities show some evidence of offense specialization. Yet, the tendency to repeat the same type of offense cannot be definitively characterized with just the data given in either Table 9.3 or 9.4. Thus, whether the tendency is strong or moderate, and whether it varies by offense type are important issues which remain unresolved. It is clear that an alternate analysis strategy is required. One such strategy is discussed and results are presented below.

Offense Transition Residuals: All Offenders

The work in the area of offense specialization of Bursik (1980), discussed in the beginning of the chapter, has moved away from the probabilistic models of Markov analyses to an approach based on contingency tables. In his approach, which has been replicated by others, the cell frequencies of the k-1 to the kth offense are analyzed instead of the cell probabilities used in Markov models. In contingency table analysis the traditional test of independence is concerned with the observed cell frequencies given the number that would be expected by chance alone (a reflection of the marginal distributions). The independence model is thus ideally suited for the analysis of offense transitions. Quite simply, the model tests the data to determine whether the k-1 and kth offenses are statistically independent. Through an analysis of the residuals (i.e., cell deviations), especially those along the main diagonal, which are a function of the difference between the observed and expected frequencies, the departure of the data (cell by cell) from independence can be investigated. Most important, the magnitude of the departure can be documented.

As noted earlier, several studies have employed the analysis of residuals to test for juvenile offense specialization. Bursik (1980), using juvenile court data, reported that white recidivists showed evidence of specializing in personal property, impersonal property, and other offenses, but not personal injury offenses. Nonwhite recidivists showed specialization for all four offense types. Rojek and Erickson (1982) have also reported for a sample of delinquents that male offenders tended to specialize in property offenses and runaway, but not for the categories of person, other crimes, and other status offenses. Separate results by race were not shown but were described as being similar to those for males generally.

Following the important precedent set by Bursik, in the analyses below we have also chosen to utilize adjusted standardized residual statistics. These cell-specific residuals are computed by taking the observed frequency minus the expected value and then adjusting by dividing by the respective standard errors. Under the assumption of a large sample size, the standardized residuals have an expected value of 0 with a variance of 1, and thus approach the standardized normal distribution.

A review of residual analysis can be found in Haberman (1973, 1978) and Bishop *et al.* (1975).

Table 9.5 reports the offense transition residuals for all offenders for the first to the ninth offense. At the outset it should be noted that all delinquents are included regardless of the number of offenses they committed. Thus, the absorbing state of desistance is included as one of the transition states. This inclusion can confound patterns of offense specialization that might be observed for the recidivists. Yet, beginning the analysis of the residuals with all offenders will allow us to focus on the movement to the state of desistance as well as to one of the five offense states. Later analyses will focus exclusively on groups of recidivist offenders and their patterns of offense specialization. For these recidivist delinquents the residuals are more reliable measures owing to the uniformity of the sample size across transitions.

Table 9.5 shows for the 1945 cohort that transitions to like-offense repeats are more frequent than would be expected by chance for the four states associated with index offenses. The residuals which lie along the main diagonal (reported here in the "same" column) are almost always positive and are generally higher than the values of the other offense pairs down the various columns of the complete K-1/K tables (not shown). Across the eight transitions, theft and combination offenders show the strongest tendency to specialize. The residuals for these offenders are usually in the range from +2.0 to +4.0. The damage-to-damage repeats show no evidence of being greater than expected. In fact, the likelihood of a damage offense seems quite independent of the k-1 offense type. Injury offense repeats show residuals that are lower than those for theft or combination. The values range from a high of +2.8 at the first transition to a low of −1.1 at the eighth transition. Thus, the evidence for injury offense specialization is only moderate at best.

With respect to a transition to the state of desistance, the residuals show a marked difference. For the first four transitions, delinquents with a nonindex offense at the k-1 are much more likely to desist at the kth offense than index offenders. The desistance residuals for nonindex offenders are considerably higher, with values of +7.6, +5.3, +3.6, and +2.9, than other types of k-1 offenders. For the later transitions, injury offenders at the k-1 offense show the greatest tendency to desist at the fifth and sixth transitions, while combination offenders exhibit this tendency at the seventh and eighth transitions.

The last important feature of the residuals given in Table 9.5 for Cohort I concerns the absence of a transition effect. That is, the residuals appear to be unrelated to transition number. The evidence of specialization does not seem to increase or decrease as rank number of offense

TABLE 9.5

Offense Transition Residuals: First Nine Offenses, by Transition Number for All Offenders by Cohort

K-1/K	1958 Cohort			1945 Cohort		
			First transition			
	N	Same	Desist	N	Same	Desist
Nonindex	2648	1.6	2.2	2275	−1.4	7.6
Injury	286	1.1	−0.8	264	2.8	−1.2
Theft	571	1.8	1.8	484	6.3	−4.5
Damage	508	2.9	−3.5	252	1.5	−2.9
Combination	302	2.6	−1.2	200	5.1	−4.3
	4315			3475		
			Second transition			
K-1/K	N	Same	Desist	N	Same	Desist
Nonindex	1506	2.7	1.4	1192	0.4	5.3
Injury	185	1.5	1.0	158	0.9	0.3
Theft	368	3.1	0.7	276	4.1	−2.5
Damage	244	3.8	−3.4	77	0.1	−2.7
Combination	208	1.7	−0.7	159	5.4	−4.3
	2511			1862		
			Third transition			
K-1/K	N	Same	Desist	N	Same	Desist
Nonindex	1031	2.1	1.2	753	0.6	3.6
Injury	142	3.2	−0.9	90	2.7	−0.4
Theft	278	2.9	1.1	232	2.1	−2.7
Damage	164	2.5	−1.9	44	−0.1	0.5
Combination	191	4.8	−0.7	93	2.6	−2.5
	1806			1212		
			Fourth transition			
K-1/K	N	Same	Desist	N	Same	Desist
Nonindex	681	2.8	−0.0	538	0.4	2.9
Injury	114	4.3	1.8	89	0.1	0.3
Theft	251	2.1	0.3	150	3.5	−2.1
Damage	108	1.7	−2.3	30	0.2	−1.8
Combination	150	3.7	−0.0	61	1.6	−1.5
	1304			868		

(*continued*)

TABLE 9.5 (continued)

| | Fifth transition | | | | | |
K-1/K	N	Same	Desist	N	Same	Desist
Nonindex	518	4.3	−1.7	375	0.3	1.5
Injury	90	2.5	1.0	57	1.2	1.4
Theft	193	3.9	1.8	114	1.4	−0.8
Damage	74	1.3	−1.8	23	−0.6	−1.9
Combination	107	4.9	1.0	58	3.1	−1.6
	982			627		

| | Sixth transition | | | | | |
K-1/K	N	Same	Desist	N	Same	Desist
Nonindex	385	3.1	−3.3	295	1.2	1.3
Injury	68	2.7	2.6	33	0.6	1.8
Theft	150	1.9	0.7	81	3.5	−2.8
Damage	69	0.2	−0.5	8	3.1	−0.6
Combination	98	1.6	2.3	39	3.0	0.4
	770			456		

| | Seventh transition | | | | | |
K-1/K	N	Same	Desist	N	Same	Desist
Nonindex	289	2.4	−0.8	205	2.4	−0.2
Injury	53	−0.1	3.0	43	1.5	1.1
Theft	121	3.3	−1.6	65	4.5	−1.4
Damage	51	1.9	0.7	18	1.3	−0.7
Combination	82	2.6	−0.1	37	−0.5	1.4
	596			368		

| | Eighth transition | | | | | |
K-1/K	N	Same	Desist	N	Same	Desist
Nonindex	204	1.8	0.6	166	1.1	−1.1
Injury	48	1.0	0.2	30	−1.1	1.9
Theft	102	3.2	−0.6	53	2.0	−1.4
Damage	51	1.1	0.9	6	−0.3	−1.2
Combination	72	2.6	−1.1	27	1.9	2.3
	477			282		

increases. Delinquents who commit like offenses in pairs appear to do so at all stages of the career. The exception as noted above concerns the fact that nonindex offenders show the strongest tendency to desist for the early transitions, while injury and combination offenders display this tendency for later transitions.

The residuals for the offense transitions of the 1958 cohort are also reported in Table 9.5. Like the Cohort I data, the residuals indicate that the type of kth offense is not statistically independent of the k-1 offense. However, the Cohort II data show this result for all five offense types. Thus, a transition to a particular state at the kth offense is greater than what would be expected by chance for offenders who had been in this particular state at the k-1 offense. Another departure from Cohort I concerns the fact that the tendency to repeat like offenses does not vary greatly by offense type. The residuals for nonindex pairs and the four pairs for index offenses generally lie in about the same range, from +2.0 to +4.0, across the various transitions.

Another finding which again confirms previous data is that the residuals for desistance in Cohort II are considerably lower than those in Cohort I. The pattern is the same with nonindex offenders showing the early tendency to desist, and then injury, theft, and combination offenders showing a greater departure from expectations in later transitions. Yet, the magnitude of the residuals shows that in Cohort II, desisting is not greatly influenced by the type of offense that a delinquent commits immediately prior to desisting.

Like Cohort I, therefore, the residuals for the 1958 cohort do not show a marked transition effect. The residuals for various offense types do vary by transition number but not systematically. Thus, the complete pool of offenders exhibits specialization patterns at all stages of the career. This finding may result from the fact that occasional and habitual offenders were included in the same analyses. Below we turn to the recidivist subsets.

Offense Transition Residuals: All Offender Recidivists

Instead of looking at delinquent careers as an absorbing Markov chain where desistance or no further arrests is one of the states of the model, we shall now examine the residuals of the offense transitions of a regular Markov chain. Because a regular Markov chain has no absorbing state and thus considers only the continuing transitions to offense states, we refer to such models in our terms as recidivism models. In the present context the recidivism model is preferable because our primary interest is the question of offense specialization. Naturally, only delinquents who commit some minimum number of offenses are candidates for specialization. For comparative purposes we consider below two sets of recidivists—delinquents with at least five offenses (the chronics) and delinquents with at least nine offenses (the chronic chronics). For the former we can analyze the residuals from four offense transitions, while for the latter we can utilize the data from eight transitions. Because the number of offenders who make the various transitions is unchanging, the residuals are less susceptible to changes in the marginal distribution which comes about when the absorbing state of desistance is included.

Table 9.6 shows the Cohort I residuals for offenders who committed five or more offenses. These data indicate for all offense types that a recidivist is more likely than expected to repeat his previous offense than to move to a different offense state. From the first to the second offense the residuals for nonindex and theft offenses show the largest departure from chance, with deviates of +3.7 and +3.5, respectively. Injury and combination offenders follow with deviates of +1.8 and +1.4, respectively. Delinquents with damage as the first offense are not very likely to repeat this offense type (residual = +.08). From the second to the third offense the residuals show a specialization ranking of combination (+3.2), nonindex (+2.6), theft (+2.2), and injury (+1.5). The damage residual is not significantly different from zero (+0.3) and shows no tendency to specialize. The third to the fourth offense follows a different pattern, with nonindex first (+2.5) followed by combination (+2.1), injury (+1.7), theft (+1.5), and damage (−0.1) last. By the fifth offense, offenders who had committed nonindex and theft offenses as their fourth offense show significant departures from expectations with deviates of +2.3 and +3.0, respectively. Combination repeats at the fourth transition (+1.3) are only slightly greater than chance. For injury and damage offenders a repeat of the offense is observed in almost perfect accord with expectations.

The Cohort II data reported in Table 9.6 also show that recidivists repeat the type of their prior offense with a frequency that exceeds the expected value. At the first transition moderate specialization is observed for combination (+2.2), nonindex (+2.0), and theft (+1.7) offenses. The residual damage (+0.9) is only slight, while the injury repeats (−0.6) are less often than expected. As we move to the third offense the residuals show moderate specialization again with nonindex offenders (+2.9) ranking first followed by damage (+2.7), theft (+2.2), and then injury (+1.0). Combination offenses are committed as a third offense only slightly more than chance would dictate. The third transition data show that as the recidivists move to the fourth offense the

TABLE 9.6

Offense Transition Residuals: First Five Offenses by
Transition Number for All Five-Time Offenders by Cohort

K-1/K	1958 Cohort		1945 Cohort	
	First transition			
	N	Same	N	Same
Nonindex	562	2.0	332	3.7
Injury	64	−0.6	52	1.8
Theft	138	1.7	121	3.5
Damage	130	0.9	57	0.8
Combination	88	2.2	65	1.4
	982		627	
	Second transition			
K-1/K	N	Same	N	Same
Nonindex	576	2.9	348	2.6
Injury	64	1.0	45	1.5
Theft	140	2.2	104	2.2
Damage	126	2.7	40	0.3
Combination	76	0.6	90	3.2
	982		627	
	Third transition			
K-1/K	N	Same	N	Same
Nonindex	555	2.7	357	2.5
Injury	77	3.0	47	1.7
Theft	138	2.5	136	1.5
Damage	104	2.3	26	−0.1
Combination	108	3.4	61	2.1
	982		627	
	Fourth transition			
K-1/K	N	Same	N	Same
Nonindex	513	3.1	370	2.3
Injury	78	4.8	63	0.1
Theft	187	2.3	119	3.0
Damage	91	1.3	26	0.0
Combination	113	3.8	49	1.3
	982		627	

tendency to repeat the third offense type is strong and covers all five offense states. Combination offenses rank first with a residual of +3.4, followed by injury (+3.0), nonindex (+2.7), theft (+2.5), and then damage (+2.3). The fourth transition shows similarly high residuals which follow another sequence. Injury is first with a residual of +4.8, followed by combination (+3.8), nonindex (+3.1), theft (+2.3), and then damage (+1.3).

In Table 9.7 we turn to the offense transition residuals for those delinquents who committed at least nine delinquent acts. With these data it is possible to investigate whether the early delinquency career is characterized by offense specialization or whether offense specialization requires the repeated recidivism of a longer career, like nine or more offenses compared to just five.

Table 9.7 shows for Cohort I that the first transition is characterized by moderate specialization for nonindex offenses (+3.9) and theft offenses (+3.3). Injury offenses show only a slight tendency to be paired, with a residual of +1.1. Damage (+0.1) and combination (−0.1) offenses are repeated with a frequency that is almost identical to that expected from the marginals. Similar data are observed for the second through the fifth transitions. As the offense number increases, different offenses show evidence of specialization.

At the second transition, combination offenses show the highest residual (+2.5) followed by injury (+1.8) and nonindex (+1.5). The third transition data show significant injury (+1.8) and nonindex (+1.7) repeats, but only slight tendencies to repeat damage (+0.5) and combination offenses (+1.0), while theft offenses are repeated less often than expected (−0.8). The fourth transition shows no evidence that the offense type committed at the fourth offense is likely to be repeated disproportionately at the fifth offense. The transition to the sixth offense is characterized by slight specialization only for injury offenses (+2.0).

The last three transitions repeat the variation observed above. From the sixth to the seventh offense, theft (+3.2), damage (+2.9), and combination (+3.3) offenses are repeated much more frequently than expected. Nonindex offenses (+1.9) are repeated more often than expected by chance. Injury offenses (−0.1) occur as seventh offenses a bit less than expected. For the seventh transition, nonindex offenses (+3.0) are likely to be repeated as are theft offenses (+2.9). Injury offenses (+1.6) show slight evidence of repetition. Damage offenses (+1.2) are repeated only slightly more than by chance, while combination offense (−0.5) repeats are underobserved. At the last transition, combination offenses emerge as moderate repeats (+2.5) and theft offenses are repeated (+1.8) slightly more often than chance.

TABLE 9.7

*Offense Transition Residuals: First Nine Offenses by
Transition Number for All Nine-Time Offenders by Cohort*

	1958 Cohort		1945 Cohort	
	First transition			
K-1/K	*N*	Same	*N*	Same
Nonindex	227	1.9	115	3.9
Injury	31	−0.7	18	1.1
Theft	48	0.8	43	3.3
Damage	58	0.0	17	0.1
Combination	39	1.3	32	−0.1
	403		225	
	Second transition			
K-1/K	*N*	Same	*N*	Same
Nonindex	227	2.5	122	1.5
Injury	24	1.9	12	1.8
Theft	60	0.7	36	0.0
Damage	62	1.9	12	0.6
Combination	30	0.6	43	2.5
	403		225	
	Third transition			
K-1/K	*N*	Same	*N*	Same
Nonindex	225	1.6	128	1.7
Injury	29	1.4	12	1.8
Theft	55	0.3	49	−0.8
Damage	54	2.1	12	0.5
Combination	40	0.3	24	1.0
	403		225	
	Fourth transition			
K-1/K	*N*	Same	*N*	Same
Nonindex	206	1.3	128	0.8
Injury	30	2.5	22	0.6
Theft	75	2.4	46	−0.2
Damage	48	0.8	12	0.2
Combination	44	0.5	17	−1.4
	403		225	

(continued)

TABLE 9.7 *(continued)*

K-1/K	*N*	Same	*N*	Same
		Fifth transition		
Nonindex	208	4.0	114	0.6
Injury	33	1.5	22	2.0
Theft	88	3.0	52	0.7
Damage	37	0.9	16	−0.7
Combination	37	2.4	21	0.9
	403		225	
		Sixth transition		
Nonindex	213	1.3	140	1.9
Injury	25	3.6	11	−0.1
Theft	78	1.5	48	3.2
Damage	38	1.2	6	2.9
Combination	49	1.6	20	3.3
	403		225	
		Seventh transition		
Nonindex	194	1.6	129	3.0
Injury	27	0.2	22	1.6
Theft	89	2.5	40	2.9
Damage	33	2.2	13	1.2
Combination	60	2.5	21	−0.5
	403		225	
		Eighth transition		
Nonindex	170	2.1	136	0.7
Injury	40	1.1	20	−0.9
Theft	88	3.1	46	1.8
Damage	41	1.2	6	−0.4
Combination	64	2.4	17	2.5
	403		225	

The offense transition residuals shown in Table 9.7 for the 1958 cohort exhibit similar variation by offense type and transition number. The first transition residuals show greater than expected repeats for nonindex offenses (+1.9) and combination offenses (+1.3). Injury, theft, and damage offenses occur with no evidence of specialization. From the second to the third offense, three offense types show the specialization tendency. The residuals for nonindex (+2.5), injury (+1.9), and damage (+1.9) are much higher than would be observed by chance. The third transition shows the same three offense types for which repeating the offense is greater than chance. Here, damage (+2.1) is first followed by nonindex (+1.6) and injury (+1.4). The fourth transition residuals indicate moderate specialization for injury (+2.5) and theft (+2.4) offenses and slight specialization for nonindex offenses (+1.3). For the transition from the fifth to the sixth offense, four offenses show departures from expected values. Nonindex (+4.0) and theft (+3.0) offenses have the highest residuals, while combination (+2.4) and injury (+1.5) offenses are repeated moderately.

The residuals for the last three offense transitions are observed to have about the same magnitudes as those of the earlier offenses. This would indicate that the strength of the tendency to repeat like offenses does not seem to increase as the career grows longer. However, unlike the earlier transitions in which at most three offense types were repeated with greater frequency than expected, the last three transitions show at least four offense types for which the observed frequency is much greater than expected.

For the sixth transition, all five offense states are repeated more than by chance. Injury offenses (+3.6) have the highest deviates followed by combination (+1.6), theft (+1.5), nonindex (+1.3), and then damage (+1.2). When delinquents move from the seventh to the eighth offense we see that only injury offenses are not repeated with sufficient frequency to indicate specialization. Theft and combination offenses show the largest residuals with a value of +2.5; they are followed by damage (+2.2) and then nonindex (+1.6). The last transition under consideration, from eighth to the ninth offense, is characterized by a tendency for offenders to repeat the type of their last offense, whichever type it is. Theft offenses (+3.1) are first, with combination (+2.4) and nonindex offenses (+2.1) exhibiting moderate specialization. Damage (+1.2) and injury (+1.1) offenses are repeated more often than expected but just slightly.

Up to this point we have presented residuals for each transition separately. This was also the case with the transition matrix probabilities presented earlier in this chapter. We showed there that because the relationship between the probability of committing a next offense of a particular type, having just committed the same type, is essentially independent of the number of the offense, it may be argued that the sequence of states is a simple, homogenous Markov chain. Consequently, an appropriate display of the transition data is the summary or generating matrix. The same argument appears valid here with the various transitions of the recidivism model. The tendency to repeat like offenses appears unrelated to transition number.

Specialization can and does occur for the various offense types at all stages of the career. Thus, as before, we present below the offense transition residuals in summary matrix form. The data are grouped by subsequent offense type, given the immediately prior offense type, without regard to the particular transition number of occurrence.

Table 9.8 reports the summary residuals for those Cohort I offenders who have committed at least five offenses and thus have made four transitions. The first panel gives the residuals. These data clearly indicate offense specialization for all offenses except damage. Nonindex pairs (+5.6) show the greatest departure from the expected frequency. Theft (+5.0) and combination offenses (+4.0) also show marked departures from expectations. Injury offense (+2.5) repeats have a lower residual, yet still reflect moderate specialization. Damage repeats (+0.9) are at best only slightly more likely than chance. In addition to the residuals, Table 9.8 gives the overall and cell-specific chi-square values for the independence model. Clearly, the chi-square of 75.0 shows that the type of next offense is not independent of the type of offense committed just prior. More important, the data show that the highest chi-square values fall along the main diagonal, thus indicating that the association between prior and subsequent offense of the same type is responsible for the departure from independence.

Table 9.8 reports the summary data for the four transitions of the Cohort II offenders who committed at least five offenses. These data show the unmistakable finding that chronic delinquents in the 1958 cohort specialize, and do so for all five offense types. Further, the residuals shown are higher than those observed in Cohort I. Nonindex (+5.5) and combination (+5.2) offenses are repeated much more often than chance and suggest strong specialization. Injury and theft offenses have the same residual, +4.5, indicating only slightly less specialization. Damage offenses (+3.8) in Cohort II, unlike Cohort I, are repeated with moderate to high specialization. The chi-square data shown in the second panel confirm the highly significant association between prior and subsequent offense types. Overall, the chi-square value is 96.2. The chi-square values along the main diagonal show that the failure of the inde-

TABLE 9.8

Offense Transition Residuals and Chi-square: Summary Transition Matrix of First Five Offenses for All Five-Time Offenders by Cohort

| | | | 1958 Cohort | | | |
| | | | Adjusted standardized deviates | | | |
K-1/K	N	I	T	D	C	Total
Nonindex	5.5	−2.0	−3.1	1.2	−2.3	2206
Injury	−0.6	4.5	−1.9	0.5	−1.2	283
Theft	−3.0	0.1	4.5	−0.7	−0.0	603
Damage	−1.9	−0.1	−0.2	3.8	−0.2	451
Combination	−2.9	−0.7	1.5	−1.7	5.2	385
						3928

| | | | Components of chi-square | | | |
K-1/K	N	I	T	D	C	Total
Nonindex	5.9	1.6	3.4	0.5	2.1	15.9
Injury	0.1	17.5	2.7	0.2	1.3	8.6
Theft	3.5	0.0	14.3	0.4	0.0	29.1
Damage	1.5	0.0	0.0	11.3	0.0	2.8
Combination	3.4	0.4	1.7	2.4	21.8	18.6
	14.4	19.4	22.2	14.9	25.3	96.2

| | | | 1945 Cohort | | | |
| | | | Adjusted standardized deviates | | | |
K-1/K	N	I	T	D	C	Total
Nonindex	5.6	−0.3	−3.7	−0.7	−3.5	1407
Injury	0.5	2.5	−2.0	0.2	−0.5	207
Theft	−4.5	−1.2	5.0	−0.5	2.4	480
Damage	−0.5	0.7	0.6	0.9	−1.2	149
Combination	−3.2	0.8	1.0	0.9	4.0	265
						2508

| | | | Components of chi-square | | | |
K-1/K	N	I	T	D	C	Total
Nonindex	5.8	0.0	5.0	0.2	4.9	15.9
Injury	0.1	5.2	3.1	0.0	0.2	8.6
Theft	7.1	1.1	16.4	0.2	4.3	29.1
Damage	0.1	0.5	0.3	0.7	1.2	2.8
Combination	3.8	0.5	0.7	0.7	12.9	18.6
	16.9	7.2	25.5	1.8	23.6	75.0

pendence model is due to like-offense repeats. For the various columns of data, the residuals along the main diagonal account for the vast majority of the chi-square for the four index offense types and the nonindex repeat value is the largest, although not as substantially as was the case for the other offense types.

In Table 9.9 we expand the summary residuals to include eight transitions or a total of nine offenses for the nine-time recidivists, or the chronic chronics as we might call them. For both Cohort I and Cohort II the data indicate evidence of offense specialization. It is certain, however, that the nine-time recidivists in Cohort II exhibit the stronger tendency to specialize.

In Cohort I the nine-time recidivists show strongest specialization for nonindex (+5.0) and theft (+3.7) offense repeats. Less specialization is evident for combination (+2.9) and injury (+2.5) offenses. Like previous Cohort I data for the five-time offenders, damage offenses (+0.9) are not repeated with sufficient departure from expectations to suggest specialization. The overall chi-square of 54.5 for the full table indicates that prior and subsequent offenses are related. The chi-square components along the diagonal are the highest, thus showing the greatest departure from independence.

The data given in Table 9.9 for the 1958 cohort show the strongest evidence of specialization in all of the analyses conducted. Each of the five offense types are characterized by main diagonal deviates that are highly reflective of specialization. Nonindex pairs depart from expectations the most (+6.2) followed closely by theft offenses (+5.7). Combination offenses with a residual of +4.8 are next. Injury and damage offenses are the lowest with residuals of +3.9 and +3.8, respectively, but these values are still high and significant. The substantial chi-square (112.5) for the prior versus subsequent offense relationship shows a very significant departure from independence. Most important, the chi-square components along the main diagonal are quite high, with index offense repeats showing the greatest share of the full chi-square.

Offense Transition Probabilities by Race

In prior sections of this volume we have shown that the two major subgroups of offenders that warrant separate attention are whites and nonwhites. Thus, it is equally important here to distinguish the race-specific offense specialization patterns. We present below the race-specific specialization analyses for the two cohorts.

The eight transitions for the first to the ninth offense are given in

TABLE 9.9

Offense Transition Residuals and Chi-square: Summary Transition Matrix of First Nine Offenses for All Nine-Time Offenders by Cohort

	1958 Cohort Adjusted standardized deviates					
K-1/K	N	I	T	D	C	Total
Nonindex	6.2	−0.3	−4.3	−1.6	−2.6	1670
Injury	−0.9	3.9	−1.2	0.6	−1.0	239
Theft	−2.1	−2.9	5.7	−0.0	−1.3	581
Damage	−3.0	−0.1	−0.5	3.8	1.7	371
Combination	−3.4	0.8	1.3	−1.9	4.8	363
						3224

	Components of chi-square					
K-1/K	N	I	T	D	C	Total
Nonindex	9.2	0.0	7.1	1.0	2.9	20.2
Injury	0.4	13.1	1.1	0.3	0.8	15.7
Theft	1.8	6.3	21.5	0.0	1.2	30.9
Damage	4.1	0.0	0.2	11.6	2.3	18.1
Combination	5.2	0.6	1.2	2.8	18.0	27.7
	20.6	20.0	31.0	15.8	25.2	112.5

	1945 Cohort Adjusted standardized deviates					
K-1/K	N	I	T	D	C	Total
Nonindex	5.0	0.5	−3.6	−1.4	−2.9	1012
Injury	−0.5	2.5	−1.6	0.3	0.4	139
Theft	−2.8	−2.2	3.7	0.2	1.6	360
Damage	−0.6	−0.2	1.2	0.9	−1.0	94
Combination	−3.5	0.1	1.5	1.1	2.9	195
						1800

	Components of chi-square					
K-1/K	N	I	T	D	C	Total
Nonindex	4.6	0.1	4.5	0.8	3.3	13.4
Injury	0.1	5.3	1.9	0.1	0.2	7.5
Theft	2.7	3.6	8.6	0.0	1.9	16.7
Damage	0.2	0.1	1.2	0.7	0.8	2.0
Combination	4.6	0.0	1.6	1.1	6.6	14.0
	12.2	9.0	17.8	2.7	12.8	54.5

Table 9.10 for white offenders in the 1945 cohort and the 1958 cohort. Whites in Cohort I show less than substantial chances of repeat index offenses (only the main diagonal entries are given) for the various transitions. Theft offenses are the most likely to be repeated, with probabilities of .12 to .18 for the first three transitions and probabilities of .23 to .30 for the fourth through the eighth transitions. Injury offense repeats are very infrequent and generally show values that vary considerably. The residual category of nonindex offenses is characterized by relatively high probabilities that have a low of .29 and a high of .51 with an average of about .42.

By comparison, whites in Cohort II show higher probabilities of like-offense repeats. Theft offenses are once again the most likely to occur in pairs. The chances range from .07 to .41 with an average of about .21. Combination and damage repeats are more likely in the second cohort. The former lie in the range of .07 to .50, while the latter fall between .09 and .14. Injury offenses are repeated the least often. These offense pairs range from a probability of .03 to a probability of .25. Like Cohort I, nonindex offenses in the 1958 cohort are repeated by whites the most often. The chances show a low of .31 to a high of .48.

The data given in Table 9.11 for nonwhites in the two cohorts show the same cohort effect. In Cohort I, nonwhites have the highest chances of repeating a theft offense. The chances range from .15 to .36. In Cohort II theft offense pairs are characterized by probabilities of .10 to .32. Combination offense repeats rank second for nonwhites in Cohort I with probabilities falling between .10 and .20. Combination offenses for Cohort II nonwhites rank the same, but show a range of .07 to .24 with more transitions at the higher end of the range. Cohort I nonwhites repeat injury offenses infrequently with chances as low as .03 and as high as .17.

Cohort II nonwhites have a higher minimum value (.05) and the same maximum (.17) but more transitions above a probability of .15 (3 to 1). Damage offense repeats are very rare for nonwhites in Cohort I. Only four transitions show a repeat damage, and the chances are less than .05 for these four transitions. Damage offense repeats are twice as frequent among the nonwhite offenders in Cohort II. The chances of a repeat are also higher and range from .03 to .08. Like whites in both cohorts nonwhites in each group display the highest probabilities of nonindex repeats. Cohort I nonwhites repeat this type of offense with probabilities of .39 to .52. Cohort II nonwhites show a more moderate tendency for nonindex pairs with values ranging from .38 to .44.

As was the case with the transition matrices for all offenders, the race-specific offense transitions appear to be the same within the limits

TABLE 9.10

Offense Transition Probabilities: First Nine Offenses, by Transition Number for White Offenders by Cohort

K-1/K	1958 Cohort			1945 Cohort		
	First transition					
	N	Same	Desist	N	Same	Desist
Nonindex	945	.3101	.5471	1412	.2960	.5956
Injury	73	.0548	.4795	120	.0667	.5083
Theft	147	.1020	.5170	247	.1255	.4291
Damage	171	.0994	.3743	160	.0375	.4250
Combination	76	.0921	.5395	80	.0500	.4250
	1412			2019		
	Second transition					
K-1/K	N	Same	Desist	N	Same	Desist
Nonindex	436	.4266	.3853	571	.3764	.4774
Injury	41	.0488	.4146	59	.0727	.4727
Theft	76	.1053	.3816	141	.1890	.3779
Damage	77	.1169	.2078	92	.0000	.3030
Combination	49	.1633	.2653	46	.1176	.2352
	679			909		
	Third transition					
K-1/K	N	Same	Desist	N	Same	Desist
Nonindex	264	.4280	.3447	336	.4331	.3866
Injury	27	.0370	.3704	29	.1429	.3333
Theft	43	.1395	.2791	79	.1771	.2291
Damage	50	.1000	.1400	23	.0526	.2631
Combination	52	.2115	.2692	39	.0385	.2307
	436			506		
	Fourth transition					
K-1/K	N	Same	Desist	N	Same	Desist
Nonindex	178	.4494	.3090	211	.4083	.4220
Injury	26	.1923	.4615	14	.0000	.3667
Theft	35	.1429	.3143	74	.3000	.2333
Damage	30	.1000	.2000	14	.0909	.2727
Combination	33	.1515	.2727	20	.1429	.2142
	302			333		

(continued)

TABLE 9.10 (continued)

K-1/K	N	Same	Desist	N	Same	Desist
			Fifth transition			
Nonindex	125	.4800	.2160	126	.4599	.3649
Injury	17	.0588	.3529	19	.1000	.6000
Theft	33	.1515	.2727	46	.2195	.3170
Damage	16	.1250	.1250	8	.0000	.1428
Combination	18	.2222	.1667	11	.2667	.1333
	209			210		
			Sixth transition			
Nonindex	93	.4731	.2206	87	.4516	.2903
Injury	11	.0909	.4545	4	.1667	.5000
Theft	19	.4118	.0588	28	.2593	.1481
Damage	23	.1429	.4286	6	.5000	.5000
Combination	16	.0714	.2143	13	.2000	.1000
	162			138		
			Seventh transition			
Nonindex	68	.4412	.2206	66	.4737	.3333
Injury	11	.0909	.4545	3	.0000	.5000
Theft	17	.4118	.0588	23	.2381	.3000
Damage	14	.1429	.4286	1	.0000	.2500
Combination	14	.0714	.2143	9	.0833	.5000
	124			102		
			Eighth transition			
Nonindex	46	.4348	.2391	38	.5116	.2558
Injury	8	.2500	.1250	4	.0000	.3333
Theft	23	.2174	.2174	14	.2308	.1538
Damage	11	.1818	.0000	3	.0000	.0000
Combination	6	.5000	.0000	6	.2000	.6000
	94			65		

TABLE 9.11

Offense Transition Probabilities: First Nine Offenses, by Transition Number
for Nonwhite Offenders by Cohort

	1958 Cohort			1945 Cohort		
			First transition			
K-1/K	N	Same	Desist	N	Same	Desist
Nonindex	1703	.3852	.3664	863	.3986	.3719
Injury	213	.0563	.3662	144	.0903	.3611
Theft	424	.1061	.4292	237	.1772	.3080
Damage	337	.0772	.3323	92	.0326	.2934
Combination	226	.0752	.3319	120	.1667	.2500
	2903			1456		
			Second transition			
K-1/K	N	Same	Desist	N	Same	Desist
Nonindex	1070	.4346	.2523	542	.4444	.2932
Injury	144	.0903	.2847	92	.0583	.3009
Theft	292	.1712	.2740	164	.2081	.2013
Damage	167	.1257	.1796	65	.0455	.1363
Combination	159	.0881	.2579	90	.1481	.1759
	1832			953		
			Third transition			
K-1/K	N	Same	Desist	N	Same	Desist
Nonindex	767	.3872	.2699	388	.4645	.2640
Injury	115	.1478	.2174	72	.1449	.2463
Theft	235	.2043	.3106	119	.1544	.1985
Damage	114	.1053	.2456	38	.0000	.3600
Combination	139	.1583	.2518	89	.1343	.1492
	1370			706		
			Fourth transition			
K-1/K	N	Same	Desist	N	Same	Desist
Nonindex	503	.4274	.2247	301	.4562	.2375
Injury	88	.1591	.2727	52	.1017	.2542
Theft	216	.1991	.2454	109	.1667	.1888
Damage	78	.0897	.1410	16	.0000	.0526
Combination	117	.1624	.2393	57	.1064	.1914
	1002			535		

(continued)

TABLE 9.11 (continued)

K-1/K	N	Same	Desist	N	Same	Desist
			Fifth transition			
Nonindex	393	.4478	.1883	244	.4832	.2310
Injury	73	.1507	.2329	44	.0851	.2765
Theft	160	.2625	.2625	73	.1644	.1780
Damage	58	.1034	.1379	18	.0000	.0625
Combination	89	.2360	.2697	38	.1163	.1860
	773			417		
			Sixth transition			
Nonindex	292	.4144	.1712	183	.4653	.1980
Injury	57	.1754	.3684	34	.1111	.2962
Theft	131	.2214	.2290	60	.2540	.0793
Damage	46	.0870	.1957	15	.1667	.0000
Combination	82	.1584	.3171	35	.2069	.2758
	608			327		
			Seventh transition			
Nonindex	221	.3756	.1765	162	.5203	.1891
Injury	42	.0714	.3333	19	.1714	.2571
Theft	104	.2500	.1635	58	.3636	.0909
Damage	37	.1622	.1622	6	.0714	.1428
Combination	68	.2353	.1912	21	.0400	.2400
	472			266		
			Eighth transition			
Nonindex	158	.3924	.1456	120	.5041	.1544
Injury	40	.1000	.1750	26	.0370	.3333
Theft	79	.3165	.1139	40	.2000	.1250
Damage	40	.1000	.2500	12	.0000	.0000
Combination	66	.2121	.1212	19	.1818	.3181
	383			217		

of chance and thus the transitions can be modeled as a simple, homogenous Markov chain. As before, the best estimate of the process of moving from one offense state to the next is the generating or summary matrix. This matrix shows the probability of following one offense type with one of five possible subsequent offense types as well as the absorbing state of desistance. The race-specific summary matrices are reported in Table 9.12.

TABLE 9.12

Summary Transition Matrix: First Nine Offenses, for All Offenders by Race and Cohort

K-1/K	N	I	T	D	C	Desist
1958 Cohort: White						
Nonindex	.4304	.0500	.0828	.0661	.0638	.3069
Injury	.3101	.0916	.1084	.0621	.0614	.3664
Theft	.3343	.0386	.1720	.1116	.0424	.3012
Damage	.3549	.0705	.1331	.1137	.1163	.2116
Combination	.3563	.0305	.1031	.0630	.1921	.2550
1945 Cohort: White						
Nonindex	.4263	.0413	.0862	.0147	.0407	.3908
Injury	.3767	.0686	.0829	.0031	.0169	.4578
Theft	.3924	.0354	.2174	.0202	.0568	.2778
Damage	.3735	.0447	.0734	.0851	.0286	.3947
Combination	.3952	.0224	.1330	.0071	.1374	.3049
1958 Cohort: Nonwhite						
Nonindex	.4081	.0740	.1441	.0612	.0882	.2244
Injury	.3459	.1189	.1070	.0602	.0866	.2813
Theft	.3284	.0538	.2164	.0603	.0875	.2535
Damage	.3620	.0527	.1664	.1063	.1070	.2055
Combination	.3172	.0741	.1382	.0572	.1657	.2475
1945 Cohort: Nonwhite						
Nonindex	.4671	.0874	.1178	.0267	.0586	.2424
Injury	.4196	.1000	.0867	.0295	.0734	.2908
Theft	.4154	.0627	.2110	.0261	.1134	.1714
Damage	.4943	.1138	.1844	.0395	.0370	.1310
Combination	.3897	.0891	.1396	.0206	.1376	.2234

White delinquents in the 1945 cohort are most likely to make a transition to a nonindex offense regardless of type of prior offense. The chances of such a transition are approximately .37 to .39 if the prior offense was an index offense and .42 if the prior offense was also non-index. If a white delinquent in Cohort I does make a transition to an index offense, it will most likely involve theft. The highest probability of committing a theft offense next occurs for white delinquents who have just committed this type of offense (.2174). This repeat probability is higher than that for the prior offense types—.07 for damage, .08 for nonindex and injury, and .13 for combination. After theft offenses, the chances are that a white delinquent will move to a combination offense. Again, the repeat probability (.1374) is the highest, while the chances of moving to this state from a noncombination prior offense are all quite low and range from .01 to .05. For the remaining two index offense types, damage and injury, the probabilities are quite low. With the exception of a specialization pair which shows a value of .08 for damage and .06 for injury, the probability of a transition to a damage or injury offense does not exceed .04.

Turning to desistance we see some variation in the likelihood of moving to this state. White injury offenders are the most likely to desist with a probability of .4578. Nonindex and damage offenders are next with a probability of .39. They are followed by combination offenders (.3049) with theft offenders showing the lowest chances of desistance (.2778).

The transition probabilities for the white offenders in Cohort II readily indicate for this group, compared to their Cohort I counterparts, that: (1) nonindex offenses are less dominant; (2) transitions to index offenses, especially repeats, are higher; and (3) the chances for desistance are lower.

Like whites in Cohort I, the most probable transition to a nonindex offense for whites in Cohort II occurs when the prior offense was non-index (.4304). A nonindex offense occurs about 35% of the time when it was preceded by a combination or damage offense. For theft and injury prior offenses the likelihood of a nonindex offense committed next is .33 for theft and .31 for injury. With the exception of a nonindex pair, the probability of a nonindex transition in Cohort II for white delinquents is lower, regardless of prior offense type, than in the 1945 cohort.

If a white offender in the 1958 cohort does move to an index offense on his next offense, it will most likely involve theft. The transition probability for this move is as low as .08 when the prior offense was non-index, and is as high as .17 when the prior offense was also theft. A transition to a theft offense occurs about 10% to 13% of the time when the prior offense was injury (.10), damage (.13), or combination (.10).

If a white Cohort II delinquent does not move to a theft offense, then the next most likely index offense transition is to combination, closely followed by damage. The probabilities range from .04 to .19 for combination and from .06 to .11 for damage. In both instances, the most probable transition is when the prior offense was the same type. Injury offenses are the most likely offense move. The chances range from .03 to .09. The upper limit, .09, for an injury-injury repeat is not that much higher than the other moves. However, for whites the transition probabilities for index offenses in Cohort II are all higher generally than the corresponding probabilities in the 1945 cohort.

Table 9.12 also demonstrates that white delinquents are less likely to desist. The highest chance is for an injury offender (.3664), but this probability is lower than the highest value obtained in Cohort I, .4578, also for injury offenders. The other desistance values are similarly lower, with a floor of .2116 in Cohort II compared to .2778 in Cohort I. For nonwhites, the transition probabilities of the summary matrix also show a cohort effect, but one that is smaller than was the case for whites.

Cohort I nonwhites are more likely to commit a nonindex offense next than to move to another state, including desistance. Delinquents moving from a damage state (.4943) show the highest probability of a nonindex transition, while offenders moving from a combination state on the prior offense (.3897) are the least likely to move to a nonindex offense. Like the white offenders in both cohorts, a Cohort I nonwhite will likely commit a theft offense when he makes a transition to an index offense. The probability is .2110 when the prior offense was theft followed by .1844 for damage, .1396 for combination, .1178 for nonindex, and .0867 for injury. If a theft transition does not occur, then the chances are close that the next offense will be combination or injury. The combination probabilities lie in the range of .03 to .13, while the injury probabilities fall between .06 and .11. Cohort I nonwhites are very unlikely to move to damage offenses. The probabilities appear to be unrelated to prior offense type and range from .0206 to .0395.

Nonwhites in the 1958 cohort show a cohort effect that is less dramatic. First, nonindex offenses are again less dominant. Second, the transition probabilities for index offenses are higher, but not by the same magnitude as was observed for whites. Third, the transition to desistance does not appear to differ by cohort for nonwhites as it did for whites.

Like all delinquents considered thus far, Cohort II nonwhites will most likely commit a nonindex offense on their next offense. The likelihood is highest if the prior offense was nonindex (.4081), and the likelihood is lowest if the prior offense was combination. For damage, theft, and injury priors, the probabilities are closely bunched between .32 and .36. As was the case for the other delinquent groups, nonwhites in the 1958 cohort are likely to commit a theft-type index offense. The probabilities range between .10 and .21 with the latter value representing a theft-theft repeat. Following theft are combination and injury offenses. The former range from .08 to .16, while the latter occur with probabilities of .05 to .11. Damage offenses show a range of .06 to .10 and are the least likely type of index offense. For all index offense types the reoccurrence of the prior type has the highest probability. The chances range from .21 for theft to .16 for combination, .11 for injury, and .10 for damage.

When the summary transition probabilities for all delinquents were presented it was suggested that the probabilities themselves do not readily point to the strength of the relationship between the k-1 and the kth offenses. What is lacking is some measure of the expected value for the relationship, a measure with which to compare the observed values. It was suggested that one possible measure is the probability of committing the same type of offense regardless of the number and type of intervening offenses. These data point to the likelihood that repeat offenses will ever occur and thus serve as one criterion for evaluating the observed transition data. We now turn to these data before considering the results of analyzing the offense transition residuals.

Table 9.13 shows that white delinquents in Cohort I are likely to commit only nonindex offenses with any frequency. A delinquent has about a 37% chance of repeating this type of offense only once and has a probability of .48 to .66 of repeating the offense two times up to nine times. The index offense data clearly show that repeat offenses in this group are infrequent. Theft repeats encompass at most three repeats and occur less than four times out of ten. Combination offenses are repeated only twice and show a maximum repeat probability of .2812. Injury and damage offenses are repeated at most once and involve only 12% of the injury offenders and only 6% of the damage offenders.

Table 9.13 shows that recidivism among the Cohort II white delinquents is more extensive. At least 40% of the nonindex offenders will commit this offense again. A second to a ninth repeat occurs with a probability of from .54 to .81. The most substantial difference between white delinquents in the two cohorts concerns index offense repeats. Theft offenses can be repeated at least nine times (compared to three in Cohort I) with a range of probabilities from .47 for two repeats to .46 for 9 repeats. Damage offenses are also repeated more often (eight times compared to once in Cohort I) and involved about one-half the damage offenders who commit a given number of prior damage offenses. Combination offenses show at most five repeats with probabilities of .33 for

TABLE 9.13

Probability of Ever Committing the Same Type of Offense Disregarding Type of Intervening Offenses for All Offenders by Race and Cohort

*k*th repeat	Nonindex	1958 Cohort: White			
		Injury	Theft	Damage	Combination
1st	.4234	.1865	.2347	.2205	.2838
2nd	.5456	.2225	.4793	.3238	.4285
3rd	.5797	.2506	.5147	.6961	.6299
4th	.6990	.0000	.6667	.4990	.5287
5th	.7009	.0000	.6843	.5000	.3333
6th	.6402	.0000	.7072	.5000	.0000
7th	.6881	.0000	.7578	.5000	.0000
8th	.8166	.0000	.6804	1.0000	.0000
9th	.8136	.0000	.4697	.0000	.0000

*k*th repeat	Nonindex	1945 Cohort: White			
		Injury	Theft	Damage	Combination
1st	.3796	.1222	.2663	.0675	.1777
2nd	.4868	.0000	.3442	.0000	.2812
3rd	.5286	.0000	.3809	.0000	.0000
4th	.5542	.0000	.0000	.0000	.0000
5th	.6068	.0000	.0000	.0000	.0000
6th	.6071	.0000	.0000	.0000	.0000
7th	.4117	.0000	.0000	.0000	.0000
8th	.8571	.0000	.0000	.0000	.0000
9th	.6666	.0000	.0000	.0000	.0000

*k*th repeat	Nonindex	1958 Cohort: Nonwhite			
		Injury	Theft	Damage	Combination
1st	.5492	.2805	.3757	.2490	.3265
2nd	.6147	.3419	.4764	.4012	.3951
3rd	.6117	.3337	.5223	.3013	.4698
4th	.6872	.4094	.5658	.4983	.5743
5th	.6850	.2214	.7199	.6400	.7414
6th	.6944	.5172	.5019	.7083	.4496
7th	.6756	.0000	.2481	.6029	.7759
8th	.6886	.0000	1.0000	.6585	.7222
9th	.7261	.0000	.0000	1.0000	.6000

*k*th repeat	Nonindex	1945 Cohort: Nonwhite			
		Injury	Theft	Damage	Combination
1st	.5653	.2620	.3920	.1255	.3285
2nd	.6488	.3771	.5277	.0000	.4434

(continued)

TABLE 9.13 (continued)

kth repeat	Nonindex	1945 *Cohort*: Nonwhite			
		Injury	Theft	Damage	Combination
3rd	.6792	.3255	.4912	.0000	.0000
4th	.6852	.0000	.4107	.0000	.0000
5th	.6794	.0000	.5217	.0000	.0000
6th	.6971	.0000	.0000	.0000	.0000
7th	.7070	.0000	.0000	.0000	.0000
8th	.7571	.0000	.0000	.0000	.0000
9th	.6037	.0000	.0000	.0000	.0000

five repeats up to .62 for three repeats. Injury offenses are repeated at most three times and occur at most 25% of the time.

Nonwhite delinquents in Cohort I show only a modest likelihood of repeating index offenses. Theft repeats occur at most five times with chances ranging from .40 to .52. Injury offenses show at most three repeats and at this point involve about one-third of the offenders that ever commit an injury offense. Combination and damage repeats are rare and occur at most twice for combination offenses and only once for damage. Like their white counterparts in Cohort I, nonwhites are likely to commit nonindex offenses most frequently. Repeat offenses of this type involve about 60% of the delinquents.

Cohort II nonwhites behave like their white counterparts in this cohort. The data show that repeat offenses are frequent and involve a substantial percentage of the offenders. Nonindex offenses are repeated up to nine times and show a probability range of .61 to .72. Most important, index offenses are repeated with regularity. Damage and combination offenses can reoccur up to nine times with great likelihood. Theft offenses show eight repeats and injury offenses can reoccur up to six times.

In sum, the two cohorts differ appreciably with respect to the number of candidates for offense specialization and the chances that such specialization will occur. Whites and nonwhites in Cohort I are unlikely to repeat index offenses except for theft. When repeats do occur, the probabilities are at best only moderate. In Cohort II, delinquents of both races show extensive recidivism including the repeating of index offenses. Further, the probability of repeats is much higher and is not substantially affected by the type of offense.

Offense Transition Residuals by Race

When we analyzed the residuals for the eight separate offense transitions and the summary matrix residuals for all delinquents by race, we found evidence of a tendency for offenders to repeat the type of prior offense. However, because the absorbing state of desistance was included in the transitions, each offense number involves a different number of offenders. Thus, the offense patterns exhibited by recidivists may be confounded with those of the less frequent delinquent. It was shown previously in the section for all offenders that one way to handle the problem is to examine the transitions of recidivists only in what was referred to as the "recidivism model." In this model the state of desistance is eliminated, thus requiring that the offender must have committed offenses for the full number of transitions examined. Earlier we examined two subsets of recidivists—offenders who had committed at least five offenses and a group of delinquents with at least nine total offenses. We continue this grouping below for whites and nonwhites in the two birth cohorts. Because the data are most effectively analyzed with respect to the summary matrices, and because our transition-by-transition analyses have not indicated that specialization is related to specific rank number of offense, our discussion below is limited to these summary matrix residuals.

Table 9.14 reports the summary matrix residuals and cell-specific components of chi-square for the first through fourth transitions for five-time white offenders in Cohort I. These data indicate that this group of white recidivists will most often repeat a theft offense. The adjusted standardized deviate for the theft-to-theft repeat is quite high (+4.8). The deviates for the other index offense types are considerably lower and represent only the slightest tendency for the type of prior offense to be repeated when it involves injury, damage, or combination. The overall chi-square for the relationship is high (44.2) and significant (.001). The cell-by-cell values, however, show that only the theft-to-theft cell with a chi-square of 14.3 is substantial.

In the 1958 birth cohort, white five-time recidivists appear to commit two offense types as repeats of the prior offense. Table 9.14 shows a substantial residual of +4.7 for the combination-to-combination pair, which indicates that such a repeat occurs much more often than expected. Theft offense repeats also show a tendency of specialization, but the value of +2.5 for this residual indicates that the tendency is only moderate. Injury (+1.1) and damage (+1.7) offense repeats are only slightly more frequent than expected. Inspection of the chi-square val-

TABLE 9.14
Offense Transition Residuals and Chi-square: Summary Transition Matrix
of First Nine Offenses for All Five-Time Offenders by Race and Cohort

K-1/K	N	I	T	D	C	Total
	1958 Cohort: White Adjusted standardized deviates					
Nonindex	4.0	−0.1	−2.1	−1.3	−2.9	488
Injury	−0.4	1.1	−0.8	0.2	0.4	49
Theft	−1.7	−0.4	2.5	−0.6	−0.2	91
Damage	−2.5	1.1	1.2	1.7	−0.0	126
Combination	−1.5	−2.0	0.1	−0.7	4.7	82
						836

K-1/K	N	I	T	D	C	Total
	Components of chi-square					
Nonindex	2.9	0.0	1.7	0.6	3.2	8.4
Injury	0.1	1.1	0.6	0.0	0.2	1.9
Theft	1.1	0.1	4.8	0.3	0.0	6.4
Damage	2.3	1.0	1.1	2.2	0.0	6.6
Combination	0.9	3.5	0.0	0.4	18.2	22.9
	7.2	5.7	8.2	3.5	21.6	46.2

K-1/K	N	I	T	D	C	Total
	1945 Cohort: White Adjusted standardized deviates					
Nonindex	3.1	−0.5	−3.2	1.6	−1.7	505
Injury	1.4	1.0	−1.3	−1.5	−0.2	46
Theft	−4.2	0.5	4.8	−1.9	1.5	175
Damage	0.7	−0.1	−1.6	1.7	−0.0	57
Combination	−1.3	−0.7	1.4	−0.3	1.0	57
						840

K-1/K	N	I	T	D	C	Total
	Components of chi-square					
Nonindex	1.5	0.1	3.3	1.0	1.0	6.9
Injury	0.7	0.9	1.3	2.0	0.0	4.9
Theft	5.3	0.2	14.3	2.9	1.6	24.3
Damage	0.2	0.0	2.0	2.5	0.0	4.6
Combination	0.6	0.4	1.5	0.1	0.9	3.5
	8.2	1.6	22.3	8.5	3.6	44.2

TABLE 9.14 *(continued)*

1958 Cohort: Nonwhite
Adjusted standardized deviates

K-1/K	N	I	T	D	C	Total
Nonindex	4.0	−2.2	−2.3	−0.7	−1.1	1718
Injury	−0.4	4.4	−1.8	0.6	−1.6	234
Theft	−2.4	0.1	3.6	−0.8	0.1	512
Damage	−0.9	−0.6	−0.6	3.1	−0.3	325
Combination	−2.5	0.2	1.6	−1.7	3.4	303
						3092

Components of chi-square

K-1/K	N	I	T	D	C	Total
Nonindex	3.3	2.0	1.9	0.2	0.5	7.9
Injury	0.1	16.2	2.5	0.3	2.0	21.2
Theft	2.2	0.0	8.7	0.5	0.0	11.5
Damage	0.3	0.3	0.2	7.8	0.1	8.7
Combination	2.5	0.0	1.9	2.2	9.2	15.9
	8.5	18.6	15.3	11.0	11.8	65.1

1945 Cohort: Nonwhite
Adjusted standardized deviates

K-1/K	N	I	T	D	C	Total
Nonindex	4.4	0.2	−2.4	−1.9	−2.9	902
Injury	0.1	1.9	−1.5	1.0	−0.8	161
Theft	−2.7	−1.6	2.5	0.8	2.1	305
Damage	−1.3	1.0	2.1	−0.2	−1.3	92
Combination	−2.6	−0.9	0.5	1.1	3.5	208
						1668

Components of chi-square

K-1/K	N	I	T	D	C	Total
Nonindex	4.0	0.0	2.2	1.6	3.4	11.1
Injury	0.0	3.0	1.6	0.8	0.5	6.0
Theft	2.7	1.8	4.3	0.5	3.2	12.6
Damage	0.7	0.9	3.4	0.0	1.4	6.5
Combination	2.7	0.7	0.2	1.1	9.5	14.1
	10.1	6.4	11.7	4.0	18.0	50.3

ues indicates that prior subsequent offense types are not statistically independent. The major portion of the total chi-square (46.2) is attributable to the combination pair (18.2). The theft-to-theft component (4.8) is noteworthy, but it is only slight in comparison to the combination component.

Nonwhites in Cohort I show evidence of repeating more offense types than their white counterparts in either cohort. Table 9.14 indicates that nonwhite recidivists in the 1945 cohort are likely to repeat combination (+3.5), theft (+2.5), and injury (+1.9) offenses more often than expected. The tendency to repeat or specialize is, however, only moderate. Further evidence of this comes from the components of chi-square. Combination pairs have the highest chi-square (9.5) followed by theft (4.3) and injury (3.0). Although significant, these chi-square values do not approach the square of the total found for the white offense repeats.

The data for nonwhites in Cohort II clearly indicate that a strong relationship exists between the type of offense just committed and the type of offense that follows. Nonwhites in the second cohort who commit at least five offenses exhibit significant residuals for all four types of index offenses. The strongest evidence of specialization occurs for injury offenses, with a residual of +4.4. The other index offenses show a smaller deviation from expectations, yet the values of +3.6 for theft, +3.4 for combination, and +3.1 for damage all indicate moderate to high departures from expected frequencies. The chi-square data provide further evidence of the relationship. The overall chi-square of 65.1 attests to the fact that prior and subsequent offense type is far from independent. Most important, the chi-square components which fall along the main diagonal are all substantial and point to the fact that it is largely the repeating of offense types that causes the independence model to fail.

The five-time offender represents only the most basic recidivist to qualify for membership in our category of chronic delinquency. The possibility of even more chronic recidivism exists for many of these delinquents. It is instructive, therefore, to examine the offense patterns when the career is extended beyond the fifth offense. We turn then to the summary matrix residuals for the first eight transitions of offenders who have committed at least nine delinquent events. These data are shown in Table 9.15.

Table 9.15 gives the residuals and chi-square data for white nine-time delinquents in Cohort I. Compared to their counterparts with at least five offenses, these recidivists show a tendency to repeat damage (+2.8) and combination (+2.1) offenses as well as theft (+3.1). These deviations are modest, but as the chi-square data indicate, the differences between the observed and expected frequencies are significant for

TABLE 9.15

*Offense Transition Residuals and Chi-square: Summary Transition Matrix
of First Nine Offenses for All Nine-Time Offenders by Race and Cohort*

K-1/K	1958 Cohort: White Adjusted standardized deviates					
	N	I	T	D	C	Total
Nonindex	3.4	0.8	−1.8	−2.7	−1.0	348
Injury	−0.6	3.7	−0.3	0.0	−1.5	36
Theft	−1.9	−1.5	2.0	2.7	−1.1	88
Damage	−2.4	−1.0	0.3	1.9	2.2	90
Combination	−0.2	−1.3	0.6	−1.0	1.6	54
						616

K-1/K	Components of chi-square					
	N	I	T	D	C	Total
Nonindex	2.3	0.3	1.3	2.8	0.4	6.9
Injury	0.2	12.0	0.1	0.0	2.0	14.2
Theft	1.4	1.8	2.9	5.3	1.0	12.4
Damage	2.2	0.9	0.1	2.7	3.6	9.4
Combination	0.0	1.4	0.3	0.8	2.2	4.7
	6.1	16.3	4.6	11.5	9.2	47.7

K-1/K	1945 Cohort: White Adjusted standardized deviates					
	N	I	T	D	C	Total
Nonindex	3.0	0.9	−3.3	−1.4	0.1	230
Injury	0.1	1.0	0.5	−0.7	−1.0	11
Theft	−2.5	−0.7	3.1	0.6	−0.1	85
Damage	0.2	−1.0	−0.1	2.8	−1.6	25
Combination	−1.7	−0.2	1.0	−0.5	2.1	33
						384

K-1/K	Components of chi-square					
	N	I	T	D	C	Total
Nonindex	1.3	0.3	3.5	0.7	0.0	5.9
Injury	0.0	0.9	0.2	0.5	0.9	2.6
Theft	1.9	0.4	6.0	0.3	0.0	8.5
Damage	0.0	0.9	0.0	6.8	2.1	9.9
Combination	1.0	0.0	0.7	0.2	3.5	5.4
	4.2	2.5	10.3	8.5	6.6	32.3

(*continued*)

TABLE 9.15 (continued)

1958 Cohort: Nonwhite
Adjusted standardized deviates

K-1/K	N	I	T	D	C	Total
Nonindex	5.1	−0.5	−3.7	−0.4	−2.3	1322
Injury	−0.6	2.8	−1.3	0.8	−0.5	203
Theft	−1.3	−2.6	5.2	−1.2	−1.0	493
Damage	−2.3	0.4	−0.6	3.2	0.9	281
Combination	−3.5	1.2	1.0	−1.5	4.4	309
						2608

Components of chi-square

K-1/K	N	I	T	D	C	Total
Nonindex	6.5	0.1	5.5	0.1	2.4	14.5
Injury	0.2	6.4	1.2	0.5	0.2	8.5
Theft	0.7	5.2	17.6	1.1	0.8	25.3
Damage	2.5	0.2	0.2	8.1	0.6	11.6
Combination	5.6	1.3	0.7	1.8	15.2	24.6
	15.4	13.1	25.2	11.6	19.2	84.4

1945 Cohort: Nonwhite
Adjusted standardized deviates

K-1/K	N	I	T	D	C	Total
Nonindex	4.0	0.4	−2.3	−0.9	−3.2	782
Injury	−0.3	1.9	−1.8	0.5	−0.6	128
Theft	−1.9	−2.0	2.4	−0.1	1.9	275
Damage	−0.9	0.2	1.5	−0.7	−0.2	69
Combination	−3.0	−0.0	1.2	1.5	2.2	162
						1416

Components of chi-square

K-1/K	N	I	T	D	C	Total
Nonindex	3.1	0.1	2.0	0.3	4.0	9.5
Injury	0.0	3.1	2.3	0.3	0.3	6.0
Theft	1.3	2.9	3.8	0.0	2.6	10.6
Damage	0.3	0.1	1.7	0.4	0.0	2.5
Combination	3.5	0.0	1.1	1.8	3.9	10.3
	8.3	6.1	10.9	2.8	10.8	30.0

the theft-to-theft, damage-to-damage, and combination-to-combination pairs.

Similarly, the white recidivists in Cohort II who have committed at least nine offenses show moderate specialization for injury (+3.7) offenses and a slight tendency to repeat theft (+2.0) and damage (+1.9) crimes. Again, the chi-square value (47.7) leads us to reject the hypothesis of independence, while the cell components point to injury repeats as the most substantial departure from independence.

Table 9.15 indicates that Cohort I nonwhite recidivists with a minimum of nine offenses have offense patterns similar to their counterparts with five offenses. Theft offenses (+2.4) show the highest deviation followed by combination (+2.2) and injury (+1.9) offenses. The overall relationship, however, is less significant for the 9+ offenses group (chi-square = 30.0) compared to the 5+ offenses group (chi-square = 50.3).

The opposite is true for the Cohort II nonwhite recidivists. The nonwhite Cohort II five-time recidivist was found to exhibit the best evidence of offense specialization. His counterpart with at least nine offenses shows even greater evidence. Overall, the prior and subsequent offense types are substantially related as shown by the chi-square of 84.4. The chi-square data along the main diagonal clearly demonstrated that the like-offense repeats are the main sources of the relationship. Theft-to-theft (+17.6) and combination-to-combination (+15.2) transitions are the strongest pairs, while damage-to-damage (+8.1) and injury-to-injury (+6.4) repeats are more moderate pairs but still comparatively large.

The residuals for the matrix of eight transitions confirm these data. Theft and combination offenses show large deviations (+5.2 and +4.4, respectively), while damage and injury repeats reflect more modest departures (+3.2 and +2.8, respectively). Clearly, the excessively chronic nonwhite recidivist in Cohort II appears to extend his pattern of repeating offenses that was established in the early transitions of his career.

Offense Escalation: All Offenders

Parallel to the question of whether like-offense repeats have a higher occurrence probability or exceed marginal expectations more often than do offense sequences that do not repeat the type of prior offense, is the issue of whether offense patterns show an increase in seriousness. That is, as the offending career progresses it is plausible to hypothesize that offenders might: (1) increasingly switch to more serious offense types, or (2) commit repeat-offense types that have a higher severity than their predecessors. Thus, for chronic recidivists in particular, who not only accumulate many offenses but also very likely repeat certain offense types like robbery or other personal injury-related offenses, we may ask the whether the juvenile career shows a pattern of increasing seriousness. This pattern may be referred to as offense severity escalation.

Most often, the topic of escalation has been operationalized in terms of whether offenders move to more serious offense types as they accumulate crimes rather than in terms of the comparative severity of offenses, especially repeat-offense sequences. The offense switching approach was used by Rojek and Erickson, and they reported that, "there is no evidence that the probability distributions of the five types of offenses shift in any way toward more serious offenses" (1982: 17). Farrington *et al.* (1988), using a similar operationalization, examined whether the frequency of serious offenses was correlated with offense transition number and found some evidence of specialization.

Cohen (1986) has thoroughly reviewed the approaches to both specialization and escalation, and regarding the latter has noted that offense switches to more serious varieties of offenses as the offending career advances is not the only way to analyze offense severity changes. She has endorsed the approach of measuring escalation that we have used in this study—an examination of the average severity of successive offenses.

We report below two related approaches to the analysis of repeat-offense seriousness. The first consists of an examination of the mean seriousness score difference between repeat offenses. The second more complex method consists of multiple regressions in which the prior offense severity and three offense-related variables are used to predict subsequent offense severity.

Table 9.16 reports the mean seriousness score differences for the offenders in Cohorts I and II by offense type. In the 1945 cohort the seriousness score is greater at almost each repetition. Only four repeats were less serious than the ones preceding—the seventh nonindex repeat was less serious than the one before, two thefts (third and sixth) and the one damage repeat.

In the 1958 cohort the pattern is much the same. The repeat-offense seriousness score is greater than the score for the prior offense in all but three instances. The eighth repeat is less serious among nonindex offenses and the fourth and fifth theft repeats are less serious than the preceding offense. It should be noted that, despite the increase in seriousness observed, the magnitude of the difference is quite small. Only the injury offense repeats show a seriousness score difference that is noteworthy.

TABLE 9.16

Mean Difference in Severity Score between
Offense Repetitions: All Offenders by Cohort

| kth | Mean severity difference | |
repeat	1958 Cohort	1945 Cohort
Nonindex		
1st	10.49	6.45
2nd	20.68	0.93
3rd	42.99	10.35
4th	1.91	0.59
5th	38.23	6.79
6th	9.57	8.05
7th	26.3	−8.75
8th	−15.74	21.12
9th	55.80	10.40
Injury		
1st	115.02	71.75
2nd	56.94	19.85
3rd	174.98	144.36
Theft		
1st	60.46	12.05
2nd	52.87	3.31
3rd	51.76	−5.78
4th	−21.80	48.79
5th	−65.19	7.63
6th	6.16	−14.29
Damage		
1st	30.09	−3.07
Combination		
1st	66.57	26.92
2nd	14.15	64.75

The mean differences in seriousness scores among the race-specific repetitions do not depart radically from the results for all offenders. The results are given in Table 9.17.

Whites in Cohort I show five instances in which the severity of the repeat is not greater than that of the prior offense. These are the second and sixth nonindex repeats, the first and third theft repeats, and the one damage repeat. Regardless of direction, the differences in seriousness scores are slight (with the exception of the injury repeat). Whites in Cohort II also show only five instances in which the severity of the repeat offense does not exceed that of the prior offense. These are the fourth and eighth nonindex repeats, the injury repeat, the third theft repeat, and the second combination repeat. The offense-to-offense dif-

TABLE 9.17
Mean Difference in Severity Score between Offense Repetitions:
All Offenders by Race and Cohort

| kth repeat | Mean severity difference | | | |
| | 1958 Cohort | | 1945 Cohort | |
	White	Nonwhite	White	Nonwhite
Nonindex				
1st	20.97	8.99	6.82	6.11
2nd	31.54	18.41	−2.23	3.15
3rd	18.71	51.48	10.74	10.14
4th	−36.29	14.19	0.58	−1.11
5th	48.96	34.81	10.75	5.23
6th	45.25	−1.56	−5.85	12.82
7th	123.90	−4.11	3.21	−11.14
8th	−105.15	10.03	0.25	25.85
9th	108.26	32.43	6.38	11.41
10th	—	18.59	—	−12.68
11th	—	−15.21	—	19.69
Injury				
1st	−151.21	139.05	127.36	58.09
2nd	—	48.37	—	37.98
3rd	—	489.37	—	144.36
Theft				
1st	98.76	49.88	−3.50	20.84
2nd	64.42	50.88	28.48	−5.96
3rd	−77.04	73.66	−28.19	0.63
4th	—	−43.19	—	43.78
5th	—	−44.47	—	1.83
Damage				
1st	10.00	32.21	−27.73	10.63
Combination				
1st	69.66	64.29	23.50	27.87
2nd	−19.92	24.14	37.89	69.49

ferences are greater in Cohort II, but they are not of sufficient magnitude to be significant.

Nonwhites in Cohort I commit repeat offenses that are higher in seriousness than the prior offense for all but four instances. Three of the exceptions occur among nonindex events (i.e., fourth, seventh, and tenth), and the other occurs for the second theft repeat. Like the previous data, the differences in severity between offenses are not large. Nonwhites in Cohort II show five instances where the repeat offense has a lower seriousness score. Three of the exceptions occur among the nonindex events (i.e., sixth, seventh, and eleventh), while the other two occur for the fourth and fifth theft repeats. Cohort II nonwhites show the greatest differences between the severity of the prior and repeat offenses. Further, the injury repeats are substantially greater than the initial injury offense seriousness.

It is difficult to offer any strong observations regarding the mean severity score differences. It is true that the repeat-offense severity is, on average, higher than that of the prior offense. Yet these simple descriptive data do not address alternative explanations. That is, repeat offense severity may be higher because it was a repeated offense but, alternatively, the severity could be higher because: (1) the repeated offense was committed at a later age, and it is this older and more mature delinquent that is driving the seriousness score; or (2) the repeat offense could have occurred much later in the career, as measured by rank number of offenses, and at this point in a career, a delinquent may be a more hardened offender.

In order to examine these possible effects on the severity of a repeat offense, we have used separate regression models for the average severity of each repeat offense by type. As predictors we used: (1) the offense severity of the immediately prior offense of the type being analyzed, (2) age-at-offense, (3) time (in months) between the two offenses, and (4) the number of intervening offenses between the prior and current commission of the designated offense type. The results are given in Tables 9.18 and 9.19.

Table 9.18 gives the regression results for all offenders in both cohorts. It is clear that some of the models are significant and some of the predictors have measurable effects, but the variance explained for both cohorts is generally very low. These results vary by offense type and repeat number, with no consistent pattern for the various coefficients.

For the 1958 cohort eight of the nine nonindex models are significant, and among these, three have an R-square greater than .10 (fourth repeat, R-square = .19; seventh repeat R-square = .12; and ninth repeat R-square = .20). For these three models the strongest predictor is the offense severity of the prior nonindex offense. All six theft offense analyses were significant, and all repeats after the first had an R-square greater than 10%. However, for these five models, prior offense severity was the strongest predictor for the third and fourth repeats, the number of intervening offenses was strongest at the second and fifth, while months between offenses was strongest at the sixth repeat. None of the injury or combination models was significant, and only one damage model (first repeat) was significant, but the R-square was only .09.

TABLE 9.18
Regression of Repeat Offense Severity on Offense Characteristics: All Offenders by Cohort

1958 Cohort

kth repeat	Standardized coefficients				F ratio	Probability	R-square	DF
	Prior offense severity	Age at offense	Months between offenses	Number of offenses between				
Nonindex								
1st	.090	.117	-.025	.088	15.29	.001	.03	1760
2nd	.162	.116	.005	.136	18.70	.001	.06	1048
3rd	.195	.077	-.051	.029	8.57	.001	.05	632
4th	.392	.145	.087	.049	26.60	.001	.19	436
5th	.211	.100	-.051	.114	5.20	.001	.06	300
6th	.256	.091	-.013	.061	4.34	.002	.08	204
7th	.351	.016	.031	.032	4.87	.001	.12	138
8th	.221	.011	.064	.123	1.54	.187	.06	99
9th	.319	.259	-.165	.143	4.47	.002	.20	74
Injury								
1st	.164	.110	.007	-.025	2.51	.042	.04	228
2nd	.061	.162	-.034	-.192	1.17	.327	.06	73
3rd	.357	.134	.349	-.195	1.22	.334	.20	23
Theft								
1st	.164	.167	.007	.044	8.24	.001	.06	424
2nd	.170	.051	-.116	.341	8.82	.001	.13	237

kth repeat	Prior offense severity	Age at offense	Months between offenses	Number of offenses between	F ratio	Probability	R-square	DF
3rd	.258	.215	.094	.098	5.71	.001	.16	123
4th	.349	.168	-.159	.187	4.18	.004	.19	71
5th	.370	-.036	.549	-.657	4.25	.005	.27	48
6th	.106	.051	.575	.033	3.96	.011	.36	32
Damage								
1st	.182	.198	-.034	.135	6.85	.001	.09	252
2nd	.131	.131	-.183	.131	1.13	.344	.04	95
3rd	.247	.015	-.465	.368	1.22	.320	.12	37
Combination								
1st	.119	.063	.026	.009	1.55	.186	.01	315
2nd	.165	.111	-.074	-.000	1.55	.191	.04	126
3rd	.031	.118	.280	-.234	.95	.440	.06	63
4th	.184	.272	-.053	.061	1.01	.412	.11	35

1945 Cohort

kth repeat	Standardized coefficients				F ratio	Probability	R-square	DF
	Prior offense severity	Age at offense	Months between offenses	Number of offenses between				
Nonindex								
1st	.075	.060	-.007	.087	5.36	.001	.01	1336
2nd	.015	.003	-.059	.052	.79	.530	.00	762
3rd	.006	-.005	.084	-.050	.68	.609	.00	470
4th	.109	.102	-.106	.179	3.15	.014	.04	300
5th	.023	.043	.097	-.078	.60	.662	.01	196

(continued)

TABLE 9.18 (continued)

1945 Cohort

kth repeat	Standardized coefficients				F ratio	Probability	R-square	DF
	Prior offense severity	Age at offense	Months between offenses	Number of offenses between				
6th	.024	.058	.032	−.064	.26	.904	.00	132
7th	−.018	−.027	−.083	.083	.18	.945	.00	83
8th	.004	.137	.375	−.309	2.62	.043	.14	64
9th	.722	.056	−.011	−.027	10.40	.001	.54	39
Injury								
1st	−.019	.142	.042	.189	1.84	.123	.05	138
2nd	−.126	.106	−.576	.793	6.03	.001	.37	44
3rd	−.004	.219	−.639	1.132	11.00	.002	.84	12
Theft								
1st	.154	.183	−.060	.100	6.05	.001	.07	308
2nd	.403	.063	−.201	.198	7.64	.001	.19	127
3rd	.361	.207	−.081	−.028	3.33	.016	.19	58
4th	−.112	.221	−.130	−.168	.55	.699	.09	26
Damage								
1st	−.098	.302	−.090	−.267	1.13	.355	.10	41
Combination								
1st	.206	.223	.090	−.056	5.77	.001	.11	181
2nd	.126	.216	.127	−.121	1.70	.158	.08	74

The results for the 1945 cohort are dissimilar to those for the 1958 cohort. Unlike Cohort II, most of the Cohort I models are not significant and have low R-squares. There are several cases, however, where the results are substantial. In the case of the ninth nonindex repeat, the R-square is .54 and the model is significant at .001. The predictor that seems to be driving the model is prior offense severity, with a coefficient of +.722. There are two injury models with substantial R-squares, the second (R-square = .37) and the third (R-square = .84). For both of these models the number of intervening offenses have very high positive coefficients and months between offenses have moderate negative coefficients, thus signifying that the greater the number of intervening offenses and the shorter the time interval over which they are committed, the greater the severity of the repeat injury offense.

The race-specific analyses displayed in Table 9.19 repeat the previous findings without exception. The models do not explain much variation in repeat-offense severity. The models are generally not significant, thus representing poor fits to the data. The regression coefficients do not follow a consistent pattern and, most important, do not indicate that the seriousness of the prior offense is the best predictor of the severity of the repeat offense.

The race-specific results, however, do clarify the few very high R-squares reported above for the 1945 cohort. Overall, the sixth nonindex repeat was found to have a high R-square (.54), and the race-specific results indicate that this holds for whites (R-square = .24) and nonwhites (R-square = .53) but is more substantial for the latter. Also, for whites it is the number of intervening offenses that is the strongest predictor, while for nonwhites it is the prior offense severity. Concerning the two substantial injury models, the race-specific data show that this result is only relevant for nonwhites.

The evidence given above concerning the relationship surrounding offense escalation does not suggest that any particular factor is responsible for the increased seriousness of repeat offenses. In some instances the effect is due to the severity of the prior offense, while in other instances it is the length of the career as measured by the number of intervening offenses that seems to be responsible for the increased severity of repeat-offense types. In any event, our results offer no conclusive support for the escalation hypothesis.

This has necessarily been a long chapter, owing primarily to the number of analyses that are associated with investigating offense specialization. Before moving on to the topic of age and delinquency in the next two chapters, we can summarize our dynamic recidivism results as follows.

TABLE 9.19

Regression of Repeat Offense Severity on Offense Characteristics: All Offenders by Race and Cohort

1958 Cohort

kth repeat	Standardized coefficients				F ratio	Probability	R-square	DF
	Prior offense severity	Age at offense	Months between offenses	Number of offenses between				
White offenders								
Nonindex								
1st	.106	.079	-.028	.032	2.48	.043	.02	483
2nd	.119	.062	-.025	100	1.77	.134	.02	263
3rd	.161	.118	-.096	.087	2.07	.087	.05	152
4th	.233	-.031	.029	.147	2.23	.070	.08	106
5th	.089	.140	-.192	.191	1.20	.314	.06	74
6th	.237	-.211	.198	.076	1.50	.218	.12	47
7th	.639	.060	-.117	.195	4.79	.004	.40	32
8th	-.006	-.200	.291	-.144	.47	.758	.07	26
Injury								
1st	-.147	.199	-.062	-.084	.49	.736	.06	35
2nd	-.168	.001	.239	-.618	.12	.966	.13	7
Theft								
1st	.151	.091	-.000	.129	.86	.490	.04	72
2nd	.097	.099	-.153	.667	4.44	.006	.37	34
Damage								
1st	.231	.018	.057	.217	2.43	.055	.12	70
2nd	.214	-.053	-.113	.006	.29	.879	.06	22
Combination								
1st	.141	.057	-.159	.289	.95	.444	.06	62
2nd	-.188	-.112	.036	-.336	.72	.587	.11	26

1945 Cohort

kth repeat	Standardized coefficients				F ratio	Probability	R-square	DF
	Prior offense severity	Age at offense	Months between offenses	Number of offenses between				
White offenders								
Nonindex								
1st	.153	.036	-.019	.121	6.44	.001	.03	644
2nd	.098	.037	.050	-.026	1.07	.371	.01	313
3rd	.186	.044	-.005	-.061	1.68	.155	.04	165
4th	.020	.107	.054	.022	.44	.779	.01	91
5th	.089	-.019	-.124	-.062	.55	.699	.04	55
6th	-.111	.179	.130	.357	2.31	.081	.24	33
Injury								
1st	.204	.031	-.115	.113	.33	.852	.05	27
Theft								
1st	.092	.081	.054	.003	.55	.699	.01	112
2nd	.144	-.030	-.407	.037	2.08	.106	.21	35
Damage								
1st	-.039	.584	-.633	-.040	.54	.713	.17	14
Combination								
1st	.297	-.005	.243	-.162	1.38	.259	.12	41
1958 Cohort								
Nonwhite offenders								
Nonindex								
1st	.068	.127	-.021	.125	14.00	.001	.04	1276
2nd	.179	.129	.023	.158	19.63	.001	.09	784
3rd	.229	.056	-.037	.018	7.94	.001	.06	479
4th	.421	.190	.098	.018	26.42	.001	.24	329

(continued)

TABLE 9.19 (continued)

1958 Cohort

kth repeat	Standardized coefficients				F ratio	Probability	R-square	DF
	Prior offense severity	Age at offense	Months between offenses	Number of offenses between				
5th	.244	.085	-.022	.096	4.56	.001	.07	225
6th	.263	.165	-.064	.069	4.79	.001	.11	156
7th	.156	.121	.165	-.013	2.20	.073	.08	105
8th	.381	.034	-.162	.279	3.98	.005	.19	72
9th	.306	.403	-.216	.205	5.74	.001	.32	52
Injury								
1st	.208	.110	.029	.005	2.99	.019	.05	192
2nd	.044	.174	-.034	-.168	.96	.436	.05	65
3rd	.303	.130	.487	-.286	1.68	.200	.28	21
Theft								
1st	.170	.179	.008	.026	7.64	.001	.06	425
2nd	.189	.034	-.124	.297	6.49	.001	.11	202
3rd	.260	.240	.105	.088	5.28	.001	.17	105
4th	.373	.190	-.206	.249	4.38	.003	.24	59
5th	.406	-.028	.548	-.528	2.85	.037	.24	40
Damage								
1st	.170	.259	-.066	.113	5.52	.001	.11	181
2nd	.119	.239	-.263	.225	1.55	.196	.08	72
3rd	.053	.080	-.402	.079	.51	.727	.10	21
Combination								
1st	.116	.067	.045	-.046	1.35	.250	.02	252
2nd	.196	.118	-.069	.022	1.55	.192	.06	99
3rd	.030	.167	.389	-.331	1.41	.245	.11	46
4th	.301	.261	-.037	.106	1.10	.381	.16	26

1945 Cohort

kth repeat	Standardized coefficients				F ratio	Probability	R-square	DF
	Prior offense severity	Age at offense	Months between offenses	Number of offenses between				
Nonwhite offenders								
Nonindex								
1st	.034	.096	.000	.055	2.35	.052	.01	691
2nd	-.006	.025	.098	.061	1.06	.373	.00	448
3rd	-.044	-.008	.137	-.074	1.22	.300	.01	304
4th	.136	.108	-.161	.225	3.20	.014	.05	208
5th	-.022	.069	.210	-.085	1.53	.194	.04	140
6th	.087	.072	.005	-.110	.57	.683	.02	98
7th	-.033	-.011	-.105	.079	.21	.932	.01	69
8th	.004	.153	.521	-.469	3.90	.008	.24	52
9th	.708	.075	-.012	-.025	7.65	.001	.53	31
Injury								
1st	-.063	.180	-.030	.211	2.10	.084	.07	110
2nd	-.187	.154	-.599	.781	6.30	.001	.41	40
3rd	.004	.219	-.639	1.130	11.00	.002	.84	12
Theft								
1st	.171	.233	-.127	.150	6.13	.001	.11	195
2nd	.468	.091	-.171	.276	7.80	.001	.26	91
3rd	.361	.182	-.270	.315	2.76	.040	.21	44
Damage								
1st	-.178	.191	.292	-.499	1.96	.134	.26	26
Combination								
1st	.194	.268	.057	-.053	4.97	.001	.12	139
2nd	.108	.252	.096	-.139	1.63	.178	.10	60

The offense patterns exhibited by the offenders in both cohorts were very much alike. The most likely transition observed was to a nonindex offense regardless of the type of prior offense. For the 1945 cohort, damage offenders were the most likely to move to a nonindex offense, while for the 1958 cohort, nonindex offenders were the most likely to commit a nonindex offense on their next offense. The next most likely transition was to the state of desistance. In both cohorts, injury offenders were the most likely to move to this state. If offenders did not move to a nonindex event or desist from further delinquency, they were likely to commit an index offense involving property theft.

When we examined the probabilities of like-offense repeats and analyzed the cell residuals to determine the extent of offense specialization, we found that like-offense repeats were evident, but the tendency to specialize was stronger for the 1958 cohort. In Cohort I, theft and combination offenders showed the strongest tendency to specialize. Injury offense repeats were moderately greater than chance. Damage offense repeats did not appear to be more frequent than expected by chance. In Cohort II, the type of subsequent offense was related to prior offense type for all offense types. For any offense type, the offender most likely to have committed it on his next offense was the one who had committed it just prior.

The strongest evidence of offense specialization was found for the recidivism models. The five-time offenders in Cohort I showed a significant tendency to repeat theft, combination, and injury offenses, while damage offense repeats were observed only slightly more often than chance. The Cohort II data presented the unmistakable finding that the five-time chronic offenders tended to specialize and did so for all offense types. Combination offenses showed the greatest repetition followed closely by injury and theft repeats. Damage offenses were repeated very often, but not with the specialization tendency evident for the other offense types.

When we expanded the delinquent career to include at least nine offenses, specialization was again observed in both cohorts but it was more pronounced in Cohort II. The nine-time offenders in the 1958 cohort had the strongest repeat tendency for theft followed closely by combination offenses. Injury and damage offense repeats were repeated less substantially but the specialization tendency was clear nonetheless.

The overall offense patterns did not show significant race effects. Whites and nonwhites in both cohorts were likely to move to a nonindex offense regardless of prior offense type. When an index transition was made, the type of offense usually committed was theft. When an offender desisted, he was most likely in a prior state of injury offense than any other offense type.

When we eliminated desisters and concentrated on the offense patterns of recidivists we found both race effects and cohort effects that were substantively important.

Five-time white offenders in Cohort I most often repeated theft offenses. The results for the other offense types showed only a slight tendency to specialize. In the 1958 cohort, the white five-time recidivists appeared to specialize strongly in two offenses (combination and theft). Damage offenses showed only slight specialization.

The five-time nonwhite chronics in Cohort I showed evidence of repeating more offense types than their white counterparts in either cohort. These offenders tended to specialize in combination, theft, and injury offenses. For Cohort II nonwhite chronics, a strong relationship was found between prior and subsequent offense type for all offenses. The strongest evidence of specialization occurred for injury offenses while the tendency to repeat theft, damage, and combination offenses, was slightly lower.

As we moved to the very chronic recidivists, those with at least nine offenses, we found that the results for five-time offenders were accentuated for all groups.

The nine-time white offenders in Cohort I specialized in theft, damage, and combination offenses compared to just theft for their five-time counterparts. The Cohort II nine-time offenders specialized in injury, theft, and damage offenses compared to combination and theft repetitions for their five-time offense counterparts.

The nine-time nonwhite offenders in Cohort I showed the same tendencies to specialize as did their five-time recidivist counterparts. They both tended to repeat theft, combination, and injury offenses. The nine-time nonwhite recidivist in Cohort II displayed the strongest evidence of offense specialization. Even when compared to his five-time offense counterpart, the evidence of offense patterning was stronger across all offense types for the nine-time nonwhite recidivist in Cohort II.

In short, we found evidence of offense specialization among recidivists (as opposed to occasional delinquents). The evidence became more pronounced as the number of offenses increased. The results were clear for both cohorts, although different patterns were found by race.

Concerning offense escalation, we found, with only a few exceptions, that when an offense was repeated the severity was greater than that of its predecessor. The exceptions were one nonindex repeat (the seventh in Cohort I and the eighth in Cohort II), two theft repeats (the third and sixth in Cohort I and the fourth and fifth in Cohort II), and one damage repeat (the first in Cohort I). Most important, the injury offenses were repeated in both cohorts with substantial increases in severity. The patterns by race did not depart from these overall patterns in any meaningful fashion.

Finally, we employed multiple regression analyses to see if we could identify factors which would explain the greater severity of repeat offenses. We used prior severity, age, time between offenses, and number of intervening offenses as predictors. Our models generally did not explain much variation in offense severity, and none of the predictors seemed to stand out.

We can only conclude that offense escalation was evident in both cohorts (and most substantial for injury offenses), but we were unable to identify possible causes.

10

Age-at-Onset and Delinquency

Introduction

Up to this point we have considered delinquency in terms of the career aspects surrounding such topics as prevalence, incidence and severity, delinquent subgroups, recidivism, offense specialization, and escalation. We have ignored the age component in the delinquency patterns in the two cohorts. In the following two chapters we take up the important issue of age and delinquency.

In *Delinquency in a Birth Cohort* it was noted that most research concerning age and delinquency has employed age as a factor antecedent to delinquency rather than as a measure of time. We have found that the analysis of age and delinquency has usually taken three major modes: (1) the distribution of delinquent acts by age-specific categories; (2) the age-at-onset of delinquency; and (3) the effect of early onset of delinquency on later delinquency. The first method provides data about the amount of delinquency at a given age, but it does not provide information about other dimensions of the relationship between age and delinquency, issues such as age-at-onset or the cumulative impact of participation in early delinquency on later behavior. The second method involves examining the extent of delinquency according to varying onset ages and essentially depicts the relationship between the amount of delinquency and time at risk. However, the number of offenses committed in a late juvenile period may not be related to the number of offenses committed in an earlier period. Thus the extent to which delinquency at the peak ages (usually 15, 16, and 17) is related to prior delinquency cannot be measured solely by the average number of offenses committed by age-at-onset categories.

With longitudinal data that are able to depict age-at-onset and the age of commission of all subsequent offenses, the third approach seems to be most fruitful. Because we can relate early delinquency to subsequent delinquency by age for the entire juvenile career, the relationship between age and delinquency becomes more susceptible to study than is possible with cross-sectional data. As noted in Chapter 3, there is a decided absence of consensus concerning the relationship between age and crime and the appropriateness of using longitudinal versus cross-sectional methods of studying age and crime. For a thorough discussion of this, the reader is again referred to Hirschi and Gottfredson (1983), Gottfredson and Hirschi (1986, 1987, 1988), and Blumstein *et al.* (1988a, 1988b).

In this chapter we report our results on the relationship between age-at-onset of delinquent behavior and various offense measures. Our goals are to describe the age-at-onset patterns across cohorts generally, and by race and SES, and to investigate the relationship between age-at-onset and delinquency patterns. In the following chapter we present data on delinquency in terms of the specific age at which the offenses are committed. These two age foci will thus allow us to compare the cohorts in terms of their similarities and differences concerning the time-based starting points of delinquency and the time trends in the commission of delinquent acts.

Age-at-Onset Percentages

The point at which a juvenile begins his or her delinquent career is, from the point of view of research on delinquent recidivism and related issues, highly significant in one crucial respect. Age-at-onset, given the fact that delinquency is limited to some maximum age by statute (age 17 for the present cohorts), forever establishes the maximum possible career length that an offender can attain as a juvenile. Because the period at risk is thus set, the extent of further delinquent behavior, or even the character and severity of the subsequent offenses, may be influenced by the offender's age-at-onset. Simply, a delinquent who begins his delinquent activities early will have a greater opportunity to commit offenses; he may accumulate more offenses; and perhaps consequently, he might exhibit the commission of a higher percentage of serious offenses because he has had a longer developmental period in which to establish a career.

In this section we analyze the relationship between delinquency and age-at-onset. Age-at-onset refers to the age at which a child designated delinquent was first taken into custody by the Philadelphia police, and thus marks the beginning of the exposure period of official delinquency. The various data presented below give, for each onset age category, the number of offenders and offenses, the average number of offenses, and the mean seriousness score. These data are given overall for the two cohorts, and for race and SES groups.

Table 10.1 indicates for Cohort I that most delinquents were initially contacted by the police between the ages of 12 and 16 (72.3%). Few contacts were incurred at ages 10 or 11 (11.9%) and only 205, or 5.9% of the offenders, initiated their delinquent careers before age 10. The modal age-at-onset for all offenders was 16, at which age 20.6% of juvenile offenders were initially taken into custody, while the next highest age-at-onset category (15) constituted 17.2%.

Table 10.1 presents similar age-at-onset data for the 1958 cohort. For this cohort, like its predecessor, the vast majority of delinquents (74%) receive their first official police contact between the ages of 12 and 16. Few delinquents (12%) begin their careers at the ages of 10 or 11, and still fewer (only 6%) initiate contact with the police before age 10. In the 1958 cohort, however, the modal age-at-onset is one year earlier, age 15 compared to age 16 in Cohort I. The next highest age-at-onset category is age 16 in Cohort II compared to age 15 in Cohort I. For both cohorts these two age-at-onset categories account for more than one-third of all delinquents (37% in Cohort I and 34% in Cohort II).

Figure 10.1a gives the distribution of the percentage of offenders at each age-at-onset category. In Cohort I the distribution of offenders by age-at-onset of delinquency shows that the proportion of offenders increases with age up to and including 16 years, but then declines at age 17. The data on age-at-onset show that only 25 delinquents, or 0.72% of the youths incur their first police contact at age 7, while the number of offenders in subsequent age categories systematically increases through age 16 to a high of 20.6%. At 17 years of age the proportion of contacts (9.96%) drops to less than half the value observed for the 16-year-olds. Figure 10.1a clearly shows the similarity between the cohorts, as the prevalence of delinquents in Cohort II increases steadily with age. In the 1958 cohort the proportion of delinquents increases from age 7 to age 15 and then declines at age 16 and again at age 17.

When race is introduced, the data for both cohorts are very similar and show a distinct race effect. Nonwhites generally incur their first police contact at an earlier age than whites. In Cohort I the respective modal age-at-onset was age 15 for nonwhites and age 16 for whites. The modal age by race for Cohort II is the same for whites and nonwhites, age 15. The data are most instructive when grouped according to ranges of age-at-onset. Thus, up to and including age 13, 48.7% of the nonwhites in Cohort I compared to 30.8% of the whites had had their first police contact. The Cohort II data show the same effect, as 41% of

TABLE 10.1

Offenders and Offenses by Age-at-Onset, Race, SES, and Cohort

1958 Cohort
Age-at-onset

	7	8	9	10	11	12	13	14	15	16	17
All offenders											
Total offenders	93	92	105	112	179	443	599	658	777	730	527
Total offenses	584	733	742	754	1145	2539	2530	2322	1922	1321	656
Mean offenses	6.3	7.9	7.1	6.7	6.4	5.7	4.2	3.5	2.5	1.8	1.2
Offenders by race											
White											
Total offenders	30	23	23	19	51	111	149	203	293	275	235
Total offenses	170	136	128	132	323	526	466	621	653	463	290
Mean offenses	5.7	5.9	5.6	6.9	6.3	4.7	3.1	3.1	2.2	1.7	1.2
Nonwhite											
Total offenders	63	69	82	93	128	332	450	455	484	455	292
Total offenses	414	597	614	622	822	2013	2064	1701	1269	858	366
Mean offenses	6.6	8.7	7.5	6.7	6.4	6.1	4.6	3.7	2.6	1.9	1.3
Offenders by SES											
Low											
Total offenders	68	74	81	89	124	306	416	429	430	423	263
Total offenses	458	624	579	624	794	1923	1806	1536	1171	788	326
Mean offenses	6.7	8.4	7.2	7.0	6.4	6.3	4.3	3.6	2.7/	1.8	1.2
High											
Total offenders	25	18	24	23	55	137	183	229	347	307	264
Total offenses	126	109	163	130	351	616	724	759	751	533	330
Mean offenses	5.0	6.1	6.8	5.6	6.4	4.5	3.9	3.3	2.2	1.7	1.3
Offenders by race and SES											
White low											
Total offenders	14	12	9	10	20	47	67	62	72	68	56

	7	8	9	10	11	12	13	14	15	16	17
Total offenses	69	60	37	81	108	263	215	204	205	119	70
Mean offenses	4.9	5.0	4.1	8.1	5.4	5.6	3.2	3.3	2.9	1.8	1.3
White high											
Total offenders	16	11	14	9	31	64	82	141	221	207	179
Total offenses	101	75	91	51	215	263	251	417	448	334	220
Mean offenses	6.3	5.9	6.5	5.7	6.9	4.1	3.1	2.9	2.1	1.7	1.2
Nonwhite low											
Total offenders	54	62	72	49	104	259	349	367	358	355	207
Total offenses	389	564	542	543	686	1660	1591	1359	966	669	256
Mean offenses	7.2	9.1	7.5	6.9	6.6	6.4	4.6	3.7	2.7	1.9	1.2
Nonwhite high											
Total offenders	9	7	10	14	24	73	101	88	126	100	85
Total ofenses	25	33	72	79	136	353	473	342	303	189	110
Mean offenses	2.8	4.7	7.2	5.6	5.7	4.8	4.7	3.9	2.4	1.9	1.3

1945 Cohort
Age-at-onset

	7	8	9	10	11	12	13	14	15	16	17
All offenders											
Total offenders	25	56	124	179	234	301	412	484	596	718	346
Total offenses	185	353	783	944	1081	1261	1406	1284	1374	1133	410
Mean offenses	7.4	6.3	6.3	5.3	4.6	4.2	3.4	2.6	2.3	1.6	1.2
Offenders by race											
White											
Total offenders	10	29	54	80	106	131	212	288	368	496	245
Total offenses	33	113	261	319	361	398	548	648	752	738	287
Mean offenses	3.3	3.9	4.8	4.0	3.4	3.0	2.6	2.2	2.0	1.5	1.2
Nonwhite											
Total offenders	15	27	70	99	128	170	200	196	228	222	101
Total offenses	152	240	522	625	720	863	858	636	622	895	123
Mean offenses	10.1	8.9	7.4	6.3	5.6	5.1	4.3	3.2	2.7	1.8	1.2

(continued)

TABLE 10.1 (continued)

1945 Cohort
Age-at-onset

	7	8	9	10	11	12	13	14	15	16	17
Offenders by SES											
Low											
Total offenders	19	35	92	132	169	211	278	275	325	356	164
Total offenses	162	242	697	753	868	950	1016	827	815	605	196
Mean offenses	8.5	6.9	7.6	5.7	5.1	4.5	3.6	3.0	2.5	1.7	1.2
High											
Total offenders	6	21	32	47	65	90	134	209	271	362	182
Total offenses	23	111	86	191	213	311	390	457	559	528	214
Mean offenses	3.8	5.3	2.7	4.1	3.3	3.4	2.9	2.2	2.1	1.4	1.2
Offenders by race and SES											
White low											
Total offenders	19	35	92	132	169	211	278	275	325	356	164
Total offenses	162	242	697	753	868	950	1016	827	815	605	196
Mean offenses	8.5	6.9	7.6	5.7	5.1	4.5	3.6	3.0	2.5	1.7	1.2
White high											
Total offenders	6	21	32	47	65	90	134	209	271	362	182
Total offenses	23	111	86	191	213	311	390	457	559	528	214
Mean offenses	3.8	5.3	2.7	4.1	3.3	3.4	2.9	2.2	2.1	1.4	1.2
Nonwhite low											
Total offenders	13	24	63	91	115	149	180	176	201	197	80
Total offenses	141	193	510	587	650	752	767	589	556	352	97
Mean offenses	10.8	8.0	8.1	6.4	5.6	5.0	4.3	3.3	2.8	1.8	1.2
Nonwhite high											
Total offenders	2	3	7	8	13	21	20	20	27	25	21
Total offenses	11	47	12	38	70	111	91	47	66	43	26
Mean offenses	5.5	15.7	1.7	4.8	5.4	5.3	4.5	2.4	2.4	1.7	1.2

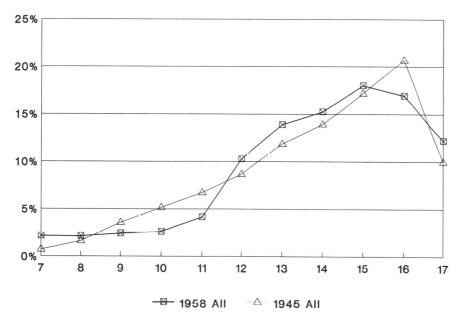

FIGURE 10.1a. Percentage of offenders by age-at-onset and cohort.

nonwhites compared to 27% of whites begin their careers before age 14. The trend is reversed between 14 and 17 years of age, where whites account for a higher percentage of their initial contacts. The discrepancy is 18 percentage points for Cohort I, and 14 points for Cohort II.

Figures 10.1b and 10.1c depict these race results. For the 1958 cohort, the prevalence of delinquency increases at about age 11 for both whites and nonwhites. Although both nonwhites and whites peak at age 15, the increasing trend is more evident for whites. By comparison, the 1945 data are very similar. The increasing trend in prevalence begins earlier, age 9 for both whites and nonwhites, but nonwhite prevalence tails off sooner, just as in Cohort I.

The age-at-onset data by SES show the same patterns as above. For the 1945 cohort low-SES boys had a sharply rising probability of first contact with a peak at age 16. The higher-SES boys showed the same trend of increasing delinquency with age, but for this group, the probabilities of first contact were much lower on the probability scale. Low-SES boys started their careers earlier than higher-SES boys. Up to and including age 14, 54% of the lower-SES delinquents compared to 42% of the higher-SES offenders had had their first police contact.

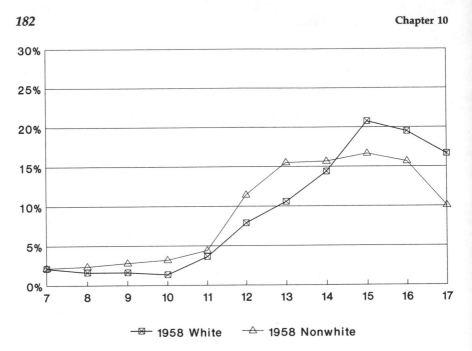

FIGURE 10.1b. Percentage of offenders by age-at-onset and race for 1958 cohort.

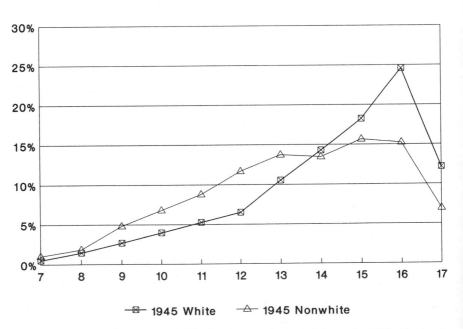

FIGURE 10.1c. Percentage of offenders by age-at-onset and race for 1945 cohort.

For the 1958 cohort the age-at-onset data are similar to those of Cohort I. For both SES groups, the probability of the first police contact increases with age. For low-SES boys, the peak occurs at age 15 with the next highest age being 14. For higher-SES boys, the modal age-at-onset is again age 15, with the next highest being age 16. When the earlier ages-at-onset are grouped, the SES disparity is most evident. Thus, up to and including age 14, 58% of the low-SES delinquents compared to 43% of their high-SES counterparts have started their delinquent careers.

Figures 10.1d and 10.1e show the age trend by cohort and SES. These graphs indicate that the shape of the curves are generally cohort related. That is, the shape of the 1958 SES curves looks like those for the 1958 race groups, and the SES and race curves in Cohort I are nearly the same. In effect, for both cohorts, nonwhites and low-SES groups have a higher prevalence of delinquency, which both begins sooner and peaks earlier than is the case for whites and high-SES delinquents.

Given these separate race and SES results, the combined race and SES data given in Table 10.1 produce age-at-onset distributions that are as expected. For the 1945 cohort the lower-SES nonwhite boys had their first police contact earlier than all other groups, with 61.9% of such contacts between ages 7 and 14. The higher-SES nonwhites and lower-

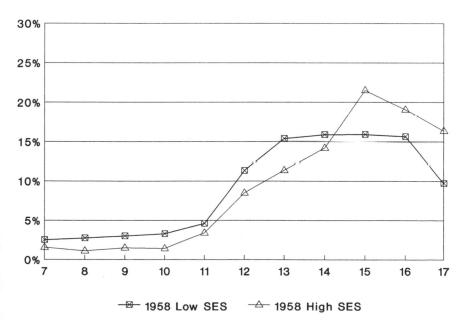

FIGURE *10.1d.* Percentage of offenders by age-at-onset and SES for 1958 cohort.

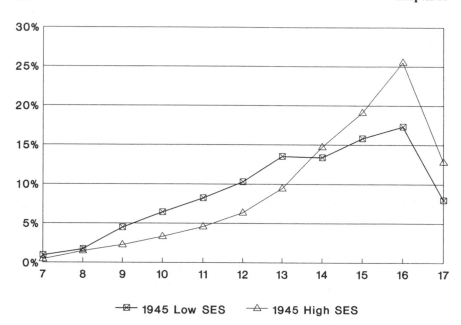

FIGURE 10.1e. Percentage of offenders by age-at-onset and SES for 1945 cohort.

SES whites were similar, with 56.3% of the former and 52.1% of the latter having their first contact at or before age 14. Finally, the higher-SES whites were the group with the lowest proportion of contacts before age 15 (40.7%).

In the 1958 cohort the data are quite similar to those above. Low-SES nonwhite delinquents have a higher proportion of delinquents (58%) that have begun their careers before age 15. They are followed by low-SES whites (55%) that have begun their careers before age 15. Next are high-SES nonwhites (51%) in terms of the cumulative proportion with a first contact by age 14. The group with the lowest probability is high-SES whites, for whom 37% of the delinquents have begun their juvenile career before age 15.

Instead of looking at the percentages of offenders by each age-at-onset category separately, it is useful to examine the cumulative percentages of delinquents that can be accounted for at each age. By examining the cumulative distributions we can determine whether the cohorts, or the demographic groups, exhibit different prevalence densities by age. These cumulative data are displayed in Figure 10.2a for the cohorts overall, and in Figures 10.2b to 10.2e for race and SES groups. We have used figures here rather than tables because the cumulative data are easier to view in graphic form.

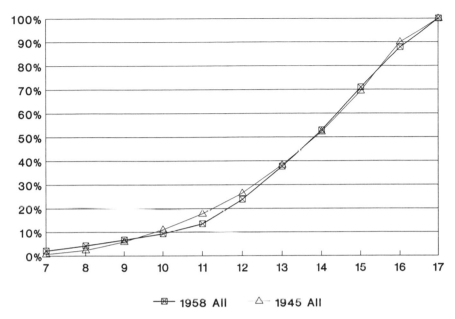

FIGURE 10.2a. Cumulative percentage of offenders by age-at-onset and cohort.

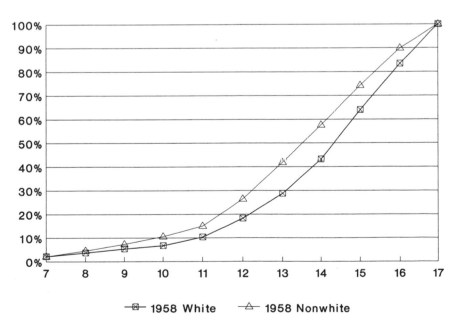

FIGURE 10.2b. Cumulative percentage of offenders by age-at-onset and race for 1958 cohort.

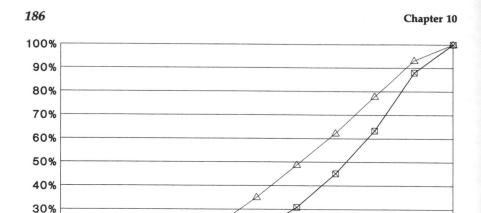

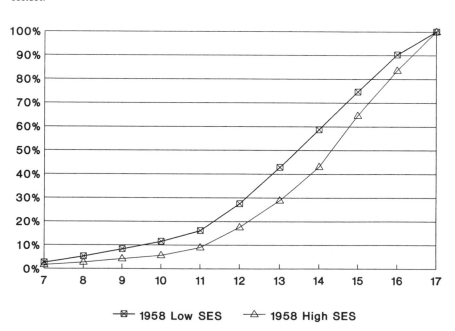

FIGURE 10.2c. Cumulative percentage of offenders by age-at-onset and race for 1945 cohort.

FIGURE 10.2d. Cumulative percentage of offenders by age-at-onset and SES for 1958 cohort.

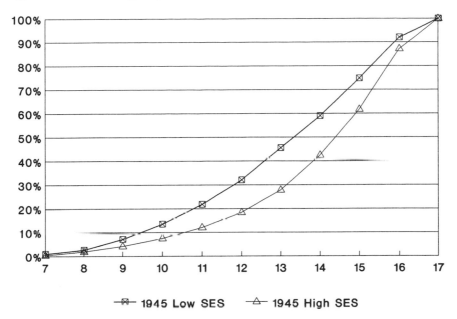

FIGURE 10.2e. Cumulative percentage of offenders by age-at-onset and SES for 1945 cohort.

Figure 10.2a indicates a very close similarity for the two cohorts. Less than 10% of the delinquents started their careers by age 10, at which point the prevalence steadily increases until it reaches the required 100% at age 17. With very little departure, the two curves are close approximations of the same distribution.

Figures 10.2b through 10.2e display the race and SES cumulative distributions for the two cohorts. In both cohorts, nonwhites have a higher percentage of delinquents accounted for at each age from 8 through 16, and the nonwhite and white curves do not begin to converge until age 16 (of course they must converge at age 17, at which point 100% of the offenders must be accounted for). By SES, low-SES delinquents show the same result as nonwhites.

Age-at-Onset and Mean Number of Offenses

In addition to looking at the distribution of delinquents by age-at-onset, it is important to consider the patterns that are exhibited when the number of offenses and offenders by age-at-onset are used to compute an average number of offenses per onset group. It might be hypothesized that the earlier the age-at-onset the higher the mean number of offenses committed, owing to the potential for a longer career among the early starters.

The data given in Table 10.1 clearly support this hypothesis for Cohort I. The earlier the age-at-onset, the larger the mean number of offenses. This fact indicates a direct negative relationship between length of exposure to arrests after the initial arrest and the mean number of arrests per age-at-onset category. That is, there is a linearly descending mean number of offenses from age 7 (mean = 7.4) to age 17 (mean = 1.2). When the data are separated by race, we observe the same pattern for nonwhites, only further emphasized, with means ranging from 10.1 at age 7 to 1.2 at age 17. The white group does not follow the general pattern but rather peaks at age 9 and then declines to age 17. The data for the two SES groups show that the inverse trend generally holds better for low-SES delinquents than those of higher SES.

The data given in Table 10.1 for Cohort II generally show a pattern of a decreasing mean number of offenses as age-at-onset increases. The average number of offenses decreases for all offenders at all ages except for age 8, which shows an increase over the previous year. When these data are viewed separately by race they indicate (like Cohort I) that whites peak at age 10 and then show a declining mean number of offenses. Nonwhites peak at age 8 and then show the inverse trend in mean number of offenses thereafter. By SES the data indicate the expected trend with the highest mean number of offenses occurring at age 8 for low-SES offenders and at age 9 for high-SES offenders.

Table 10.2 reports the rank order correlations between age-at-onset and the mean number of offenses by race and SES for the two cohorts. In Cohort I the relationship is strongest for low-SES nonwhites, correlation = −.991, followed by high-SES whites, correlation = −.920. The same is true for Cohort II as well. Here the correlation is −.972 for low-SES nonwhites and −.881 for high-SES whites. The group with the weakest

TABLE 10.2
Rank Order Correlations between Age-at-Onset and Mean Number of Offenses by Race, SES, and Cohort

	1958 Cohort		1945 Cohort	
	Low SES	High SES	Low SES	High SES
White	−.727	−.881	−.898	−.920
Nonwhite	−.972	−.645	−.991	−.743

correlation is the same for both cohorts—high-SES nonwhites, with a correlation of −.743 in Cohort I and −.645 in Cohort II.

The age-at-onset and mean number of offenses data are graphed in Figures 10.3a to 10.3e. In Figure 10.3a we see that after the initial onset year, age 7, both cohorts exhibit a negative relationship between age-at-onset and mean number of offenses. In the two race figures (10.3b, 10.3c) we observe clearly that the inverse trend is strong for nonwhites in both cohorts, is weak for whites in Cohort I, and is inconsistent for Cohort II whites until age 10, at which point the inverse trend takes over. By SES the figures (10.3d, 10.3e) indicate that the negative relationship is strongest in both cohorts for low-SES offenders, while it is weak for high SES in Cohort I and initially inconsistent for high SES in Cohort II (just as was the case for whites).

Age-at-Onset and Offense Severity

Another important relationship to be examined is that between age-at-onset and the mean seriousness score for the offenses ultimately committed by a specific age-at-onset group. Simply, data of this sort show

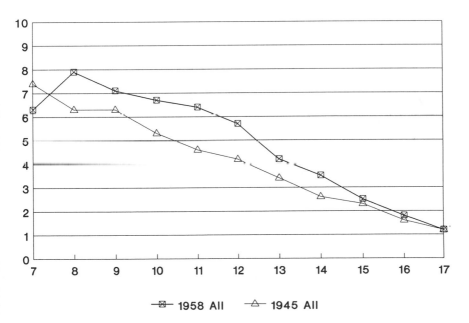

FIGURE 10.3a. Mean number of offenses by age-at-onset and cohort.

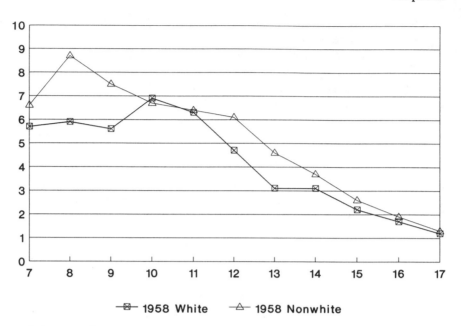

FIGURE 10.3b. Mean number of offenses by age-at-onset and race for 1958 cohort.

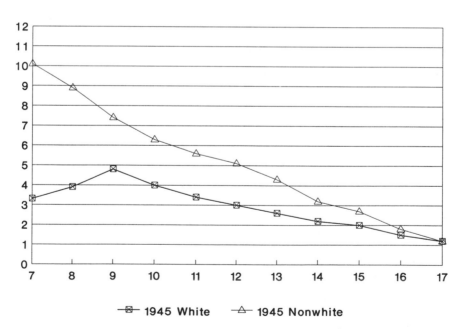

FIGURE 10.3c. Mean number of offenses by age-at-onset and race for 1945 cohort.

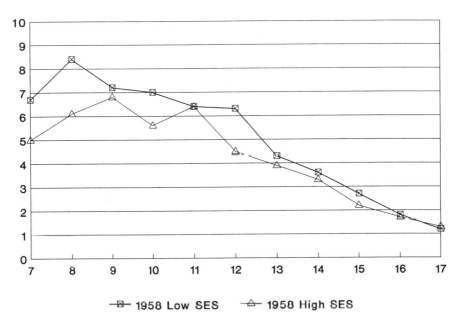

FIGURE 10.3d. Mean number of offenses by age-at-onset and SES for 1958 cohort.

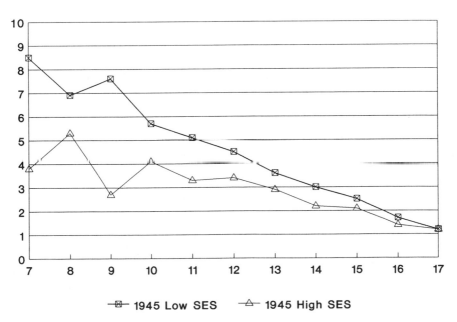

FIGURE 10.3e. Mean number of offenses by age-at-onset and SES for 1945 cohort.

whether delinquent careers which are begun at early ages show a more serious set of delinquencies than careers which are started at later points on the age continuum. For convenience, these data are reported in graphic form in Figure 10.4a for the 1945 and 1958 cohorts.

Overall, the chart shows almost no relationship between age-at-onset and average career severity. Both curves are flat with no clear trends. With respect to the data underlying the graph, several general findings emerge for all offenders in the 1945 cohort. First, the 12-year-old age-at-onset group had the highest mean offense seriousness score (123.89). Second, the average seriousness score for the offenses committed during the onset year was lower than the overall mean seriousness score for each age-at-onset category. Third, the range of mean seriousness scores across all onset categories was 35.8 points and was reduced to 21.7 points if the lowest mean score (age 16) was eliminated. Fourth, there seems to be only a moderate (at best) negative relationship between age-at-onset and the mean seriousness score.

Figure 10.4a also displays the mean seriousness score data by age-at-onset for the 1958 birth cohort. Overall, offenders in the later cohort attain their highest mean offense seriousness score in the 9-year-old onset group compared to age 12 in Cohort I. Also, the range of mean

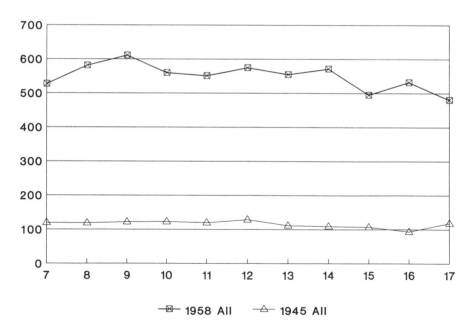

FIGURE 10.4a. Mean severity score by age-at-onset and cohort.

seriousness scores in Cohort II is over 3 times greater than in Cohort I (116.3 points vs. 35.8 points). Further, the Cohort I finding showing a negative relationship between age-at-onset and mean seriousness scores does not obtain in Cohort II. In the later cohort the mean severity scores fluctuate up and down across the age-at-onset categories.

Figures 10.4b and 10.4c report age-at-onset and offense seriousness score means for nonwhites and whites by cohort. In Cohort I, nonwhites had their highest mean offense severity at age 17, with an overall range of 50.3. They also exhibited higher offense means in all onset-age categories. The white offense mean seriousness scores had their highest value at age 9, with a range of 31.7. Whites consistently had mean offense seriousness scores which were lower than that for the total cohort and therefore lower than that for nonwhites.

The results by race are also dissimilar in Cohort II compared to Cohort I. In the 1958 cohort, whites attain their highest mean serious-ness score in the age-10 onset group compared to age 9 for nonwhites. These data represent a difference of 1 year later for whites and 8 years earlier for nonwhites compared to their counterparts in the 1945 cohort. The range of mean seriousness scores in Cohort II by race reverses that observed for Cohort I. Whites in the second cohort exhibit the greater

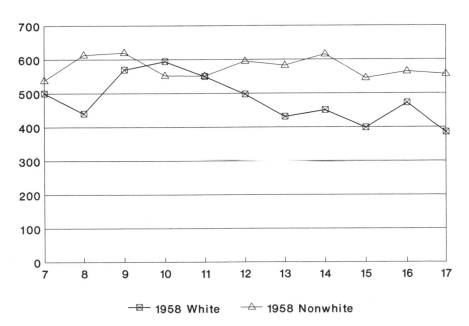

FIGURE 10.4b. Mean severity score by age-at-onset and race for 1958 cohort.

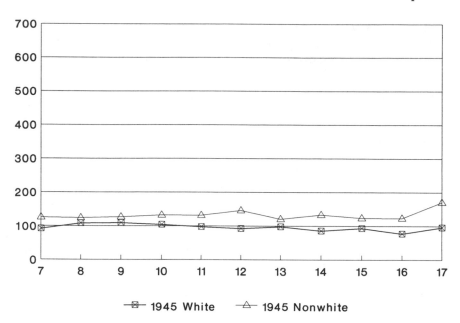

FIGURE 10.4c. Mean severity score by age-at-onset and race for 1945 cohort.

range (208.7 points) compared to nonwhites (81.5 points). Further, the white range in Cohort II is 6.5 times greater than the range for whites in the earlier cohort, but the nonwhite difference in range of mean seriousness scores is only greater by a factor of 1.5 for the 1958 cohort.

The seriousness score data by age-at-onset and SES shown in Figures 10.4d and 10.4e also show clear differences. In Cohort I the lower-SES groups had consistently higher average seriousness scores than high-SES offenders across all age-at-onset categories. The range of mean seriousness scores was more narrow for low-SES delinquents (30.1 points) compared to that for higher-SES offenders (46.6 points). A major similarity, however, was that the highest average seriousness score for both levels of SES occurred at the same age-at-onset category (age 12).

Like the 1945 cohort, the relationship between age-at-onset and mean seriousness scores for the 1958 cohort shows an SES effect. Generally, low-SES offenders have higher mean seriousness scores than high-SES delinquents across age-at-onset categories. Exceptions to this occur at ages 9 and 11, where the higher-SES offender shows the greater mean seriousness score. Like Cohort I the mean seriousness scores vary more across age-at-onset categories for high-SES delinquents (219.5 points) than for low-SES delinquents (104.5).

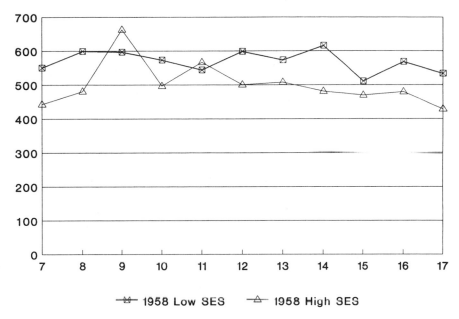

FIGURE 10.4d. Mean severity score by age-at-onset and SES for 1958 cohort.

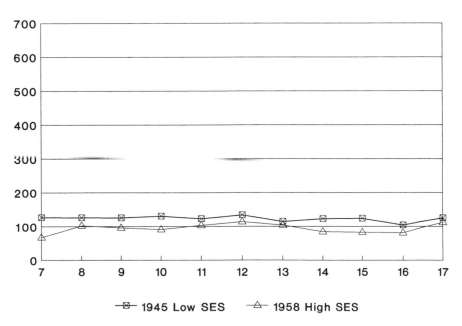

FIGURE 10.4e. Mean severity score by age-at-onset and SES for 1945 cohort.

In sum, these data indicate that both race and SES affect the relationship between age-at-onset and average career seriousness for both cohorts. In Cohort I the effects appear to approach additivity, but in Cohort II the conjoint influence is less additive, especially as evidenced by the data for whites.

Age-at-Onset and Offense Types

Because the mean offense seriousness scores by age-at-onset groups do not make provisions for the type of offenses that occur for each onset group, Table 10.3 presents data on the number and percentage of offenses and the mean seriousness score by the Sellin-Wolfgang offense types (nonindex, injury, theft, damage, or combination) for the race-

TABLE 10.3
Number, Percentage, and Mean Severity for Offense Types by Race and Cohort

| | 1958 Cohort | | | | | |
| | White | | | Nonwhite | | |
	N	Percentage	Mean	N	Percentage	Mean
Age 7						
Nonindex	99	58.2	244.1	221	53.4	195.4
Injury	8	4.7	874.8	31	7.5	1621.4
Theft	25	14.7	831.8	57	13.8	900.5
Damage	20	11.8	513.9	60	14.5	488.1
Combination	18	10.6	1266.4	45	10.9	1081.3
	170			414		
Age 8						
Nonindex	77	56.6	259.0	310	51.9	202.4
Injury	7	5.1	685.6	52	8.7	1792.5
Theft	17	12.5	712.1	108	18.1	934.7
Damage	24	17.6	373.3	68	11.4	475.2
Combination	11	8.1	1270.6	59	9.9	1303.6
	136			597		
Age 9						
Nonindex	64	50.0	265.9	289	47.1	161.3
Injury	6	4.7	1171.5	61	9.9	1666.5
Theft	20	15.6	878.7	112	18.2	871.8
Damage	23	18.0	549.7	80	13.0	469.8
Combination	15	11.7	1242.2	72	11.7	1345.9
	128			614		

TABLE 10.3 (continued)

	1958 Cohort					
	White			Nonwhite		
	N	Percentage	Mean	N	Percentage	Mean
Age 10						
Nonindex	54	40.9	130.0	303	48.7	165.1
Injury	5	3.8	1539.8	42	6.8	1103.5
Theft	34	25.8	884.4	144	23.2	871.3
Damage	23	17.4	642.0	54	8.7	491.9
Combination	16	12.1	1175.8	79	12.7	1202.0
	132			622		
Age 11						
Nonindex	157	48.6	213.3	446	54.3	197.2
Injury	34	10.5	1034.6	57	6.9	1182.8
Theft	44	13.6	943.6	121	14.7	927.5
Damage	55	17.0	525.0	97	11.8	530.9
Combination	33	10.2	1166.2	101	12.3	1325.9
	323			822		
Age 12						
Nonindex	302	57.4	239.8	1009	50.1	185.0
Injury	33	6.3	827.4	167	8.3	1251.4
Theft	56	10.6	860.0	393	19.5	951.7
Damage	80	15.2	560.7	192	9.5	461.8
Combination	55	10.5	1246.8	252	12.5	1345.2
	526			2013		
Age 13						
Nonindex	292	62.7	179.9	1076	52.1	161.0
Injury	30	6.4	1146.0	184	8.9	1480.1
Theft	45	9.7	788.5	370	17.9	914.6
Damage	63	13.5	506.3	212	10.3	536.8
Combination	36	7.7	1290.0	222	10.8	1368.9
	466			2064		
Age 14						
Nonindex	400	64.4	204.2	940	55.3	199.2
Injury	42	6.8	935.4	181	10.6	1539.7
Theft	71	11.4	857.0	261	15.3	920.7
Damage	61	9.8	485.9	128	7.5	513.4
Combination	47	7.6	1447.0	191	11.2	1440.1
	621			1701		
Age 15						
Nonindex	451	69.0	186.5	716	56.4	147.3
Injury	30	4.6	977.0	112	8.8	1490.7
Theft	62	9.5	857.2	232	18.3	890.9
Damage	56	8.6	440.8	82	6.5	475.6
Combination	54	8.3	1271.7	127	10.0	1358.5
	653			1269		

(continued)

TABLE 10.3 (continued)

	1958 Cohort					
	White			Nonwhite		
	N	Percentage	Mean	N	Percentage	Mean
Age 16						
Nonindex	311	67.2	228.3	452	52.7	174.6
Injury	31	6.7	1074.2	67	7.8	1384.1
Theft	58	12.5	914.5	190	22.1	869.8
Damage	25	5.4	520.0	56	6.5	607.3
Combination	38	8.2	1263.7	93	10.8	1221.8
	463			858		
Age 17						
Nonindex	210	72.4	200.1	210	57.4	182.0
Injury	13	4.5	960.8	27	7.4	1356.5
Theft	31	10.7	830.6	73	19.9	889.9
Damage	18	6.2	545.6	15	4.1	565.5
Combination	18	6.2	1197.2	41	11.2	1348.5
	290			366		

	1945 Cohort					
	White			Nonwhite		
	N	Percentage	Mean	N	Percentage	Mean
Age 7						
Nonindex	17	51.5	31.9	71	46.7	40.5
Injury	1	3.0	207.0	13	8.6	246.5
Theft	7	21.2	164.9	33	21.7	158.9
Damage	6	18.2	99.3	6	3.9	103.7
Combination	2	6.1	266.0	29	19.1	244.0
	33			152		
Age 8						
Nonindex	65	57.5	25.7	122	50.8	33.1
Injury	2	1.8	150.0	19	7.9	313.4
Theft	26	23.0	209.5	48	20.0	155.9
Damage	8	7.1	159.3	14	5.8	56.9
Combination	12	10.6	289.8	37	15.4	270.8
	113			240		
Age 9						
Nonindex	138	52.9	25.2	260	50.3	29.1
Injury	15	5.7	228.9	60	11.6	395.3
Theft	67	25.7	188.2	101	19.5	155.6
Damage	25	9.6	176.6	37	7.2	135.3
Combination	16	6.1	278.3	59	11.4	253.5
	261			517		

TABLE 10.3 (continued)

	1945 Cohort					
	White			Nonwhite		
	N	Percentage	Mean	N	Percentage	Mean
Age 10						
Nonindex	186	58.3	23.1	33	53.0	26.8
Injury	23	7.2	313.7	74	11.9	441.1
Theft	49	15.4	183.7	125	20.0	161.7
Damage	30	9.4	141.9	35	5.6	150.1
Combination	31	9.7	272.7	60	9.6	259.1
	319			327		
Age 11						
Nonindex	226	63.0	23.8	400	55.5	33.2
Injury	15	4.2	280.0	68	9.4	420.9
Theft	60	16.7	222.8	130	18.1	161.8
Damage	31	8.6	152.2	27	3.8	161.7
Combination	27	7.5	279.4	95	13.2	295.3
	359			720		
Age 12						
Nonindex	254	63.7	28.5	494	57.5	35.9
Injury	22	5.5	283.1	101	11.8	409.4
Theft	68	17.0	171.2	142	16.5	188.7
Damage	27	6.8	160.6	40	4.7	167.2
Combination	28	7.0	268.5	82	9.5	397.0
	399			859		
Age 13						
Nonindex	370	67.4	22.8	529	61.4	31.0
Injury	36	6.6	355.8	85	9.8	381.2
Theft	81	14.8	203.0	146	16.9	180.5
Damage	30	5.5	187.3	23	2.7	182.0
Combination	32	5.8	326.8	79	9.2	307.9
	549			862		
Age 14						
Nonindex	456	70.2	24.8	398	62.7	34.7
Injury	47	7.2	297.3	79	12.9	443.1
Theft	91	14.0	204.8	98	15.4	191.6
Damage	36	5.5	179.0	20	3.2	165.0
Combination	20	3.1	274.3	40	6.3	340.5
	650			635		
Age 15						
Nonindex	540	71.8	22.1	402	62.7	36.5
Injury	43	6.4	437.1	66	12.9	413.3
Theft	107	14.2	204.1	81	15.4	201.4
Damage	23	3.1	193.4	23	3.2	154.3
Combination	34	4.5	329.5	53	6.3	293.0
	752			625		

(continued)

TABLE 10.3 (continued)

			1945 Cohort			
	White			Nonwhite		
	N	Percentage	Mean	N	Percentage	Mean
Age 16						
Nonindex	588	80.0	21.0	263	66.4	32.8
Injury	35	4.8	427.9	37	9.3	392.3
Theft	77	10.5	188.0	55	13.9	213.1
Damage	17	2.3	205.9	13	3.3	154.2
Combination	18	2.4	626.6	28	7.1	428.1
	735			396		
Age 17						
Nonindex	218	75.7	32.6	73	58.4	70.1
Injury	17	5.9	470.6	16	12.8	446.3
Theft	34	11.8	243.9	22	17.6	207.0
Damage	9	3.1	111.1	5	4.0	160.0
Combination	10	3.5	320.0	9	7.2	344.4
	288			125		

specific age-at-onset categories. These data essentially involve two major issues: (1) the distribution of offense types by age-at-onset and (2) the seriousness score patterns by offense type and age-at-onset.

Considering first the distribution of nonindex offenses within age-at-onset categories, we note that the two cohorts differ concerning the relationship between age-at-onset and the proportionate share of nonindex offenses. For Cohort I, Table 10.3 and Figure 10.5b show that the earlier the age-at-onset the lower the proportion of nonindex offenses for both races. Thus, boys who began their delinquency careers early were more likely to have those careers characterized by a higher percentage of index offenses. For the Cohort II data, however, this result is much less characteristic of the careers. Table 10.3 and Figure 10.5a show that whites exhibit a slight tendency to have an increasing percentage of nonindex offenses as age-at-onset increases; nonwhite delinquents show a much more even distribution across the age-at-onset categories.

Among index offenses, the theft category accounts for the largest proportion for all age-at-onset groups for both cohorts. Differences appear, however, with respect to the trend in theft offenses by age. That is, in Cohort I, theft offenses showed a declining percentage of the index total as age-at-onset increased for both races. In Cohort II the proportion is stable for whites but increases with age for nonwhites.

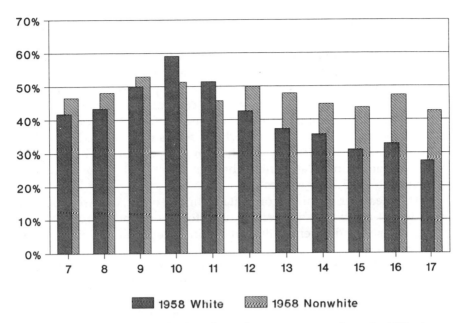

FIGURE 10.5a. Percentage of index offenses by age-at-onset and race for 1958 cohort.

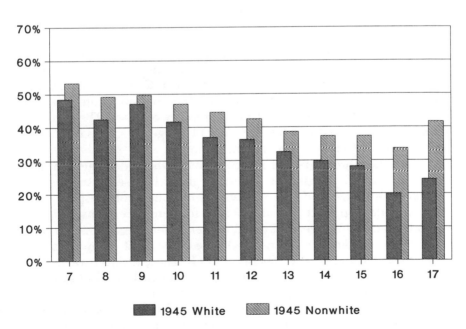

FIGURE 10.5b. Percentage of index offenses by age-at-onset and race for 1945 cohort.

The injury offenses show a much more stable pattern across age-at-onset categories in both cohorts. The ranges of high to low percentages for whites and nonwhites in Cohort I were 5.4% and 4.9%, respectively. The ranges in Cohort II are 6.7% for whites and 3.8% for nonwhites. The increased range for whites in Cohort II is accompanied by an increase in the relative proportion of injury offenses compared to Cohort I. That is, in the 1945 cohort, injury offenses accounted for a high of 12.9% for nonwhites compared to 7.2% for whites across onset ages. In the 1958 cohort the races are virtually identical in the peak of the injury share across all age-at-onset categories. The peak share is 10.6% for nonwhites compared to 10.5% for whites.

The mean seriousness score data by age-at-onset, offense type, and race do not exhibit a consistent pattern for the offender groups in the two cohorts. The differences that are attained depend more on race than any age effect.

Concerning the nonindex offense seriousness scores, the distribution across age-at-onset categories for the two cohorts show very little variation (for either race), thus indicating the absence of an age effect. There is, however, a cohort-specific race effect in the mean seriousness scores across age-at-onset categories. In Cohort I, nonwhite males had higher average scores for all age groups. On the other hand, Cohort II data show that whites have the higher scores in all but one instance (age 10).

The seriousness scores for injury offenses show a cohort effect for age, but a race effect for all groups. That is, the injury offense mean scores are strongly positively related with age in Cohort I but are generally weak in Cohort II. The data also indicate that nonwhite offenders have higher mean seriousness scores for injury offenses. The nonwhite scores exceeded those of whites in 8 out of 11 age categories in Cohort I and in 10 out of 11 age categories in Cohort II.

The other three types of index offenses (theft, damage and combination) show no consistent pattern of increasing seriousness scores with age-at-onset. The data do, however, indicate a cohort-specific race effect, an effect opposite to that observed for nonindex offenses. For the Cohort I data, whites generally had higher seriousness scores for theft, damage, or combination offenses. On the other hand, nonwhites have about the same scores as whites in Cohort II. These results reverse those obtained for the nonindex offense category, for which whites had higher average severity scores.

The data pertaining to age-at-onset and offense type by SES are given in Table 10.4 and in Figures 10.5c and 10.5d. These data show very similar patterns for both cohorts. In Cohort I the low-SES offenders showed a trend in which the percentage of offenses that are nonindex

TABLE 10.4

Number, Percentage, and Mean Severity for Offense Types by SES and Cohort

	1958 Cohort					
	Low SES			High SES		
	N	Percentage	Mean	N	Percentage	Mean
Age 7						
Nonindex	244	53.3	213.1	76	60.3	202.4
Injury	34	7.4	1505.3	5	4.0	1217.4
Theft	67	14.6	887.8	15	11.9	844.5
Damage	59	12.9	500.9	21	16.7	480.1
Combination	54	11.8	1108.4	9	7.1	1293.3
	458			126		
Age 8						
Nonindex	320	51.3	202.0	67	61.5	267.4
Injury	55	8.8	1663.6	4	3.7	1630.5
Theft	110	17.6	926.1	15	13.8	749.7
Damage	78	12.5	476.3	14	12.8	297.2
Combination	61	9.8	1285.6	9	8.3	1392.6
	624			109		
Age 9						
Nonindex	269	46.5	168.9	84	51.5	220.3
Injury	56	9.7	1483.5	11	6.7	2329.5
Theft	106	18.3	867.7	26	16.0	898.8
Damage	82	14.2	465.7	21	12.9	576.8
Combination	66	11.4	1319.2	21	12.9	1357.9
	579			163		
Age 10						
Nonindex	299	47.9	168.0	58	44.6	116.1
Injury	39	6.3	1231.8	8	6.2	753.5
Theft	148	23.7	884.4	30	23.1	824.3
Damage	60	9.6	562.0	17	13.1	447.9
Combination	78	12.5	1209.8	17	13.1	1143.0
	794			351		
Age 11						
Nonindex	432	54.4	200.3	171	48.7	205.2
Injury	59	7.4	1178.6	32	9.1	1035.8
Theft	110	13.9	932.6	55	15.7	931.5
Damage	101	12.7	527.0	51	14.5	532.9
Combination	92	11.6	1305.2	42	12.0	1247.9
	794			351		
Age 12						
Nonindex	971	50.5	205.8	340	55.2	176.0
Injury	156	8.1	1236.4	44	7.1	988.4
Theft	354	18.4	956.0	95	15.4	882.7
Damage	198	10.3	490.7	74	12.0	494.8
Combination	244	12.7	1323.8	63	10.2	1343.2
	1923			616		

(*continued*)

TABLE 10.4 (continued)

| | 1958 Cohort | | | | | |
| | Low SES | | | High SES | | |
	N	Percentage	Mean	N	Percentage	Mean
Age 13						
Nonindex	961	53.2	167.9	407	56.2	161.0
Injury	166	9.2	1470.0	48	6.6	1307.1
Theft	309	17.1	909.5	106	14.6	878.6
Damage	181	10.0	498.3	94	13.0	590.8
Combination	189	10.5	1373.0	69	9.5	1315.9
	1806			724		
Age 14						
Nonindex	865	55.3	203.2	475	62.6	197.2
Injury	159	10.2	1545.4	64	8.4	1131.7
Theft	246	15.7	929.0	86	11.3	844.7
Damage	126	8.1	517.9	63	8.3	479.4
Combination	167	10.7	1476.0	71	9.4	1359.1
	1563			759		
Age 15						
Nonindex	697	59.5	156.5	470	62.6	171.3
Injury	99	8.5	1454.0	43	5.7	1217.7
Theft	195	16.7	889.2	99	13.2	874.9
Damage	80	6.8	472.8	58	7.7	448.6
Combination	100	8.5	1339.7	81	10.8	1325.5
	1171			751		
Age 16						
Nonindex	429	54.4	178.3	334	62.7	220.6
Injury	61	7.7	1477.2	37	6.9	972.1
Theft	166	21.1	868.5	82	15.4	905.8
Damage	49	6.2	630.0	32	6.0	505.3
Combination	83	10.5	1279.7	48	9.0	1157.8
	788			533		
Age 17						
Nonindex	198	60.7	185.1	222	67.3	197.0
Injury	22	6.7	1608.8	18	5.5	763.5
Theft	64	19.6	910.6	40	12.1	811.9
Damage	15	4.6	506.6	18	5.5	595.5
Combination	27	8.3	1331.2	32	9.7	1278.5
	326			330		

| | 1945 Cohort | | | | | |
| | Low SES | | | High SES | | |
	N	Percentage	Mean	N	Percentage	Mean
Age 7						
Nonindex	71	43.8	39.6	17	79.9	36.0
Injury	12	7.4	247.8	1	4.6	220.0

TABLE 10.4 (continued)

	1945 Cohort					
	Low SES			High SES		
	N	Percentage	Mean	N	Percentage	Mean
Theft	38	23.5	159.9	3	13.0	179.7
Damage	10	6.2	104.4	2	8.7	87.0
Combination	31	19.1	245.4	0	0.0	0.0
	162			23		
Age 8						
Nonindex	120	49.6	32.5	67	60.3	26.9
Injury	14	5.8	324.8	7	6.3	243.9
Theft	62	25.6	178.8	12	10.8	157.8
Damage	14	5.8	149.7	8	7.2	171.8
Combination	32	13.2	276.8	17	15.3	273.1
	242			111		
Age 9						
Nonindex	351	50.4	28.9	51	59.3	18.0
Injury	67	9.6	375.3	8	9.3	250.9
Theft	156	22.4	166.0	13	15.1	198.1
Damage	50	7.2	147.5	12	14.0	170.7
Combination	73	10.5	256.3	2	2.3	350.0
	697			86		
Age 10						
Nonindex	407	54.1	26.4	110	57.6	21.9
Injury	85	11.3	452.0	12	6.3	117.8
Theft	133	17.7	161.5	41	21.5	188.6
Damage	49	6.5	142.1	16	8.4	159.2
Combination	79	10.5	262.2	12	6.3	276.1
	753			191		
Age 11						
Nonindex	490	56.4	30.2	138	64.7	28.0
Injury	69	8.0	401.5	14	6.7	307.6
Theft	161	18.6	178.5	29	13.6	195.3
Damage	46	5.3	148.0	13	6.1	190.3
Combination	102	11.8	291.3	19	8.9	299.4
	868			213		
Age 12						
Nonindex	560	59.0	31.6	191	61.4	38.2
Injury	101	10.6	401.6	22	7.1	318.6
Theft	151	15.9	185.5	59	19.0	180.8
Damage	48	5.0	169.7	18	5.2	150.7
Combination	90	9.5	363.3	21	6.8	367.9
	950			311		
Age 13						
Nonindex	630	62.0	26.4	264	67.7	29.6
Injury	93	9.2	484.3	28	7.2	338.4
Theft	173	17.1	181.5	54	13.0	207.4

(continued)

TABLE 10.4 (continued)

	1945 Cohort					
	Low SES			High SES		
	N	Percentage	Mean	N	Percentage	Mean
Damage	32	3.2	176.8	21	5.4	197.3
Combination	88	8.7	306.8	23	5.9	338.2
	1016			390		
Age 14						
Nonindex	542	65.5	33.8	313	68.5	22.0
Injury	95	11.5	425.3	30	6.6	282.5
Theft	118	14.3	198.4	69	15.4	199.3
Damage	31	3.8	175.8	25	5.5	171.8
Combination	41	5.0	342.4	20	4.4	263.4
	827			457		
Age 15						
Nonindex	524	64.3	33.4	415	74.2	20.7
Injury	85	10.4	444.4	29	5.2	361.4
Theft	113	13.9	200.9	75	13.4	205.9
Damage	29	3.6	155.9	17	3.0	204.4
Combination	64	7.8	287.2	23	4.1	363.4
	815			559		
Age 16						
Nonindex	432	71.4	29.8	420	79.6	19.5
Injury	47	7.8	418.5	26	4.9	381.5
Theft	78	12.9	210.2	55	10.1	180.1
Damage	20	3.3	170.2	10	1.5	210.0
Combination	28	4.6	370.1	17	3.2	747.1
	605			528		
Age 17						
Nonindex	127	64.8	54.9	161	75.2	32.1
Injury	18	9.2	353.3	15	7.0	606.7
Theft	34	17.4	215.5	22	10.3	250.9
Damage	9	4.6	144.4	5	2.3	100.0
Combination	8	4.1	325.4	11	5.1	336.4
	196			214		

increases from the age of 7 through age 16. For high-SES delinquents the trend was not evident, and the percentage of offenses that are nonindex was much higher for this group across the onset ages. In Cohort II the proportion of nonindex offenses, although not stable, does not indicate a consistent trend for either SES group, thus showing no age effect. Like Cohort I, the nonindex offenses represent a greater share of high-SES delinquency regardless of age-at-onset.

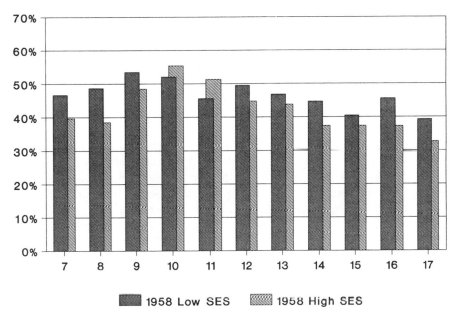

FIGURE 10.5c. Percentage of index offenses by age-at-onset and SES for 1958 cohort.

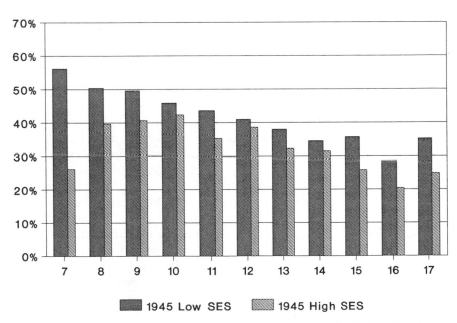

FIGURE 10.5d. Percentage of index offenses by age-at-onset and SES for 1945 cohort.

With respect to injury offenses, both cohorts show that the proportion fluctuates across age-at-onset categories for both SES levels. In both cohorts, low-SES delinquents have the greater share of injury offenses. The same can be said of theft and combination offenses as well. In both cohorts, lower-status delinquents are more likely to engage in these acts than delinquents of higher SES. On the other hand, the data indicate that higher-status offenders are more likely to engage in damage-related offenses.

Turning to the issue of the relationship between age-at-onset and mean seriousness by SES, we observe that the data for both cohorts are quite similar. The results indicate that age-at-onset is not consistently related to mean seriousness. Thus, for both cohorts and SES levels, the age at which a delinquent begins his career does not appear to be related to average seriousness. The mean seriousness scores fluctuate up and down, thus showing no age effect.

Second, the data also indicate that there is no consistent pattern of an SES effect on mean seriousness. At some age-at-onset levels, low-SES delinquents exhibit higher scores across the offense types, while high-SES delinquents predominate at others. In general, for Cohort I the magnitude of the mean seriousness scores for nonindex and injury offenses tended to be greater for the lower-SES boys, while the magnitude of the mean seriousness scores for theft, damage, and combination offenses tended to be greater for the higher-SES boys. The pattern is different in the 1958 cohort. Here, low-SES delinquents seem to have higher scores for injury, theft, and combination offenses, while high-SES delinquents exhibit higher mean scores for nonindex and damage offenses. These data do not point to a consistent SES effect but, rather, show cohort-specific differences.

The last step in the presentation of descriptive data for age-at-onset is a display in Table 10.5 of the distribution of delinquents and mean number of offenses by age-at-onset, race, and type of offender, as measured by the commission of a certain number (i.e., chronic delinquents) of offenses or offense types (i.e., injury offenses or UCR index offenses). As a whole, the data show great similarities both across and within cohorts by race.

First, the modal age-at-onset for chronic offenders differs only slightly: age 14 for whites and age 13 for nonwhites in Cohort II; and age 13 for whites and a tie between the ages of 11 and 12 for nonwhites in Cohort I. Second, the delinquents in both cohorts exhibit about the same race and age effects for injury offenders. Cohort I whites had age 15 as the peak year, while nonwhites began their injury offenses 2 years earlier. In Cohort II, nonwhites again begin at age 13, but whites begin 3

TABLE 10.5
Mean Number of Offenses for Select Offenders, by Age at Onset, Race, and Cohort

		1958 Cohort							
		All offenders		Chronic offenders		Injury offenders		UCR index offenders	
Age	Race	N	Mean	N	Mean	N	Mean	N	Mean
10	W	95	5.96	33	13.39	24	10.96	48	9.96
10	NW	307	7.32	156	12.26	125	11.58	226	9.27
11	W	51	6.33	28	9.71	20	10.45	36	8.03
11	NW	128	6.42	72	9.58	57	9.07	100	7.46
12	W	111	4.74	35	10.66	27	7.96	68	6.57
12	NW	332	6.06	162	10.10	152	8.95	249	7.29
13	W	149	3.13	28	8.18	33	4.94	87	4.94
13	NW	450	4.59	168	8.79	164	5.63	279	4.57
14	W	203	3.06	42	7.52	44	4.64	87	4.57
14	NW	455	3.74	127	7.93	160	5.63	279	4.94
15	W	293	2.23	30	6.73	36	3.83	104	3.37
15	NW	484	2.62	64	6.70	125	3.96	287	3.33
16	W	275	1.68	11	6.36	38	2.50	86	2.29
16	NW	455	1.89	22	6.68	88	2.85	240	2.37
17	W	235	1.23	2	5.50	14	1.86	56	1.48
17	NW	292	1.25	2	13.50	38	1.50	120	1.49
All	W	1412	2.77	209	9.16	236	5.56	551	4.63
All	NW	2903	3.91	773	9.48	909	6.76	1803	5.28
All	Both	4315	3.53	982	9.41	1145	6.51	2354	5.12
		1945 Cohort							
		All offenders		Chronic offenders		Injury offenders		UCR index offenders	
Age	Race	N	Mean	N	Mean	N	Mean	N	Mean
10	W	174	4.19	61	8.49	37	5.16	82	6.56
10	NW	210	7.30	119	11.13	109	10.02	151	9.29
11	W	104	3.43	30	7.20	17	3.05	50	5.10
11	NW	130	5.56	71	8.32	55	7.20	97	6.54
12	W	131	3.03	23	7.91	20	5.80	57	4.35
12	NW	169	5.08	71	8.97	69	6.78	117	6.30
13	W	213	2.58	31	6.48	34	4.52	71	3.88
13	NW	200	4.30	68	8.42	76	6.38	119	5.84
14	W	289	2.23	28	6.89	43	3.20	81	3.54
14	NW	196	3.26	43	7.37	67	4.89	101	4.10
15	W	369	2.04	26	6.26	48	2.95	115	2.91
15	NW	227	2.72	33	7.63	61	4.75	94	3.98

(continued)

TABLE 10.5 (continued)

		\multicolumn{8}{c}{1945 Cohort}							
		All offenders		Chronic offenders		Injury offenders		UCR index offenders	
Age	Race	N	Mean	N	Mean	N	Mean	N	Mean
16	W	494	1.48	11	5.27	35	2.25	78	2.06
16	NW	223	1.78	12	6.58	42	2.66	65	2.60
17	W	245	1.17	—	—	19	1.42	46	1.26
17	NW	101	1.21	—	—	17	1.58	33	1.45
All	W	2019	2.20	210	7.29	253	3.55	580	3.72
All	NW	1456	3.95	417	9.05	494	6.45	777	5.76
All	Both	3475	2.93	627	8.46	747	5.47	1357	4.89

years later at age 16. Last, the UCR offender data show nonwhites begin earlier than whites (13 vs. 15 in Cohort I and 13 vs. 15/16 in Cohort II).

These data also indicate that the offenders who fall into the injury and/or UCR index offense groups exhibit the declining offense pattern reported previously for total offenses. That is, for both cohorts, the average number of offenses declines with age for both UCR index and Sellin-Wolfgang injury offenders. The chronic offenders are a special case. Because at least five offenses are required in order for an offender to be classified as chronic in the first place, the mean number of offenses by age does not exhibit the same degree of decline as the other groups.

Our data indicate that the 1958 cohort had higher rates of delinquency, especially the most serious offenses, compared to Cohort I. We looked to the age-at-onset data as one possible explanation for the cohort offense differences. The results pertaining to age-at-onset did not offer a definitive explanation.

We found that the proportions of delinquents who began their careers at various ages from 7 through 17 were about the same for both cohorts. From age 7 through age 9, 6.6% of the Cohort II delinquents and 5.8% of the Cohort I delinquents had started their careers. From ages 10 through 14, 56.1% of the delinquents in the 1945 cohort and 45.8% of the delinquents in the 1958 cohort had initiated their involvement in delinquency. For the late starters, ages 15, 16, and 17, we found that 47% of delinquents in both cohorts were so classified. These findings were generally repeated when race, SES, and chronic offender status were examined.

The two cohorts were also alike with respect to the finding that age-at-onset was inversely related to mean number of offenses. On average, the earlier an offender started, the more offenses he accumulated. The correlation between age-at-onset and mean number of offenses was strong for both races and both SES levels in each cohort. The highest correlation was the same in both cohorts, low-SES nonwhites, with values of −.97 in Cohort II and −.99 in Cohort I. The weakest correlation obtained was also for the same group in the two cohorts, high-SES nonwhites, with values of −.64 in the 1958 cohort and −.74 in the 1945 cohort.

The assumption that a delinquency career started early will produce severe delinquency was not confirmed. The mean severity of delinquency was only moderately related to age-at-onset in Cohort I, while for Cohort II the severity scores fluctuated across the age-at-onset categories. Although the measured severity of offenses was not strongly related to age-at-onset, we found that age-at-onset was related to the type of offenses that were committed. That is, the earlier an offender began his career, the more likely he was to engage in index offenses compared to those offenders who began at the tail end of the age continuum.

On the whole, age-at-onset was not strongly related to offense severity. Most important, the cohorts were sufficiently similar with respect to age-at-onset so that the starting points of the delinquent careers in the two cohorts did not explain the greater severity of delinquency in the later cohort.

11

Delinquency and Age-at-Offense

Distribution of Offenses by Age

This chapter concerns the age at which the offenses in the two cohorts were committed. Thus, these data are akin to the age-specific arrest rates published in the FBI's *Uniform Crime Reports*. As such, these data represent the distribution of offenses by age for the complete juvenile career, and although our research is longitudinal, the present data are generally comparable to other police-based age-at-offense data, whether cross-sectional or longitudinal.

The data describing the distribution of offenses by age, given in Table 11.1, show a close similarity between the two cohorts. Referring first to the total columns for the cohorts overall, we observe that except for age 10, which is a composite of age 10 and under, the proportion of offenses increases with age up to 16 and then declines at age 17. The peak age at which offenses are committed is 16 for both cohorts. The two cohorts are also very similar in that a majority of the delinquent acts were committed toward the end of the period at risk. In the 1958 cohort, 64% of the offenses were committed by delinquents of ages 15, 16, and 17, while in the 1945 cohort 60% of the offenses were committed by delinquents at these three ages. Thus, both cohorts show the familiar age and delinquency curve which rises from age 11 through age 16 and then declines.

When race is introduced, the overall patterns described above hold for Cohort I, but differ slightly in the 1958 cohort. Table 11.1 indicates that in Cohort I, the percentage of offenses increased from age 11 through age 16 and then declined at age 17 for nonwhites and whites. The peak age (16) was the same regardless of race, although whites showed the more pronounced peak at this age (28.4% vs. 22.1%). Similarly, white delinquents showed the higher percentage (66%) of offenses committed in the last 3 years at risk compared to nonwhites (55%). In fact, the trend of decreasing nonwhite involvement versus an increasing white involvement by age was evident throughout the age

TABLE 11.1
Offenses by Age, Race, and Cohort

| | 1958 Cohort | | | | | |
| | White | | Nonwhite | | Total | |
Age	N	Percentage	N	Percentage	N	Percentage
LE 10[a]	123	3.2	518	4.6	641	4.2
11	94	2.4	286	2.5	380	2.5
12	200	5.1	691	6.1	891	5.8
13	355	9.1	1250	11.0	1605	10.5
14	477	12.2	1476	13.0	1953	12.8
15	809	20.1	2266	19.9	3075	20.1
16	917	23.5	2688	23.7	3605	23.6
17	933	23.9	2165	19.1	3098	20.3
All	3908	100.0	11,340	100.0	15,248	100.0

| | 1945 Cohort | | | | | |
| | White | | Nonwhite | | Total | |
Age	N	Percentage	N	Percentage	N	Percentage
LE 10[a]	208	4.7	376	6.5	584	5.7
11	156	3.5	284	4.9	440	4.3
12	225	5.5	442	7.7	667	6.5
13	339	7.6	620	10.8	959	9.4
14	569	12.8	826	14.4	1395	13.7
15	878	19.7	1118	19.4	1996	19.4
16	1269	28.4	1269	22.1	2538	24.8
17	814	18.3	821	14.3	1635	16.0
All	4458	100.0	5756	100.0	10,214	100.0

[a]LE 10 = age 10 and under.

distribution. At age 10, 65% of the offenses were committed by nonwhites compared to 35% by whites. As age increased, the nonwhite proportion steadily decreased, while that for whites increased. In the last 2 years at risk (ages 16 and 17), there was virtual parity between the races.

In the 1958 cohort, the nonwhite data show the increasing percentage of offenses from age 11 to age 16 and then a decline at age 17; however, the data for whites show a continuing increase from age 11 through the last year of the juvenile period (age 17). This trend produces a slight discrepancy in the percentage of delinquent acts that are committed in the later stage of the juvenile career. For whites 68% of the acts are committed after age 14, while for nonwhites the figure is 62%. In spite of the age trend and the concentration of offenses at the end of the career, the data indicate that nonwhite offenses predominate throughout the age distribution. The discrepancy is greatest at the initial year (age 10), where 80% of the offenses belong to nonwhites, while the race difference is lowest at the final year (age 17), where nonwhites are responsible for about 70% of the delinquency.

The number of offenders in each age category is another important aspect of the relationship between age and delinquency. Table 11.2 shows the number and percentage of offenders at specific ages and the mean number of offenses committed. An individual offender can appear

TABLE 11.2
Offenders by Age, Race, and Cohort

					1958 Cohort				
	White			Nonwhite			Total		
Age	N	Percentage	Mean	N	Percentage	Mean	N	Percentage	Mean
LE 10[a]	106	4.2	1.16	375	5.6	1.38	481	5.2	1.33
11	69	2.7	1.36	191	2.9	1.50	260	2.8	1.46
12	146	5.7	1.37	465	6.9	1.49	611	6.6	1.46
13	233	9.1	1.52	736	11.0	1.70	969	10.5	1.66
14	326	12.8	1.46	942	14.1	1.57	1268	13.8	1.54
15	502	19.7	1.61	1242	18.6	1.82	1744	18.9	1.76
16	576	22.6	1.59	1444	21.7	1.86	2020	21.9	1.78
17	594	23.3	1.57	1272	19.1	1.70	1866	20.2	1.66
All	2552	100.0		6667	100.0		6653	100.0	
					1945 Cohort				
	White			Nonwhite			Total		
Age	N	Percentage	Mean	N	Percentage	Mean	N	Percentage	Mean
LE 10[a]	186	5.6	1.12	256	7.7	1.47	442	6.6	1.32
11	135	4.1	1.12	194	5.8	1.46	329	4.9	1.34
12	178	5.4	1.26	282	8.5	1.57	460	6.9	1.45
13	278	8.4	1.22	297	8.9	2.09	575	8.6	1.68
14	423	12.8	1.34	496	14.9	1.67	919	13.8	1.52
15	627	18.9	1.40	620	18.6	1.80	1247	18.7	1.60
16	881	26.6	1.44	693	20.8	1.83	1574	23.7	1.61
17	608	18.3	1.34	499	14.9	1.64	1107	16.6	1.48
All	3316	100.0		3337	100.0		6653	100.0	

[a]LE 10 = age 10 and under.

in each age category, but he can be counted only once within a specific age (i.e., a multiple count of offenders would be equivalent to an offense count).

In Cohort I the total distribution of delinquents by age was nearly the same as that of offenses. The general pattern reflects increasing proportions to age 16, then a decrease at age 17. The same trend is shown in Table 11.2 for the offenders in Cohort II. The major difference between the cohorts concerns the average number of offenses for each age category. We reported in a previous chapter that the Cohort II males had generally higher offense rates than their counterparts in the 1945 cohort. It is important, therefore, to note here that, with the exception of age 13, the Cohort II males have a higher mean number of offenses for each age than that of Cohort I.

The offender and age data by race closely resemble that of the total offender category. The proportion of offenders increased with age (up to 16) for both races in Cohort I and for nonwhites in Cohort II. Whites in Cohort II show an increasing offender involvement through age 17. The mean scores, however, confirm the cohort effect reported earlier in this volume. That is, for Cohort I, nonwhites had a higher mean number of offenses than whites at each age-specific category (a difference of from .3 to .4 offenses, usually). However, in Cohort II, although the means for nonwhites are still higher, the difference for almost all ages is about .2 offenses, or close to one-half the difference of Cohort I.

Offense Rates by Age

In Table 11.3 we turn to a presentation of crude and weighted offense rates by age and race. The crude offense data mirror the frequency data reported previously. In Cohort I the crude delinquency rates increased from age 11 through age 16 and then declined for both races. In Cohort II this is true for nonwhites but not for whites. For the latter, the rates increase consistently as age increases. These crude offense rates by race are depicted in Figures 11.1a and 11.1b.

The ratio of the nonwhite to white crude rates reflects the smaller race difference in the 1958 cohort than in its predecessor. That is, for tne 1945 cohort there was an overall ratio of 3.1, which began at 4.5 to 1 at age 10 or under and declined to 2.4 to 1 at the last year of delinquency. In the 1958 cohort the ratio is smaller overall (2.6 to 1), starts out smaller (3.8 to 1), and is smaller at every age except age 16.

In light of data presented in earlier sections of this volume, especially those pertaining to the severity differences between the races, the

TABLE 11.3
Crude and Weighted Rates of Delinquency by Age, Race, and Cohort

	1958 Cohort					
	White		Nonwhite		NW to W ratio	
Age	Crude	Weighted	Crude	Weighted	Crude	Weighted
LE 10[a]	19.79	59.95	74.60	263.16	3.8	4.4
11	15.12	71.55	41.19	210.30	2.7	2.9
12	32.18	130.59	99.51	438.96	3.1	3.4
13	57.11	227.95	180.01	714.50	3.2	3.1
14	76.74	338.20	212.56	1107.49	2.8	3.3
15	130.15	611.75	326.32	1915.53	2.5	3.1
16	147.52	717.73	387.10	2581.47	2.6	3.6
17	150.10	746.19	311.78	2259.47	2.1	3.0
All	628.71	2903.93	1633.07	9490.88	2.6	3.3
	1945 Cohort					
	White		Nonwhite		NW to W ratio	
Age	Crude	Weighted	Crude	Weighted	Crude	Weighted
LE 10[a]	7.33	7.33	32.39	83.32	4.5	11.4
11	22.15	17.82	97.86	112.80	4.4	6.3
12	31.95	37.93	152.31	170.30	4.8	4.5
13	48.13	43.34	213.65	241.66	4.5	5.6
14	80.79	72.24	284.63	345.68	3.5	4.8
15	124.66	120.79	385.25	445.01	3.1	3.6
16	180.18	143.65	437.28	633.49	2.4	4.4
17	115.58	122.50	282.91	503.34	2.4	4.1
All	632.97	587.84	1633.07	9490.88	3.1	4.4

[a]LE 10 = age 10 and under; the rates for this composite age category are expressed as the mean of the individual rates of the four ages, from 7 to 10 years of age.

weighted rates by age are especially significant. The data for Cohort I show a wide disparity in offense severity by race. Overall, nonwhite delinquency was 4.4 times as serious as that of white delinquency. The data by age generally showed, however, that the race difference was greater in the early ages of offending and then declined as the delinquents age. For example, the ratio of the nonwhite weighted rate to that for whites was a factor of over 11 times for offenses committed at ages 10 and under and was a factor of about 6 times for offenses committed at age 11. On the other hand, the nonwhite to white ratio for weighted rates was 4.4 at age 16 and 4.1 at age 17.

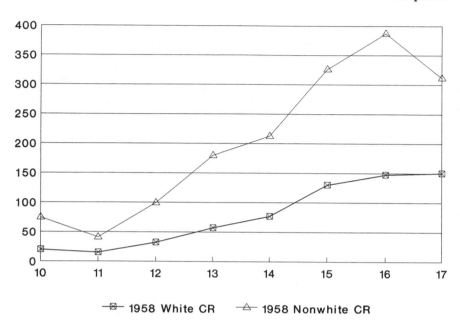

FIGURE 11.1a. Crude delinquency rates by age-at-offense and race for 1958 cohort.

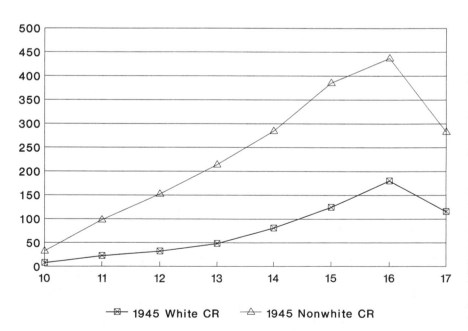

FIGURE 11.1b. Crude delinquency rates by age-at-offense and race for 1945 cohort.

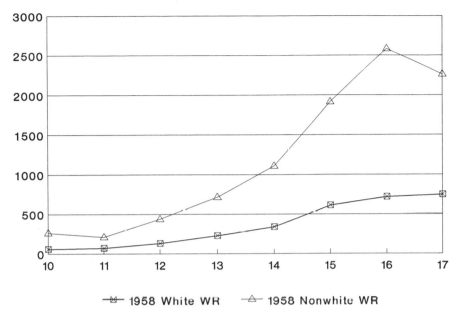

FIGURE 11.1c. Weighted delinquency rates by age-at-offense and race for 1958 cohort.

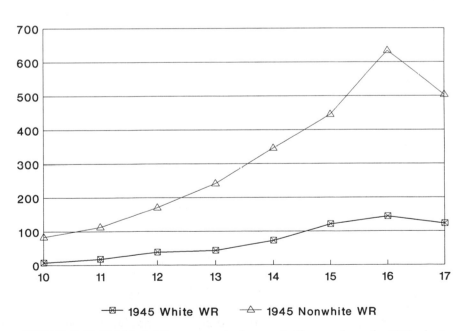

FIGURE 11.1d. Weighted delinquency rates by age-at-offense and race for 1945 cohort.

Although the trend in the data (see Figure 11.1d) shows a declining difference with age, it is unmistakable that nonwhite delinquents in Cohort I had a much greater seriousness in their delinquency. Thus, for the single year when nonwhites in this cohort were 16 years old, their weighted rate of delinquency (633.49) was higher than the rate for whites over their entire juvenile careers (587.84).

The situation in Cohort II is different, as we have continually noted. Although nonwhites still have higher weighted rates than whites for all age categories, the differences are not so great as those observed for the first cohort. Overall, the ratio of weighted rates is reduced from a factor of 4.4 in Cohort I to a factor of 3.3 in Cohort II. More important, the age data for Cohort II generally indicate that the difference between the races is relatively stable by age (see Figure 11.1c).

Presentation of the crude offense rates by age and race controlling for SES, shown in Table 11.4, does not affect previous findings. Regardless of SES level, the crude offense rates increase for both races in Cohort I, and increase for nonwhites in Cohort II from age 11 to age 16, and then show a decline at age 17. Whites in Cohort II show a monotonic increase in offense rate with age. Also, regardless of SES, nonwhite rates are higher than white rates for all age categories in both cohorts.

The introduction of SES does, however, point out the relative difference between the two cohorts. For Cohort I the nonwhite to white ratio for the offense rates averages 2.3 among low-SES delinquents and 2.4 among high-SES delinquents, or almost no SES effect. In Cohort II, however, the nonwhite to white ratio differs by SES. At the lower level, the nonwhite to white ratio of 1.7 is less than the ratio (2.3) at the higher level of SES.

Offense Types by Age

When the offenses are separated by our harm-based index versus nonindex dichotomy, the same pattern emerges as that observed previously for offenses overall. Table 11.5 indicates for Cohort I that the proportion of both index and nonindex offenses increased after age 10 to a peak at age 16 and then declined. The data also show that nonindex offenses predominated at all ages, but especially late in the juvenile career. Table 11.5 shows the same age trend in Cohort II as above. The proportion of both serious and trivial offenses increases as delinquents age. The data also show, however, that in the 1958 cohort nonindex offenses are far from the dominant type of offense. In fact, nonindex offenses represent the larger percentage of delinquency at only ages 10

TABLE 11.4
Crude Rates of Delinquency by Age, Race, SES, and Cohort

| | 1958 Cohort | | | | | |
| | Low SES | | High SES | | NW to W ratio | |
Age	White	Nonwhite	White	Nonwhite	Low SES	High SES
LE 10[a]	40.21	92.23	14.29	25.97	2.3	1.8
11	32.63	49.84	10.41	17.32	1.5	1.7
12	70.56	113.03	21.85	62.23	1.6	2.8
13	135.05	200.55	36.14	123.38	1.5	3.4
14	131.26	235.09	62.07	150.43	1.8	2.4
15	209.41	357.14	108.82	241.34	1.7	2.2
16	230.65	428.96	125.15	271.65	1.9	2.2
17	235.96	333.40	126.99	252.16	1.4	1.9
All	1085.73	1810.24	505.72	1144.48	1.7	2.3

| | 1945 Cohort | | | | | |
| | Low SES | | High SES | | NW to W ratio | |
Age	White	Nonwhite	White	Nonwhite	Low SES	High SES
LE 10[a]	12.97	35.90	4.94	13.39	2.8	2.7
11	39.72	103.93	14.48	65.50	2.6	4.5
12	58.88	157.12	20.19	126.64	2.7	6.3
13	81.78	230.36	33.45	124.45	2.8	3.7
14	116.35	301.55	65.27	194.32	2.6	2.9
15	172.43	417.35	103.81	213.97	2.4	2.1
16	239.25	473.40	154.40	244.54	1.9	1.6
17	146.73	296.24	101.98	211.79	2.0	2.1
All	907.01	2123.57	513.36	1235.81	2.3	2.4

[a]LE 10 = age 10 and under; the rates for this composite age category are expressed as the mean of the individual rates of the four ages, from 7 to 10 years of age.

and under, 13, 14, and 15. In the other instances (ages 11, 12, 16, and 17) index offenses show the greater share. Further, there does not appear to be an age trend in these data. Cohort II offenses are more serious than those committed by the first cohort regardless of the age at which the offenses are committed.

Table 11.6 presents the frequency of index and nonindex offenses by age and race. Like the overall data presented above, there are distinct race effects by cohort. For the 1945 cohort, the percentage of index offenses increased with age to a peak at age 16 for nonwhites and at age 15 for whites. In the second cohort, nonwhites again peak at age 16, but

TABLE 11.5
Index and Nonindex Offenses by Age and Cohort

	1958 Cohort					
	Index		Nonindex		Total	
Age	N	Percentage	N	Percentage	N	Percentage
LE 10[a]	305	4.0	336	4.4	641	4.2
11	238	3.1	142	1.9	380	2.5
12	481	6.3	410	5.4	891	5.8
13	698	9.2	907	11.8	1605	10.5
14	893	11.8	1060	13.8	1953	12.8
15	1497	19.7	1578	20.6	3075	20.2
16	1838	24.2	1767	23.1	3605	23.6
17	1636	21.6	1462	19.1	3098	20.3
All	7586	100.0	7662	100.0	15248	100.0
	1945 Cohort					
	Index		Nonindex		Total	
Age	N	Percentage	N	Percentage	N	Percentage
LE 10[a]	284	7.4	300	4.7	584	5.7
11	217	5.7	223	3.5	440	4.3
12	355	9.3	312	4.9	667	6.5
13	417	10.9	542	8.5	959	9.4
14	536	14.1	859	13.4	1395	13.7
15	693	18.2	1303	20.4	1996	19.5
16	737	19.3	1801	28.1	2538	24.8
17	574	15.1	1061	16.6	1635	16.0
All	3813	100.0	6401	100.0	10214	100.0

[a]LE 10 = age 10 and under.

whites show a continuing increase through age 17. Thus, nonwhites peak at age 16, regardless of birth year, while whites peak early, age 15, in the 1945 cohort and do not peak in the 1958 cohort.

Concerning the nonindex offenses, both whites and nonwhites in Cohort I committed the highest percentage of their nonindex offenses at age 16. For Cohort II the nonindex offenses follow the previous pattern index pattern with a nonwhite peak at age 16 and no decline by age for whites.

The average severity of the index and nonindex offenses is displayed in line charts in Figures 11.2a through 11.2d. These data show a distinct difference in the average seriousness of offenses by age, race,

TABLE 11.6
Index and Nonindex Offenses by Age, Race, and Cohort

1958 Cohort

| | Index | | | | Nonindex | | | |
| | White | | Nonwhite | | White | | Nonwhite | |
Age	N	Percentage	N	Percentage	N	Percentage	N	Percentage
LE 10[a]	65	3.9	240	4.0	58	2.6	278	5.1
11	53	3.2	185	3.1	41	1.8	101	1.9
12	100	6.0	381	6.4	100	4.4	310	5.7
13	150	9.1	548	9.2	205	9.1	702	12.9
14	208	12.6	685	11.5	269	11.9	791	14.6
15	335	20.2	1162	19.6	474	21.0	1104	20.4
16	369	22.3	1469	24.8	548	24.3	1219	22.5
17	375	22.7	1261	21.3	558	24.8	904	16.7
All	1655	100.0	5931	100.0	2253	100.0	5409	100.0

1945 Cohort

| | Index | | | | Nonindex | | | |
| | White | | Nonwhite | | White | | Nonwhite | |
Age	N	Percentage	N	Percentage	N	Percentage	N	Percentage
LE 10[a]	100	7.1	184	7.6	108	3.5	192	5.7
11	59	4.2	158	6.5	97	3.2	126	3.8
12	126	9.0	229	9.5	99	3.2	213	6.4
13	125	8.9	292	12.1	214	6.9	328	9.8
14	203	14.5	333	13.8	366	11.9	493	14.7
15	287	20.5	406	16.8	591	19.3	712	21.3
16	277	19.8	460	19.1	992	32.4	809	24.2
17	223	15.9	351	14.5	591	19.3	470	14.1
All	1400	100.0	2413	100.0	3058	100.0	3343	100.0

[a]LE 10 = age 10 and under.

and cohort. Figure 11.2b shows that for both nonwhites and whites in Cohort I, the mean severity of index offenses increased from age 11 onward. The average severity of nonwhite index offenses increased from a low of 182.3 to a high of 341.7, or a difference of 159.4 seriousness points. For whites index offenses ranged from a low of 181.9 to a high of 294.7, or a difference of 112.8 seriousness points.

Figure 11.2a shows that in the second cohort the average seriousness for index offenses also increases with age regardless of race. As the

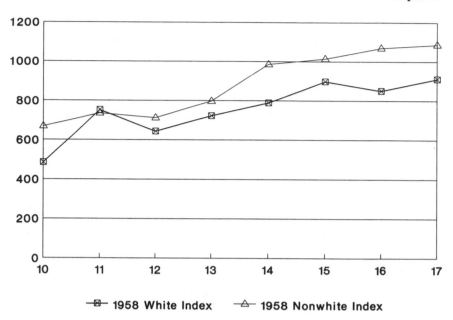

FIGURE 11.2a. Mean severity of index offenses by age-at-offense and race for 1958 cohort.

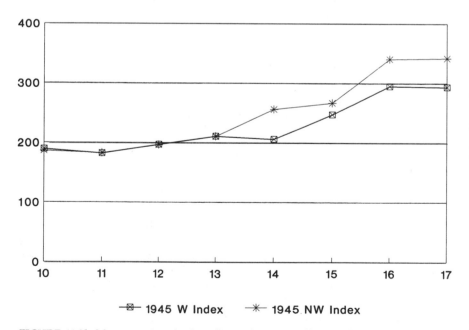

FIGURE 11.2b. Mean severity of index offenses by age-at-offense and race for 1945 cohort.

nonwhites age, their seriousness scores range a total of 417.6 points (1,085.9 − 668.3). Whites also show a considerable increase in mean severity as they age. From a low of 484.4 at age 10 or under, the mean seriousness of white offenses increases to a peak of 911.0 at age 17, for a difference of 426.6 points.

The data relative to nonindex offenses do not exhibit these clear trends. Figure 11.2d shows in Cohort I that the average seriousness of both nonwhite and white nonindex events fluctuated with age. For nonwhites the mean seriousness by age was at or below the grand mean except at age 17, where the mean (55.6) was 22 points higher than the overall average (33.2). Similarly, for whites most age-specific mean scores were at or well below the grand mean (24.0), except at age 17 where the mean (35.3) was much higher. On the other hand, the Cohort II data in Figure 11.2c differ by race. White nonindex offenses are higher than those committed by nonwhites at all ages except age 17, where the nonwhite rate is slightly higher (220.9 vs. 219.1). The white scores increase from age 10 and under to age 12 but are then relatively flat until ages 16 and 17, where the means show sharp increases relative to the other age categories. Nonwhite offenses tend to increase in seriousness

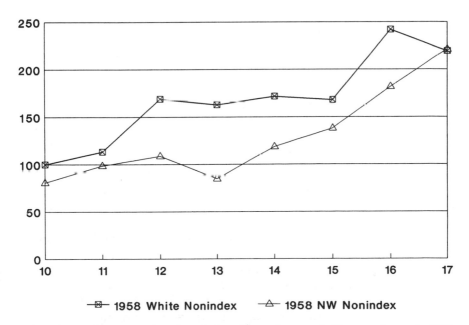

—⊠— 1958 White Nonindex   —△— 1958 NW Nonindex

FIGURE 11.2c. Mean severity of nonindex offenses by age-at-offense and race for 1958 cohort.

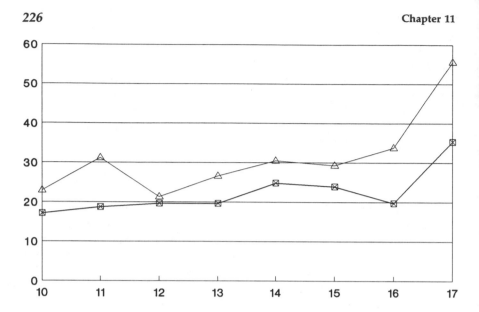

FIGURE 11.2d. Mean severity of nonindex offenses by age-at-offense and race for 1945 cohort.

with age from age 10 to 17, with a dip at age 13 being the only break in the pattern.

Thus, the two cohorts are quite similar concerning index offenses. For this type of delinquency, average seriousness increases with age regardless of race. The cohorts are dissimilar concerning nonindex behaviors. The 1945 cohort shows no trend for either race in the mean seriousness of nonindex crimes by age. As usual, nonwhite seriousness scores were higher than those for whites. In Cohort II the white scores for nonindex events are higher and show sharp increases late in the career. The nonwhite scores follow the index pattern of increasing seriousness with age.

Table 11.7 presents the crude and weighted offense rates for index and nonindex offenses by age and race. These data replicate the previous findings concerning the rates of all delinquent events without regard to index versus nonindex type. We see that all rates, crude or weighted, in Cohort I were higher for nonwhites. The greatest differential was for index offenses at age 11, where the nonwhite rates were 6.6 times higher than white rates. The lowest differential was at age 17 for nonindex offenses, where the crude rate for nonwhites was only 1.9

TABLE 11.7

Crude and Weighted Rates of Index and Nonindex Offenses by Age, Race, and Cohort

	1958 Cohort							
	Index				Nonindex			
	White		Nonwhite		White		Nonwhite	
Age	CR	WR	CR	WR	CR	WR	CR	WR
LE 10[a]	10.46	50.65	34.56	230.98	9.33	9.30	40.03	32.27
11	8.53	64.08	26.64	195.95	6.60	7.47	14.54	14.34
12	16.09	103.35	54.87	390.94	16.09	27.16	44.64	48.53
13	24.13	174.35	78.92	628.81	32.98	53.62	101.09	85.63
14	33.46	263.95	98.65	972.46	43.28	74.26	113.91	135.10
15	53.89	483.76	167.34	1696.15	76.25	128.03	158.99	219.40
16	59.36	504.53	211.55	2262.10	88.16	213.17	175.55	319.14
17	60.33	549.49	181.60	1971.95	89.77	196.68	130.18	287.58
All	266.25	2194.16	854.13	8349.34	362.46	709.69	778.93	1141.99

	1945 Cohort							
	Index				Nonindex			
	White		Nonwhite		White		Nonwhite	
Age	CR	WR	CR	WR	CR	WR	CR	WR
LE 10[a]	3.55	6.70	15.85	29.53	3.83	.65	16.54	3.79
11	8.38	15.24	54.45	99.25	13.77	2.58	43.42	13.55
12	17.89	35.17	78.91	154.67	14.06	2.76	73.40	15.63
13	17.75	37.38	100.62	211.60	30.38	5.96	113.03	30.06
14	28.82	59.35	114.75	293.87	51.97	12.89	169.88	51.81
15	40.75	100.73	139.90	373.12	83.91	20.06	245.35	71.89
16	39.33	115.90	158.51	539.26	140.85	27.75	278.77	94.23
17	31.66	92.96	120.95	413.29	83.91	25.94	161.96	90.05
All	198.78	483.63	831.50	2203.46	434.19	104.21	1151.96	382.45

[a]LE 10 = 10 and under; the rates for this composite age category are expressed as the mean of the individual rates of the four ages, from 7 to 10 years of age.

times as great and the weighted rate 3.4 times as great as the respective white rates.

The major pattern revealed by these data is that the highest crude rates occurred among the nonindex offenses at ages 16, 15, and 14, in that order for nonwhites, and at age 16, then with a tie between ages 15 and 17 for whites. Weighted rates followed essentially the same pattern with age 16 being the peak year. The one exception is found among white nonindex rates: at age 16 the crude rate was 140.85 and the weighted rate was 27.75, while at age 17 the crude rate was much lower, 83.91, and the weighted rate about the same, 25.94. The greater number of nonindex offenses committed by whites at age 16 ($n = 992$) compared to their nonindex offenses at age 17 ($n = 591$) is offset by the lower mean seriousness score of these offenses at age 16 (mean $= 19.7$) compared to age 17 (mean $= 35.3$).

As we have seen before, the rates generally increase with age up to age 16 and then decline at age 17. This is true for all of the nonwhite rates, the rates for whites for nonindex offenses, and the weighted rates for white index offenses. The exception is found for whites at age 15 among index events where the crude rate peaks at this age rather than at age 16. With this one noted exception it seems clear that delinquency of both types seems to reach a peak at age 16.

As an aid to the reader, the Cohort I index rates are graphed in Figures 11.3b (crude index) and 11.3d (weighted index), while the non-index rates are given in Figures 11.4b (crude nonindex) and 11.4d (weighted nonindex).

Table 11.7 also presents the data for the 1958 cohort. Without exception, the crude and weighted rates for nonwhites are higher than those for whites regardless of age or offense category. The peak age for non-

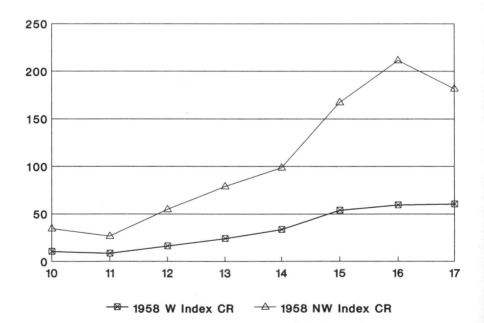

FIGURE 11.3a. Crude index offense rates by age-at-offense and race for 1958 cohort.

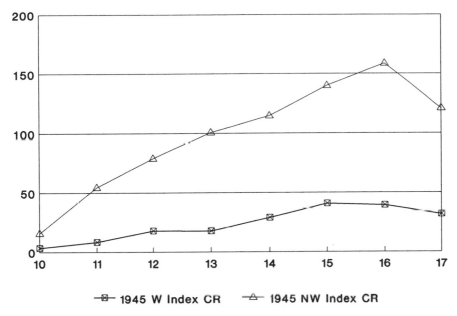

FIGURE 11.3b. Crude index offense rates by age-at-offense and race for 1945 cohort.

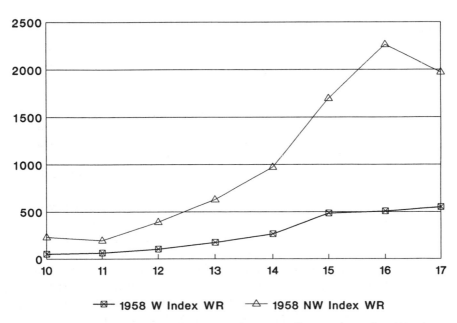

FIGURE 11.3c. Weighted index offense rates by age-at-offense and race for 1958 cohort.

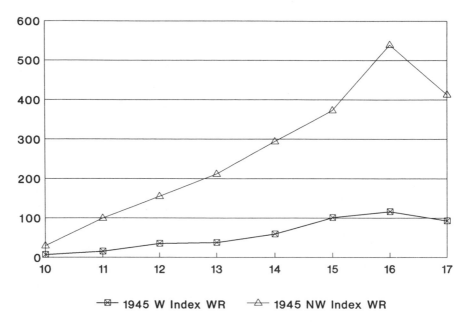

FIGURE 11.3d. Weighted index offense rates by age-at-offense and race for 1945 cohort.

whites is age 16, where the crude rate is 211.55 and the weighted rate is 2,262.10 for index offenses and 175.55 and 319.14, respectively, for non-index offenses. Whites reach their apparent peak 1 year later, age 17, and show index rates of 60.33 (crude) and 549.49 (weighted) and non-index rates of 89.77 (crude) and 196.68 (weighted). Comparing the races at their peak ages we see that for index offenses, the nonwhite crude rate is 3.5 times as great and the weighted rate is 4.1 times as great as the white rates, while the nonindex offenses show nonwhite to white ratios of 1.9 for crude rates and 1.5 for weighted rates.

Like Cohort I, the Cohort II rates are sensitive to age for both offense types. The index rates increase to age 16 for nonwhites and to age 17 for whites. The nonindex rates are the same pattern for nonwhites, while whites show an increasing crude rate to age 17, but an increasing weighted rate to age 16. Regardless of these slight differences, it is clear that the rate and severity of delinquency in Cohort II is much different in the later stage of the career than it is in the early ages. This is also true in Cohort I, but the age difference is not as great. Like the Cohort I rates discussed above, the index rates are displayed in Figures 11.3a and 11.3c, while the nonindex data are shown in Figures 11.4a and 11.4c for Cohort II.

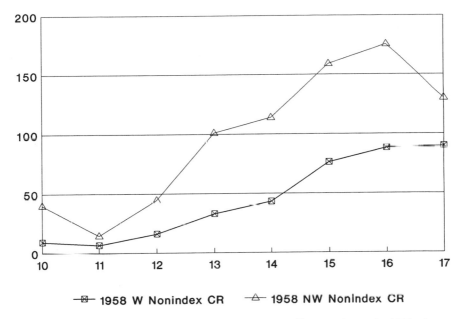

FIGURE 11.4a. Crude nonindex offense rates by age-at-offense and race for 1958 cohort.

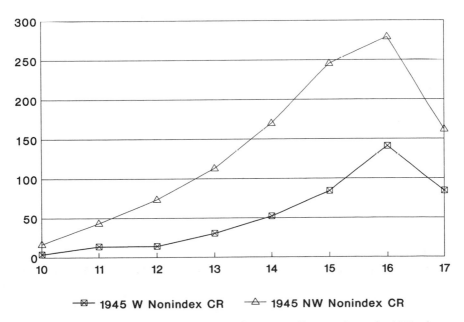

FIGURE 11.4b. Crude nonindex offense rates by age-at-offense and race for 1945 cohort.

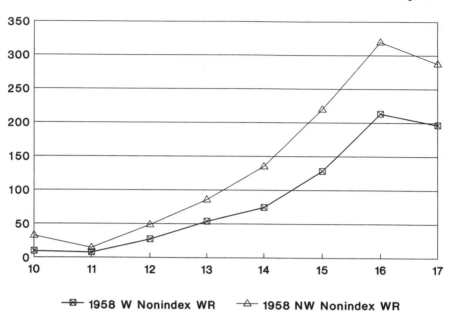

FIGURE 11.4c. Weighted nonindex offense rates by age-at-offense and race for 1958 cohort.

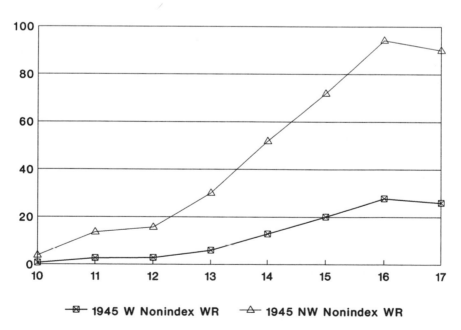

FIGURE 11.4d. Weighted nonindex offense rates by age-at-offense and race for 1945 cohort.

In Table 11.8 we break down index offenses into the four categories of violence, robbery, property, and other index offenses. The violence category includes homicide, rape, aggravated and simple assault, and battery. Property offenses include burglary, larceny, and auto theft. Robbery has been retained as a separate category because it is in the anomalous position of being an offense against the person and/or against property.

The Cohort I data displayed in Table 11.8 indicate that these specific index offenses tend to vary by age. Crimes of violence increased steadily from age 10 and under (3.6%) to age 16, where the percentage reached a high of 24.8%. Robbery events showed a sharp increase from age 12 (7.2%) to age 13 (19.69%) and then fluctuated to age 17 with no apparent trend. Like crimes of violence, the property offenses increased from age 10 to age 15 (except at age 13) and then declined at ages 16 and 17. The other offense category followed no discernible age pattern. Beyond the composite category of 10 and under, the residual offenses peak at age 15. The single generalization that can be offered from these data is that violence, robbery, and property offenses are more likely to occur late in the juvenile career, but only violent offenses showed a clear and direct relationship with age.

The Cohort II data reported in Table 11.8 are quite dissimilar from those of Cohort I. A clear age effect is evident for all index offenses except for those in the "other" index offenses category. Crimes of violence show a steady increase from age 11 (1.9%) to age 17 (26.2%), for a range of 24% across age. Both robbery and property offenses increase to age 16 and then decline at age 17. Robbery shows a low to high range of 27.9%, while property offenses exhibit a range of 20.9%. The concentration of these offenses late in the offense career is also noteworthy. In the last 3 years of delinquency, 75% of the robberies and 66% of the property offenses are committed. Like Cohort I, the "other" index offense category does not follow an age pattern. The offenses cluster in the middle of the age range but fluctuate up and down yearly. Thus, in the second cohort, the serious index offenses, especially violence, follow a pattern of increasing with age.

When the type of offense by age data are examined by race the results are similar to the overall patterns discussed above. For the 1945 cohort we see in Table 11.9 that violent offenses increased with age for nonwhites through age 16 and for whites through age 17. Whites not only showed a longer-lasting trend but also committed a greater share of their violent offenses (71%) after age 14 than was the case for nonwhites after this age (64%). For property offenses, whites peaked earlier, age 15, compared to nonwhites, who peaked at age 16. Robbery and the other index offenses did not show age effects for either race. There was a

TABLE 11.8
Index Offenses by Type, Age, and Cohort

1958 Cohort

Age	Violence N	Violence Percentage	Robbery N	Robbery Percentage	Property N	Property Percentage	Other N	Other Percentage	Total N	Total Percentage
LE 10[a]	32	2.3	10	0.8	164	4.1	99	11.0	305	4.0
11	28	1.9	17	1.3	137	3.4	56	6.2	238	3.1
12	72	5.1	60	4.7	241	6.1	108	12.0	481	6.3
13	119	8.4	94	7.3	316	7.9	169	18.8	698	9.2
14	166	11.7	139	10.8	478	12.0	110	12.3	893	11.8
15	262	18.5	303	23.5	797	20.0	135	15.1	1497	19.7
16	366	25.9	371	28.8	968	24.3	133	14.8	1838	24.2
17	370	26.2	296	22.9	883	22.2	87	9.7	1636	21.6
All	1415	100.0	1290	100.0	3984	100.0	897	100.0	7586	100.0

1945 Cohort

Age	Violence N	Violence Percentage	Robbery N	Robbery Percentage	Property N	Property Percentage	Other N	Other Percentage	Total N	Total Percentage
LE 10[a]	29	3.6	10	5.2	154	6.8	91	16.6	284	7.4
11	31	3.8	10	5.2	131	5.8	45	8.2	217	5.7
12	34	4.2	14	7.2	250	11.1	57	10.4	355	9.3
13	63	7.7	38	19.7	248	10.9	68	12.4	417	10.9
14	111	13.6	34	17.6	315	13.9	76	13.8	536	14.1
15	160	19.6	23	11.9	426	18.9	84	15.4	693	18.2
16	202	24.8	38	19.7	425	18.8	72	13.2	737	19.3
17	184	22.6	26	13.5	310	13.7	54	9.8	574	15.1
All	814	100.0	193	100.0	2259	100.0	547	100.0	3813	100.0

[a]LE 10 = age 10 and under.

slight tendency for whites to commit these offenses later than did non-whites. Whites committed 40% of their robberies and 35% of their "other" index offenses after the age of 15 compared to 32% and 22%, respectively, for nonwhites.

In the 1958 cohort the data are dissimilar for whites and nonwhites across offense types. For nonwhites the percentage of violent offenses, robberies, and property offenses increases up to age 16 and then declines at age 17. For whites the percentage of these three offense types increases to age 17 without any decline. As we have seen before, the other index offenses do not obey an age trend but rather rise and fall across age categories for both races.

Unlike Cohort I, race has little effect on the relative proportion of offenses which are committed late in the delinquency career (after age 14). For violent offenses, the nonwhites show a percentage of 70% while whites show 71%. Robbery events predominate for nonwhites (75% vs. 73%) but property offenses are higher for whites (68% vs. 65%). In sum, as delinquents age, regardless of race, the proportion of the more serious offenses increases but the trend is more consistent for whites than for nonwhites.

Up to this point we have used our crime severity scale to classify offenses into index versus nonindex categories on the basis of whether particular types of social harm were inflicted on victims. We then grouped index events into four subcategories of harm. It should be noted that this scheme is but one method of classifying events. Another

TABLE 11.9

Index Offenses by Type, Age, Race, and Cohort

| | 1958 Cohort: White | | | | | | | |
| | Violence | | Robbery | | Property | | Other | |
Age	N	Percentage	N	Percentage	N	Percentage	N	Percentage
LE 10[a]	6	1.9	0	0.0	28	2.9	31	10.2
11	5	1.6	1	1.3	28	2.9	19	6.3
12	17	5.5	6	7.5	44	4.6	33	10.9
13	27	8.7	4	5.0	68	7.1	51	16.8
14	32	10.3	10	12.5	131	13.6	35	11.5
15	54	17.4	18	22.5	216	22.5	47	15.5
16	78	25.2	18	22.5	223	23.2	50	16.5
17	91	29.4	23	28.8	223	23.2	38	12.5
All	310	100.0	80	100.0	961	100.0	304	100.0

(continued)

TABLE 11.9 (continued)

	1958 Cohort: Nonwhite							
	Violence		Robbery		Property		Other	
Age	N	Percentage	N	Percentage	N	Percentage	N	Percentage
LE 10[a]	26	2.4	10	0.8	136	4.5	68	11.5
11	23	2.1	16	1.3	109	3.6	37	6.2
12	55	4.9	54	4.4	197	6.5	75	12.7
13	92	8.3	90	7.4	248	8.2	118	19.9
14	134	12.1	129	10.7	347	11.5	75	12.7
15	208	18.8	285	23.6	581	19.2	88	14.8
16	288	26.1	353	29.2	745	24.6	83	14.0
17	279	25.3	273	22.6	660	21.8	49	8.3
All	1105	100.0	1210	100.0	3023	100.0	593	100.0

	1945 Cohort: White							
	Violence		Robbery		Property		Other	
Age	N	Percentage	N	Percentage	N	Percentage	N	Percentage
LE 10[a]	7	3.2	3	15.0	43	4.9	100	7.1
11	6	2.8	0	0.0	28	3.2	59	4.2
12	9	4.2	0	0.0	87	9.9	126	9.0
13	11	5.1	2	10.0	75	8.6	125	8.9
14	29	13.4	4	20.0	126	14.4	203	14.5
15	48	22.1	3	15.0	197	22.5	287	20.5
16	48	22.1	6	30.0	185	21.2	277	19.8
17	59	27.2	2	10.0	133	15.2	223	15.9
All	217	100.0	20	100.0	874	100.0	1400	100.0

	1945 Cohort: Nonwhite							
	Violence		Robbery		Property		Other	
Age	N	Percentage	N	Percentage	N	Percentage	N	Percentage
LE 10[a]	22	3.7	7	4.1	111	8.1	44	17.1
11	25	4.2	10	5.8	103	7.4	20	7.8
12	25	4.2	14	8.1	163	11.8	27	10.5
13	52	8.7	36	20.8	173	12.5	31	12.0
14	82	13.7	30	17.3	189	13.6	32	12.4
15	112	18.8	20	11.6	229	16.5	45	17.4
16	154	25.0	32	18.5	240	17.3	34	13.2
17	125	20.9	24	13.9	177	12.8	25	9.7
All	597	100.0	173	100.0	1385	100.0	258	100.0

[a]LE 10 = age 10 and under.

and widely used method is the UCR designations employed by the FBI. Because of the widespread use of this method we have analyzed our offense data by age in terms of this scheme as well. Thus, data are given below drawing first on the UCR designation of index versus nonindex and then, second, separating the index offenses by type. It must be noted that unlike our crime severity scheme which labels an event index if and only if the offense produced injury, theft, damage, or some combination of these, the UCR method uses a crime code or legal-label hierarchy only, and does not necessarily reflect actual social harm committed. The best example of this difference is that an offender could be charged with the index offense of robbery, even if it was only an attempt at committing robbery.

TABLE 11.10
UCR Index and Nonindex Offenses by Age and Cohort

| | 1958 Cohort | | | | | |
| | UCR index | | UCR nonindex | | Total | |
Age	N	Percentage	N	Percentage	N	Percentage
LE 10[a]	183	3.1	458	4.9	641	4.2
11	167	2.8	213	2.3	380	2.5
12	316	5.3	575	6.2	891	5.8
13	457	7.6	1148	1.2	1605	10.5
14	699	11.7	1254	13.6	1953	12.8
15	1237	20.7	1838	19.9	3075	20.2
16	1545	25.8	2060	22.3	3605	23.6
17	1387	23.2	1711	18.5	3098	20.3
All	5991	100.0	9257	100.0	15248	100.0
	1945 Cohort					
	UCR index		UCR nonindex		Total	
Age	N	Percentage	N	Percentage	N	Percentage
LE 10[a]	168	6.2	416	5.6	584	5.7
11	148	5.4	292	3.9	440	4.3
12	268	9.8	399	5.3	667	6.5
13	302	11.1	657	8.8	959	9.4
14	375	13.8	1020	13.6	1395	13.7
15	499	18.3	1497	20.0	1996	19.5
16	552	20.2	1986	26.5	2538	24.9
17	416	15.2	1219	16.3	1635	16.0
All	2728	100.0	7486	100.0	10214	100.0

[a]LE 10 = age 10 and under.

Our first display consists of index versus nonindex offenses by age. These data are given in Table 11.10. The column percentages for Cohort I and Cohort II mirror the overall age distribution. The proportion of index and nonindex offenses increases to age 16 and then declines. Although the row percentages (not shown) indicate that nonindex offenses constitute the higher proportion of offenses at any given age, the data also reflect cohort and sex differences for this finding. That is, for Cohort I offenders, index offenses constituted no more than 40% of the offenses committed at any given age, and the proportion usually ranged from 23% to 28%. Thus nonindex offenses represent the vast majority of the delinquencies committed for all age categories.

For the delinquents in the 1958 birth cohort, however, nonindex offenses still constitute the greater proportion at each age, but the proportionate difference between index and nonindex is considerably smaller than in Cohort I. For example, index offenses in the later cohort can be seen to be as high as 45% (age 17) and generally fall in a range of from 35% to 40%. The gap between the two types of offenses is especially smaller at the higher age levels compared to Cohort I.

When the index and nonindex offense data are examined by both age and race (Table 11.11), the results consistently follow those reported above. For both races in the 1945 cohort, offenses of both types increased with age and nonindex offenses predominated at any given age. Nonwhites committed proportionately more of their index offenses earlier compared to whites (e.g., before age 14, nonwhites committed 36% while whites committed 25%). On the other hand, the white index offenses appeared to cluster at the later ages, where from age 15 upward whites committed 60% compared to 50% for nonwhites.

The data for Cohort II exhibit two crucial departures from these findings. For nonwhite males, index offenses do not constitute the minority offense type for all age categories; at age 17 the index offenses constitute the higher share of the total offenses committed at this age. Second, the racial difference in the age base for Cohort I index offenses disappears. That is, both white and nonwhite delinquents in Cohort II commit approximately 70% of their index offenses from age 15 up compared to 60% and 50% for whites and nonwhites, respectively, in Cohort I.

Although reflective of some degree of offense seriousness, the index versus nonindex dichotomy is not altogether sufficient for our purposes. There are considerable differences among the index offenses in the severity of the crimes included in the group. Thus we have broken down the index offenses into four main categories as follows: (1) violence (homicide, rape, and aggravated assault); (2) robbery; (3) burglary;

TABLE 11.11
UCR Index and Nonindex Offenses by Age, Race, and Cohort

	1958 Cohort							
	UCR index				UCR nonindex			
	White		Nonwhite		White		Nonwhite	
Age	N	Percentage	N	Percentage	N	Percentage	N	Percentage
LE 10[a]	28	2.4	155	3.2	95	3.5	363	5.6
11	31	2.7	136	2.8	63	2.3	150	2.3
12	54	4.7	262	5.4	146	5.3	429	6.6
13	82	7.1	375	7.7	273	9.9	875	13.5
14	151	13.1	548	11.3	326	11.9	928	14.3
15	255	22.0	982	20.3	554	20.1	1284	19.7
16	268	23.2	1277	26.4	649	23.6	1411	21.7
17	288	24.9	1099	22.7	645	23.4	1066	16.4
All	1157	100.0	4834	100.0	2253	100.0	6506	100.0

	1945 Cohort							
	UCR index				UCR nonindex			
	White		Nonwhite		White		Nonwhite	
Age	N	Percentage	N	Percentage	N	Percentage	N	Percentage
LE 10[a]	47	5.0	121	6.8	161	4.6	255	6.4
11	29	3.1	119	6.7	127	3.6	165	4.2
12	87	9.3	181	10.1	138	3.9	261	6.6
13	80	8.5	222	12.4	259	7.4	398	10.0
14	132	14.1	243	13.6	437	12.4	583	14.7
15	209	22.3	290	16.2	669	19.0	828	20.9
16	203	21.6	349	19.5	1066	30.3	920	23.2
17	152	16.2	264	14.8	662	18.8	557	14.0
All	939	100.0	1789	100.0	3519	100.0	3967	100.0

[a]LE 10 = age 10 and under.

and (4) larceny/auto theft. These data are given in Table 11.12 for the overall age distribution, while the distribution by age and race is examined in Table 11.13.

Table 11.12 clearly indicates that crimes of violence predominated at the later stage of delinquency for both cohorts. In each case the vast majority of violent offenses are committed from the age of 15 and beyond. The Cohort II delinquents exhibit the lower percentage (76%) compared to Cohort I offenders (79%). For robbery, only the Cohort II

TABLE 11.12
UCR Index Offenses by Type, Age, and Cohort

1958 Cohort

Age	Violence N	Violence Percentage	Robbery N	Robbery Percentage	Burglary N	Burglary Percentage	Larceny/Auto N	Larceny/Auto Percentage	Total N	Total Percentage
LE 10[a]	9	1.3	10	0.8	71	4.2	93	4.0	183	3.1
11	13	1.8	17	1.3	69	4.1	68	2.9	167	2.8
12	15	2.1	60	4.7	120	7.2	121	5.2	316	5.3
13	47	6.6	94	7.3	157	9.4	159	6.9	457	7.6
14	82	11.4	139	10.8	218	13.0	260	11.3	699	11.7
15	137	19.1	303	23.5	325	19.4	472	20.4	1237	20.6
16	206	28.7	371	28.8	286	23.1	582	25.2	1545	25.8
17	208	29.0	296	22.9	327	19.6	556	24.1	1387	23.2
All	717	100.0	1290	100.0	1673	100.0	2311	100.0	5991	100.0

1945 Cohort

Age	Violence N	Violence Percentage	Robbery N	Robbery Percentage	Burglary N	Burglary Percentage	Larceny/Auto N	Larceny/Auto Percentage	Total N	Total Percentage
LE 10[a]	6	2.2	10	5.2	52	8.1	100	6.2	168	6.2
11	7	2.5	10	5.2	31	4.8	100	6.2	148	5.4
12	4	1.4	14	7.2	75	11.7	175	10.8	268	9.8
13	16	5.8	38	19.7	92	14.3	156	9.7	302	11.1
14	26	9.4	34	17.6	96	14.9	219	13.6	375	13.8
15	50	17.9	23	11.9	122	19.0	304	18.8	499	18.3
16	89	32.0	38	19.7	108	16.8	317	19.6	552	20.2
17	80	28.8	26	13.5	66	10.3	244	15.1	416	15.2
All	278	100.0	193	100.0	642	100.0	1615	100.0	2728	100.0

[a]LE 10 = age 10 and under.

males show the same tendency (75%) to commit this offense in the later ages compared to the 1945 cohort (45%). Much the same pattern is observed for burglary as well. Relative to larceny and auto theft, Cohort II offenders tend to commit this offense at the later ages (70% vs. 54%), while the males in Cohort I tended to begin this set of offenses proportionately at the earlier ages (about 33% at or below age 13 compared to 19% for Cohort II offenders). Despite these differences it is interesting to note that the modal age of offenses is the same in Cohort II as for Cohort I (age 16), except for violent index offenses, which peak later in Cohort II (age 17).

Reviewing the index offense types by age and race (Table 11.13) does not produce many appreciable race differentials. For violence the

TABLE 11.13
UCR Index Offenses by Type, Age, Race, and Cohort

				1958 Cohort: White				
	Violence		Robbery		Burglary		Larceny/Auto	
Age	N	Percentage	N	Percentage	N	Percentage	N	Percentage
LE 10[a]	0	0.0	0	0.0	9	2.2	19	3.5
11	2	1.7	1	1.3	16	3.9	12	2.2
12	4	3.5	6	7.5	22	5.3	22	4.0
13	10	8.6	4	5.0	34	8.3	34	6.2
14	10	8.6	10	12.5	53	12.9	78	14.2
15	21	18.1	18	22.5	111	26.9	105	19.1
16	27	23.3	18	22.5	85	20.6	138	25.1
17	42	36.2	23	28.8	82	19.9	141	25.7
All	116	100.0	80	100.0	412	100.0	549	100.0
				1958 Cohort: Nonwhite				
	Violence		Robbery		Burglary		Larceny/Auto	
Age	N	Percentage	N	Percentage	N	Percentage	N	Percentage
LE 10[a]	9	1.5	10	0.8	62	4.9	74	4.2
11	11	1.8	16	1.3	53	4.2	56	3.2
12	11	1.8	54	4.5	98	7.8	99	5.6
13	37	6.2	90	7.4	123	9.8	125	7.1
14	72	11.9	129	10.7	165	13.1	182	10.3
15	116	19.3	285	23.6	214	16.9	367	20.8
16	179	29.8	353	29.2	301	23.9	444	25.2
17	166	27.6	273	22.6	245	19.4	415	23.6
All	601	100.0	1210	100.0	1261	100.0	1762	100.0

(continued)

TABLE 11.13 (continued)

	Violence		Robbery		Burglary		Larceny/Auto	
				1945 *Cohort*: White				
Age	N	Percentage	N	Percentage	N	Percentage	N	Percentage
LE 10[a]	1	2.2	3	15.0	16	6.5	27	4.3
11	1	2.2	0	0.0	11	4.4	17	2.7
12	0	0.0	0	0.0	38	15.3	49	7.8
13	3	6.7	2	10.0	38	15.3	37	5.9
14	2	4.4	4	20.0	27	10.9	99	15.8
15	9	20.0	3	15.0	48	19.4	149	23.8
16	12	26.7	6	30.0	43	17.3	142	22.6
17	17	37.8	2	10.0	27	10.9	106	16.9
All	45	100.0	20	100.0	248	100.0	626	100.0

	Violence		Robbery		Burglary		Larceny/Auto	
				1945 *Cohort*: Nonwhite				
Age	N	Percentage	N	Percentage	N	Percentage	N	Percentage
LE 10[a]	5	2.2	7	4.1	36	9.1	73	7.4
11	6	2.6	10	5.8	20	5.1	83	8.4
12	4	1.7	14	8.1	37	9.4	126	12.7
13	13	5.6	36	20.8	54	13.7	119	12.0
14	24	10.3	30	17.3	69	17.5	120	12.1
15	41	17.6	20	11.6	74	18.8	155	15.7
16	77	33.1	32	18.5	65	16.5	175	17.7
17	63	27.0	24	13.8	39	9.9	138	13.9
All	233	100.0	173	100.0	394	100.0	989	100.0

[a]LE 10 = age 10 and under.

tendency for both races, regardless of cohort, is to commit this type of offense in the later ages at risk. The modal age is 16 for nonwhite males and 17 for white males in both cohorts. For robbery, however, the nonwhites in the 1945 cohort began much earlier and had a lower modal age (13) than white males (age 16). This difference does not exist between the races in the later cohort. In Cohort I regardless of age, nonwhites exhibited a much greater tendency to engage in violent and robbery offenses, while whites had proportionately more burglary and theft offenses. For the later cohort, nonwhites commit proportionately more robbery offenses, slightly more violent offenses, and fewer burglary and theft offenses than whites. The age distribution does little to affect these results.

We may summarize the age-at-offense data as follows. Concerning the age distribution of offenses, regardless of type, there were two major results. First, the age distribution of delinquency was similar for both cohorts—the percentage of offenses increased with age to a peak generally at age 16. Thus, most offenses were committed late in the delinquency career—64% of Cohort II offenses and 60% of Cohort I offenses were committed at age 15 or later.

Second, there were distinct race effects by cohort. In Cohort I both whites and nonwhites followed an increasing offense frequency to a peak at age 16; in Cohort II the nonwhite data followed this trend, while the white offenses continued to increase through age 17 and perhaps beyond. Similarly, the crude and weighted offense rates showed wide race disparities in Cohort I of about 3 to 1 and 4.4 to 1 for nonwhites versus whites. These race effects were reduced to about 2.6 for crude rates and 3.3 for weighted rates in Cohort II. Further, unlike the Cohort I data for which the rates were most discrepant at the early ages, the rates by race in Cohort II were closer overall and across the age continuum.

With respect to the age distribution by type of offense there were also two main findings. First, the age distribution of index and nonindex offenses differed for the two cohorts. In Cohort I, the proportion of both index and nonindex offenses increased from age 10 or 11 to a peak at age 16, and nonindex offenses predominated at all ages. In Cohort II, the proportion of serious and nonindex offenses increased, but nonindex offenses did not predominate at all ages, only at 10 or under, 13, 14, and 15. Second, when index events were grouped by type, there was again a cohort effect. In the 1945 cohort only crimes of violence showed consistent increases from age 10 or under through age 16. In the 1958 cohort a clear age effect was evident for all the serious index offenses—violence, robbery, and property.

Finally, it must be noted the age-at-offense data generally indicate that delinquents in Cohort II were still active beyond the age when Cohort I offenders had peaked, thus allowing for a greater utilization of the period at risk. This may partially explain: (1) why overall the Cohort II incidence and offense rates were higher than those in Cohort I; (2) why the concentration of serious offenses was greater in the 1958 cohort, since index offenses are likely to occur at later ages; and (3) why the race disparity in Cohort II was smaller than in Cohort I, since whites in Cohort II were active longer than nonwhites, whereas whites stopped earlier than nonwhites in Cohort I.

12

Police and Court Dispositions

This chapter will address the police and juvenile court dispositions applied to the offenses in the cohorts. Before discussing the disposition findings, however, it is necessary to review the procedures surrounding the police handling of juveniles in Philadelphia. When a juvenile in Philadelphia is apprehended for a delinquent act, the initial disposition of the offense is handled by the Juvenile Aid Division officer. Like most jurisdictions, Philadelphia police officers confronted with a juvenile delinquent have wide discretion in choosing a disposition. That is, the police officer can let the offender go with a warning, or the police can make an official arrest. Unlike other jurisdictions, however, the two particular choices open to the Philadelphia police officer—"remedial" (no official arrest, no further processing in the juvenile justice system) or "arrest"—allow the officer to be lenient, but still preserve a record of the case. Thus, remedial processing is a way of "letting the offender go," but at the same time making note of the contact for future use.

In Philadelphia the decision to remedial or arrest the juvenile is governed by five official criteria, as set forth in departmental communications, and three other, informal criteria, which are nonetheless important. These eight criteria are as follows:

1. The number of previous police contacts as determined by a record check
2. Type of current and prior offenses and the role which the juvenile has played
3. Attitude of the victim or complainant
4. Family situation of the offender
5. Community resources which might be utilized
6. General appearance and attitude/demeanor of the offender toward the police
7. Possible overcrowding at the Youth Study Center (the detention facility)
8. The police officer's anticipation of eventual juvenile court action should an arrest be made

Before the initial disposition decision is made, the line officer calls headquarters to check on the previous record of the offender as recorded in a master file. The disposition decision is removed from the officer's hands when offenders have what is called a "remedial stop" attached to their Juvenile Aid Division record (JAD record). Such a designation, made by the Juvenile Aid Division staff in the case of some of the more persistent or serious offenders, requires that the next officer handling the juvenile make an arrest. This is the most significant manner in which a prior record can influence the disposition decision. When there is no remedial stop, it is general policy that the officer consider such things as number and seriousness of prior offenses in particular in making his or her decision.

Disposition Distributions

The frequency distributions of the police and subsequent court dispositions for the offenses in the 1945 and 1958 birth cohorts are shown in Table 12.1. Immediate differences between the two cohorts can be seen with respect to the overall disposition of offenses and the distributions by race. Concerning the overall data, the Cohort II results show that 20.5% of the offenses were remedialed compared to 63.8% in Cohort I. Before assuming, however, that the Cohort I offenders were treated much more leniently, it is important to note the large number of "unknowns" in Cohort II.

For this cohort, about 21% of the offenses are listed as unknown compared to just 2.5% in Cohort I. The disposition is not completely unknown, however. We know for sure that the offense handling did not progress beyond the police stage (there was no record in the court file), but because the police record was incomplete, we were unable to determine whether the offense was given a remedial or an arrest. If we combine the three categories of remedial, arrest only, and unknown (no further processing beyond the police stage), then 59% of the Cohort II offenses and 68% of the Cohort I offenses were disposed of by the police without a court referral.

With respect to the other dispositions, it seems that initially, without regard to type of offense or offender status, the 1958 cohort had somewhat more lenient dispositions than did the 1945 cohort. That is, for the 1958 cohort, more cases were adjusted/discharged at the time of court appearance (25% vs. 14%); slightly more cases proportionately were given probation (13% vs. 11%); and fewer cases proportionately were sentenced to institutional care (2% vs. 6%). Given the previous

TABLE 12.1
Number and Percentage of Dispositions by Race and Cohort

| | 1958 Cohort | | | | | |
| | White | | Nonwhite | | Total | |
Disposition	N	Percentage	N	Percentage	N	Percentage
Remedial	1179	30.2	1961	17.3	3125	20.5
Arrest only	562	14 4	2034	17.9	2611	17.1
Adjusted or discharged	932	23.8	2881	25.4	3813	25.0
Probation	471	12.1	1534	13.5	2005	13.1
Institution	43	0.1	321	2.8	364	2.3
Adult court	2	0.0	59	0.0	61	0.0
Unknown	719	18.4	2550	22.5	3269	21.4
Total	3908	100.0	11,340	100.0	15,248	100.0

| | 1945 Cohort | | | | | |
| | White | | Nonwhite | | Total | |
Disposition	N	Percentage	N	Percentage	N	Percentage
Remedial	3339	74.9	3176	55.2	6515	63.8
Arrest only	90	2.0	168	2.9	258	2.5
Adjusted or discharged	453	10.2	982	17.1	1435	14.0
Probation	360	8.1	734	12.8	1094	10.7
Institution	116	2.6	538	9.3	654	6.4
Adult court	—	—	—	—	—	—
Unknown	100	2.2	158	2.7	258	2.5
Total	4458	100.0	5756	100.0	10,214	100.0

results in this volume concerning the greater recidivism, and especially index recidivism of the 1958 cohort, this differential in dispositions was unexpected.

Another important substantive difference in the distribution of offense dispositions between the cohorts pertains to race. In the 1945 cohort, nonwhites were much more likely to have their offenses disposed of beyond the police stage. Thus, 39% of the offenses by nonwhites were adjusted, given probation, or resulted in a commitment to a delinquent institution compared to 21% of the offenses by whites. In the 1958 cohort, this race effect is much less pronounced. About 42% of the offenses by nonwhites compared to about 37% of the offenses by whites progressed beyond the police stage and could have received a severe court disposition.

In sum, offenses committed by the offenders in the 1958 cohort were less likely to terminate with the police disposition than offenses in Cohort I. However, this greater number of cases that did reach the juvenile court were handled more leniently than those in Cohort I. Further, the wide race disparity in Cohort I was greatly diminished in Cohort II.

In order to simplify the analyses we have grouped the various disposition categories into the following three: (1) remedial—the unofficial action of the police; (2) adjustment—meaning that after arrest the case was terminated at the Youth Study Center or was otherwise adjusted or discharged, either before reaching the judge (screening by an intake worker), or at the court hearing before a judge; and (3) court penalty—those cases in which a relatively severe penalty was imposed, such as probation or commitment to an institution.

In addition to race we have included other variables that may be associated with offense disposition. These are (1) one-time offenders versus recidivists; (2) nonindex offenders versus index offenders; (3) offenders that committed trivial offenses (seriousness scores under 100) versus delinquents with more serious offenses (scores above 100); and (4) lower-SES boys versus higher-SES boys.

Table 12.2 displays data for a simple dichotomy of remedial versus all other dispositions. For both cohorts, whites, boys of higher SES, nonindex offenders, and the low-seriousness offenders are more likely than their counterparts to be given a remedial disposition. The two cohorts are also similar in that the seriousness score comparison produces the sharpest contrast of dispositions. Thus, 91% of the offenses under a seriousness score of 100 in Cohort II were remedialed, and 86% of these offenses were remedialed in Cohort I. By comparison, 29% of the more serious offenses in Cohort II and 35% in Cohort I were given remedial dispositions. The nonindex comparisons show similar findings.

The two cohorts differ with respect to the likelihood of remedial dispositions by race (noted earlier) and SES. Cohort I shows a distinct differential for race and SES. In the 1945 cohort, whites have a probability of .76 of being remedialed compared to .56 for nonwhites; high-SES boys have a remedial probability of .76, while lower-SES boys show a probability of .60. In Cohort II these differences are considerably lessened. The probabilities of a remedial disposition by race are .48 for whites and .40 for nonwhites, and by SES the values are .46 for high-SES boys and .40 for low-SES boys.

We know from previous analyses that the race and SES combined distributions are uneven, and we also know that the distributions of index versus nonindex offenses and one-time versus recidivist offenders

TABLE 12.2

Number and Percentage of Remedial versus Other Dispositions
by Race, SES, Offense Type, and Cohort

| | 1958 Cohort | | | |
| | Remedial | | All others | |
	N	Percentage	N	Percentage
White	1898	48.6	2010	51.4
Nonwhite	4550	40.1	6790	59.9
Low SES	4300	40.4	6356	59.6
High SES	2148	46.8	2444	53.2
Nonindex	5396	64.3	2993	35.7
Index	1052	15.3	5807	84.7
Offense severity				
<100	3013	91.3	288	8.7
>100	3435	28.8	8512	71.2

| | 1945 Cohort | | | |
| | Remedial | | All others | |
	N	Percentage	N	Percentage
White	3339	76.6	1019	23.4
Nonwhite	3176	56.7	2422	43.3
Low SES	4215	60.7	2726	39.3
High SES	2310	76.3	715	23.7
Nonindex	5133	82.8	1070	17.2
Index	1382	36.8	2371	63.2
Offense severity				
<100	5091	86.3	809	13.7
>100	1424	35.1	2632	64.9

differ by race. Thus, bivariate displays are insufficient alone to uncover the possible relationships. Thus, we present in the following four sets of tables (Tables 12.3 to 12.6) the basic multivariate arrays of the remedial versus other dispositions.

Table 12.3 displays the disposition dichotomy by SES and race. For the 1945 cohort the data clearly indicate that regardless of SES, whites are more likely to be given a remedial disposition. The difference is less at the lower level of SES, where 72% of whites compared to 57% of nonwhites are remedialed. The race effect is greater among higher-SES boys, where 80% of the whites compared to 59% of the nonwhites are remedialed. This pattern is repeated for the 1958 cohort data but with

TABLE 12.3

Number and Percentage of Dispositions by Race, SES, and Cohort

	1958 Cohort				1945 Cohort			
	Remedial		All others		Remedial		All others	
	N	Percentage	N	Percentage	N	Percentage	N	Percentage
Low SES								
White	674	47.1	757	52.9	1351	71.8	531	28.2
Nonwhite	3626	39.3	5599	60.7	2854	56.5	2195	43.5
High SES								
White	1224	49.4	1253	50.6	1988	80.3	488	19.7
Nonwhite	924	43.7	1191	56.3	322	58.7	227	41.3

the smaller differences we have seen before. For Cohort II, nonwhites are less likely to receive a remedial disposition regardless of SES compared to whites. The contrasts are 39% versus 47% among low-SES boys, and 44% versus 49% among high-SES boys. Thus, the pronounced race effects in the two cohorts are not spurious and do not depend on SES, although the race effect in Cohort I is more pronounced than in Cohort II.

Like SES, whether the offender was a one-time delinquent or whether he was a recidivist could be a factor behind the race effect shown above. But we see from Table 12.4 that offender status does not explain the race differential. For the 1945 cohort, the greater likelihood

TABLE 12.4

Number and Percentage of Dispositions for One-Time and Recidivist Offenders by Race and Cohort

	1958 Cohort				1945 Cohort			
	Remedial		All others		Remedial		All others	
	N	Percentage	N	Percentage	N	Percentage	N	Percentage
One-time								
White	470	64.1	263	35.9	963	86.9	145	13.1
Nonwhite	574	53.6	497	46.4	352	70.1	150	29.9
Recidivist								
White	1428	44.9	1747	55.1	2376	73.1	874	26.9
Nonwhite	3976	38.7	6293	61.3	2824	55.4	2272	44.6

for white boys to be handled informally by the police persists for both offender groups. There is a difference of about 16 percentage points (86.9% vs. 70.1%) for one-time offenders and a difference of about 17 percentage points (73.1% vs. 55.4%) for recidivists in favor of whites being remedialed. For the 1958 cohort the race effect is also maintained but is once again less pronounced. Remedial dispositions favor whites by about 10 percentage points (64.1% vs. 53.6%) among one-time delinquents and by 6 points among the recidivists (44.9% vs. 38.7%). The observed pattern of 16 points, 17 points, 10 points, and 6 points does suggest that remedial decisions are less likely to be based on race in Cohort II, and this seems especially so when the delinquent is a recidivist.

We have seen that index offenses are more likely to result in arrest, adjustment, or court penalty than are nonindex offenses. In Cohort I about 37% of index offenses were given remedials, while in Cohort II only 15% of the index offenses were given a remedial disposition. Our interest now focuses on whether there is a difference in disposition between whites and nonwhites when type of offense is included in the analysis. Table 12.5 reports these data.

It is clear again from Table 12.5 that in Cohort I, nonwhite boys are more frequently arrested or further disposed beyond a remedial disposition than are white boys, even when the category of offenses is held constant. Only 48.1% of whites who had committed index offenses were arrested, compared to 68.4% of nonwhites. For nonindex offenses, the arrest percentages were 9.3 for whites and 20.8 for nonwhites.

TABLE 12.5

Number and Percentage of Dispositions for Index and Nonindex Offenses by Race and Cohort

| | 1958 Cohort | | | | 1945 Cohort | | | |
| | Remedial | | All others | | Remedial | | All others | |
	N	Percentage	N	Percentage	N	Percentage	N	Percentage
Nonindex								
White	1533	63.4	884	36.6	2665	90.7	274	9.3
Nonwhite	3863	64.7	2109	35.3	2468	79.2	650	20.8
Index								
White	365	24.5	1126	75.5	674	51.8	626	48.1
Nonwhite	687	12.8	4681	87.2	708	31.6	1536	68.4

Table 12.5 shows for Cohort II that the race difference only pertains to index offenses. For the nonindex offense category, whites (36.6%) and nonwhites (35.3%) are arrested, or exposed to further processing, in nearly equal proportions. For index offenses, however, nonwhites (87.2%) are still more likely to be arrested, compared to white boys (75.5%). The reason for this disparity could depend on the relative severity of white and nonwhite index offenses, such as the propensity of nonwhites to commit violent index offenses. Nevertheless, because nonwhites are more likely to be arrested for their index crimes, and because they commit more index offenses, nonwhites are more likely to show up in previous analyses as having been arrested. This partially explains the race effect for the disposition data in the 1958 cohort.

Another way of examining the association between offense severity and disposition is to group the offenses by seriousness score. Table 12.6 reports the disposition dichotomy by two levels of seriousness, by race, and by SES (a four-way relationship).

Table 12.6 shows for the 1945 cohort that, within each seriousness category, nonwhites still receive more severe dispositions than do whites. For offenses with a seriousness score below 100, 92% of whites and 84% of nonwhites are remedialed. For offenses with scores of 100 or more, 50% of whites and 30% of nonwhites are remedialed (computed from Table 12.6). The data given in Table 12.6 for the 1958 cohort repeat the earlier finding for index offenses, namely, that only for more serious offenses do we find a race effect. Thus, for offenses of less severity about 10% of white boys are arrested, while about 8% of nonwhite boys are arrested. The race difference is again only slight and here favors whites, not nonwhites. For the more serious offenses, however, the race effect for an arrest disposition is larger and favors nonwhites. For offenses with a seriousness score of 100 or better, 60% of the whites are arrested, or further processed, compared to 75% of the nonwhite boys (computed from Table 12.6).

Socioeconomic status does not greatly affect these results. For the 1945 cohort the race differences persist regardless of SES level. For white boys whose offenses were minor (score less than 100), 91% of those in the lower-SES level and 93% of those in the higher-SES level were remedialed; for nonwhite boys, 84% were remedialed for both levels of SES. For white boys whose offenses were more serious (score of 100 or more), 45% of those in the lower-SES level and 56% of those in the higher-SES level were remedialed; for nonwhites, 30% of the lower-SES boys and 33% of the higher-SES boys were given a remedial disposition.

The same situation obtains in Cohort II when SES is controlled. For trivial or minor offenses, 89.3% of whites as against 91.5% of nonwhites

TABLE 12.6

Number and Percentage of Dispositions by Race, SES, and Cohort

Severity/ SES/Race	1958 Cohort				1945 Cohort			
	Remedial		All others		Remedial		All others	
	N	Percentage	N	Percentage	N	Percentage	N	Percentage
<100								
Low-SES W	266	89.3	32	10.7	1057	90.7	109	9.3
Low-SES NW	1919	91.5	179	8.5	2195	83.9	421	16.1
High-SES W	360	90.5	38	9.5	1594	93.4	113	6.6
High-SES NW	468	92.3	39	7.7	245	83.6	48	16.4
>100								
Low-SES W	408	36.0	725	64.0	294	44.7	364	55.3
Low-SES NW	1707	23.9	5420	76.1	659	29.7	1558	70.3
High-SES W	864	41.6	1215	58.4	394	55.6	314	44.4
High-SES NW	456	28.4	1152	71.6	77	32.6	159	67.4

are remedialed at low-SES levels and 90.5% of whites and 92.3% of nonwhites are remedialed at the higher level of SES. These differences are very slight and show that nonwhites, not whites, are favored with a remedial disposition. For the more serious offenses, at the lower level of SES 36% of whites versus 24% of nonwhites are remedialed; at the higher level of SES 41% of whites and 28% of nonwhites are remedialed. Thus, for serious offenses, whites are more likely to be favored with a remedial disposition, regardless of SES.

Disposition Contingencies

At this point in the analysis of the disposition data we turn to a more dynamic view of the relationship between offenses and the various dispositions. We have classified all of the first through fourth offenses as either index or nonindex and their possible dispositions as remedial or court. We have then traced for each offense number the probability of each subsequent offense type and disposition. We thus can attempt a more dynamic assessment of the impact of disposition on offense type probabilities.

For this purpose we have altered the clustering of disposition categories but still retain a simple dichotomy for most analyses. With remedial, we here include every other kind of disposition except a juvenile court penalty. In the previous analyses we were concerned with whether the police directly and finally decide the disposition informally, and hence, we divided cases into remedial versus all other forms. Here we are concerned principally with whether a court penalty, such as probation, probation and fine, probation and restitution, or institutional commitment, which is tantamount to conviction in criminal court, is related to subsequent delinquency.

Tables 12.7 and 12.8 present the probability of disposition and the probability of committing a subsequent offense, given the type of previous disposition for index and nonindex offenses, respectively. The basic layout of these tables is as follows. First, the N and the probability for total (T) and index (I) or nonindex (NI) (Table 12.8) offenses are shown. Second, from here, the data branch to show the offenses (and the probability values) that received either a remedial or court disposition. Third, for the next offense rank, the data branch again showing the number and probability of total and index offenses for the two prior offense dispositions that we are examining, remedial and court. This process continues for the third and fourth offenses, with more branching of course.

The data for the 1945 cohort given in Tables 12.7 and 12.8 indicate

TABLE 12.7

Probability of Disposition for Index Offenses by Offense Number and Cohort

1958 Cohort

First offense[a] Base		Disposition		Second offense Base		Disposition	
N	Probability	N	Probability	N	Probability	N	Probability
4315	.3278 (T)			841	.6211 (T)		
1667	.3863 (I)	1354 R	.8122	369	.2725 (I)	273 R	.7398
						96 C	.2601
		313 C	.1878	163	.5207 (T)		.5384
				78	.2492 (I)	42 R	.4615
						36 C	

Third offense[a] Base		Disposition		Fourth offense Base		Disposition	
N	Probability	N	Probability	N	Probability	N	Probability
213	.7802 (T)			67	.8170 (T)		
107	.3919 (I)	82 R	.7663	43	.5243 (I)	33 R	.7674
						10 C	.2325
		25 C	.2336	20	.8000 (T)		
				9	.3600 (I)	7 R	.7777
						2 C	.2222
72	.7500 (T)						
38	.3958 (I)	21 R	.5526	14	.6666 (T)		
				7	.3333 (I)	5 R	.7142
						2 C	.2857
		17 C	.4473	12	.7058 (T)		
				7	.4117 (I)	3 R	.4285
						4 C	.5714
28	.6666 (T)			4	.4444 (T)		
14	.3333 (I)	9 R	.6428	3	.3333 (I)	2 R	.6666
						1 C	.3333
		5 C	.3571	5	1.0000 (T)		
				4	.8000 (I)	3 R	.7500
						1 C	.2500
23	.6388 (T)			4	.8000 (T)		
12	.3333 (I)	5 R	.4166	1	.2000 (I)	1 R	1.0000
						0 C	.0000
		7 C	.5833	7	1.0000 (T)		
				2	.2857 (I)	2 R	1.0000
						0 C	.0000

(continued)

TABLE 12.7 (continued)

1945 Cohort

First offense[a]				Second offense			
Base		Disposition		Base		Disposition	
N	Probability	N	Probability	N	Probability	N	Probability
3475	.3494 (T)			589	.6116 (T)		
1200	.3453 (I)	963 R	.8025	244	.2534 (I)	170 R	.6967
						74 C	.3033
		237 C	.1975	160	.6751 (T)		
				75	.3164 (I)	35 R	.4667
						40 C	.5333

Third offense[a]				Fourth offense			
Base		Disposition		Base		Disposition	
N	Probability	N	Probability	N	Probability	N	Probability
134	.7882 (T)			27	.7941 (T)		
58	.3412 (I)	34 R	.5862	19	.5588 (I)	9 R	.4737
						10 C	.5263
		24 C	.4138	18	.7500 (T)		
				8	.3333 (I)	5 R	.6250
						3 C	.3750
60	.8108 (T)						
33	.4459 (I)	13 R	.3939	12	.9231 (T)		
				5	.3846 (I)	4 R	.8000
						1 C	.2000
		20 C	.6061	14	.7000 (T)		
				8	.4000 (I)	2 R	.2500
						6 C	.7500
26	.7429 (T)			9	1.0000 (T)		
15	.4286 (I)	9 R	.6000	4	.4444 (I)	1 R	.2500
						3 C	.7500
		6 C	.4000	6	1.0000 (T)		
				3	.5000 (I)	1 R	.3333
						2 C	.6667
31	.7750 (T)			2	.6667 (T)		
16	.4000 (I)	3 R	.1875	2	.6667 (I)	1 R	.5000
						1 C	.5000
		13 C	.8125	13	1.0000 (T)		
				10	.7692 (I)	1 R	.1000
						9 C	.9000

[a]T, total offenses; I, index offenses; R, remedial; C, court.

TABLE 12.8

Probability of Disposition for Nonindex Offenses by Offense Number and Cohort

1958 Cohort

First offense[a]				Second offense			
Base		Disposition		Base		Disposition	
N	Probability	N	Probability	N	Probability	N	Probability
4315	.3278 (T)			1456	.5694 (T)		
2648	.6136 (NI)	2557 R	.9656	916	.3582 (NI)	874 R	.9541
						42 C	.0458
		91 C	.0343	51	.5604 (T)		
				33	.3626 (NI)	26 R	.7878
						7 C	.2121

Third offense[a]				Fourth offense			
Base		Disposition		Base		Disposition	
N	Probability	N	Probability	N	Probability	N	Probability
595	.6807 (T)			255	.7183 (T)		
378	.4324 (NI)	355 R	.9391	148	.4169 (NI)	138 R	.9324
						10 C	.0675
		23 C	.0608	12	.5217 (T)		
				6	.2608 (NI)	4 R	.6666
32	.7619 (T)					2 C	.3333
21	.5000 (NI)	18 R	.8571	14	.7777 (T)		
				9	.5000 (NI)	9 R	1.0000
						0 C	.0000
		3 C	.1428	1	.3333 (T)		
				1	.3333 (NI)	1 R	1.0000
						0 C	.0000
14	.5384 (T)			3	.5000 (T)		
7	.2692 (NI)	6 R	.8571	1	.1667 (NI)	1 R	1.0000
						0 C	.0000
		1 C	.1428	1	1.0000 (T)		
				1	1.0000 (NI)	0 R	.0000
5	.7142 (T)					1 C	1.0000
4	.5714 (NI)	4 R	1.0000	3	.7500 (T)		
				2	.5000 (NI)	0 R	.0000
						2 C	1.0000
		0 C	.0000	0	.0000 (T)		
				0	.0000 (NI)	0 R	.0000
						0 C	.0000

(continued)

TABLE 12.8 (continued)

1945 Cohort

First offense[a]				Second offense			
Base		Disposition		Base		Disposition	
N	Probability	N	Probability	N	Probability	N	Probability
3475	.3494 (T)			1083	.4894 (T)		
2275	.6547 (NI)	2231 R	.9727	741	.3348 (NI)	720 R	.9717
						21 C	.0283
		62 C	.0273	30	.4839 (T)		.8571
				21	.3387 (NI)	18 R	
							.1429
						3 C	

Third offense[a]				Fourth offense			
Base		Disposition		Base		Disposition	
N	Probability	N	Probability	N	Probability	N	Probability
427	.5762 (T)			190	.6463 (T)		
304	.4103 (NI)	294 R	.9671	123	.4184 (NI)	114 R	.9268
						9 C	.0732
		10 C	.0329	6	.6000 (T)		
				6	.6000 (NI)	6 R	1.0000
9	.4286 (T)					0 C	.0000
6	.2857 (NI)	6 R	1.0000	2	.3333 (T)		
				2	.3333 (NI)	2 R	1.0000
						0 C	.0000
		0 C	.0000	0	.0000 (T)		
				0	.0000 (NI)	0 R	.0000
						0 C	.0000
14	.7778 (T)			6	1.0000 (T)		
8	.4444 (NI)	6 R	.7500	5	.8333 (NI)	4 R	.8000
						1 C	.2000
		2 C	.2500	0	.0000 (T)		.0000
				0	.0000 (NI)	0 R	.0000
2	.6667 (T)					0 C	.0000
2	.6667 (NI)	0 R	.0000	0	.0000 (T)		
				0	.0000 (NI)	0 R	.0000
						0 C	.0000
		2 C	1.0000	1	.5000 (T)		
				1	.5000 (NI)	1 R	1.0000
						0 C	.0000

[a]T, total offenses; I, index offenses; R, remedial; C, court.

that, in general, the probability of committing a subsequent offense increases consistently from the second through the fourth offense (these probabilities are similar to the probability of a like-offense repeat as described in Chapter 9). Most important, the data show that the more severe the disposition, the higher is the probability of committing a subsequent offense. Thus, for example, if an offender receives a remedial for his first index offense, the probability that he will commit a second offense, regardless of type, is .6116; whereas if he receives a court disposition of at least probation for his first index offense, the likelihood of a second offense of any type is higher, .6751. Similarly, the probability of committing another index offense increases and it is higher for offenders given a court penalty. Thus, at the second offense, offenders who were remedialed for their first index offense show a probability of .2534 of committing a second index crime, but offenders who were given a court penalty for their first index offense have a probability of .3164 of committing a second index offense. Similar trends are observed with respect to nonindex offenses (Table 12.8), but the number of cases given a court penalty is too small for reliable conclusions.

The data reported in Tables 12.7 and 12.8 for the 1958 cohort show that court penalty is more effective than in Cohort I, especially at the situation of the first offense. Among the 1,667 index offenders at the first offense, 313 or 18% were given a court penalty, and, of these offenders, 52% committed a second offense of any type, and 24% committed a second index offense. On the other hand, the 1,354 index offenders who were remedialed at the first offense were more likely to commit a second offense (p. = .6211) and a second index offense (p. = .2725). As we move to the third offense, we see that the remedial first offenders, regardless of how they were disposed of at the second offense (remedial or court), have a greater chance of committing a third offense (.7802 for remedial at second offense, and .7500 for court at second offense), and a greater likelihood of committing a third index offense (.3919 for remedial seconds and .3958 for court seconds) compared to the first-offense court cases. For the latter, the chances of committing the third offense are .6666 for the second-offense remedials and .6388 for the second-offense court cases, and with respect to index recidivism, the first-offense court cases show a probability of .3333 of committing a third offense regardless of the second-offense disposition.

These data point out the interesting results that the likelihood of a third offense, whether it be index or not, is more sensitive to the disposition at the first offense than how the offender was handled at his second offense. Thus, given a remedial at the first offense, offenders who move on to a third do so in about the same proportions regardless of whether they were remedialed or given a court penalty for their second offenses. The same is true for the delinquents exposed to court processing and sanctioned at their first index offense.

For the Cohort II nonindex offenses, the data resemble the Cohort I findings. From the first to the second offense, the chances of general recidivism, or a nonindex offense repeat, are about the same for the first-offense remedials and court penalty cases. After the second offense, the data indicate that a court penalty is associated with a greater likelihood of recidivism than is the case for remedial dispositions.

Tables 12.7 and 12.8 contain data showing the disposition probabilities as well as the recidivism probabilities. Thus, we can tentatively point out the disposition contingencies for both cohorts.

In Cohort I the decision of a court penalty for a repeat of the same type of offense is most often influenced by previous decisions, the decision immediately preceding the offense having the maximum impact. For example, if a delinquent receives a court disposition for his first index offense (see Table 12.7) the probability (.5333) that he will receive similar treatment for his second index offense is greater than the probability (.4667) of being remedialed for his second index offense. Similarly, there is a strong indication that an offender remedialed for his first index offense will again be given this disposition on his second index offense compared to receiving a court penalty (.6967 vs. .3033). After the second offense, the probability of a third and fourth court disposition increases to .8125 and .9000 respectively, while repeat remedial dispositions drop to .5862 at the third offense and .4737 at the fourth. For the mixed combinations of remedial followed by court penalty, or court penalty followed by remedial, the data show an increasing reluctance to remedial the offender as rank number of offense increases.

Table 12.9 presents data on the pattern of offenses from first to fourth, the disposition between the two most recent offenses, the probability of the most recent offense type, time interval to this most recent offense, and the desistance probability. Although this table presents a wealth of data, we can greatly simplify the discussion with a few general observations.

First, the offense probabilities show considerable variation thus indicating much offense switching. We know from Chapter 9 that the most likely next offense is always a nonindex offense, and the data here confirm this fact even when disposition between offenses is known.

Second, the time between offenses, as expected, becomes shorter as offense number increases. The interval does not seem to be related to prior offense disposition in any consistent way.

Third, although court penalties do not appear to have a substantial

TABLE 12.9

Contingent Probability and Mean Time between Offenses by Type of Prior Offense, Type of Disposition Immediately Prior to Offense, and Cohort

Offense number	Type/disp/type[a]	N	Probability	Mean time	Type/disp/type	N	Probability	Mean time	Desist probability
					1958 Cohort				
1st	I(R)–I	254	.2957	23.3	I(R)–N	313	.3644	25.4	.3399
	I(C)–I	78	.2492	8.8	I(C)–N	85	.2716	9.3	.4792
	I(O)–I	115	.2323	12.6	I(O)–N	159	.3212	14.1	.4465
to	N(R)–I	481	.2189	16.3	N(R)–N	799	.3637	17.4	.4174
2nd	N(C)–I	18	.1978	11.9	N(C)–N	33	.3626	8.7	.4396
	N(O)–I	55	.1639	14.1	N(O)–N	117	.3250	11.6	.5111
	I-I(R)–I	74	.4157	11.2	I-I(R)–N	68	.3820	15.6	.2022
	I-I(C)–I	50	.3788	6.3	I-I(C)–N	45	.3409	9.5	.2803
	I-I(O)–I	47	.3431	8.9	I-I(O)–N	52	.3796	11.4	.2774
2nd	N-I(R)–I	88	.4018	12.2	N-I(R)–N	83	.3790	13.3	.2192
	N-I(C)–I	46	.3046	8.8	N-I(C)–N	52	.3444	8.1	.3510
to	N-I(O)–I	53	.2819	8.9	N-I(O)–N	80	.4255	10.1	.2926
3rd	I-N(R)–I	128	.3005	9.4	I-N(R)–N	197	.4621	10.9	.2371
	I-N(C)–I	11	.3793	7.4	I-N(C)–N	12	.4133	6.0	.2069
	I-N(O)–I	42	.4118	5.7	I-N(O)–N	32	.3137	9.9	.2745
	N-N(R)–I	182	.2514	10.5	N-N(R)–N	322	.4448	10.4	.3039
	N-N(C)–I	12	.2449	6.6	N-N(C)–N	25	.5102	8.1	.2449
	N-N(O)–I	42	.2386	8.8	N-N(O)–N	63	.3580	7.3	.4034
3rd	I-I-I(R)–I	37	.6066	6.7	I-I-I(R)–N	14	.2295	13.5	.1639
	I-I-I(C)–I	22	.4074	6.4	I-I-I(C)–N	22	.4074	4.5	.1852
to	I-I-I(O)–I	17	.3036	7.0	I-I-I(O)–N	21	.3750	6.5	.3214
4th[b]	N-I-I(R)–I	31	.4493	6.9	N-I-I(R)–N	27	.3913	9.2	.1594
	N-I-I(C)–I	17	.2656	6.1	N-I-I(C)–N	27	.4229	9.7	.3125
	N-I-I(O)–I	20	.3704	6.9	N-I-I(O)–N	13	.2407	6.4	.3889

(continued)

TABLE 12.9 (continued)

1945 Cohort

Offense number	Type/disp/type[a]	N	Probability	Mean time	Type/disp/type	N	Probability	Mean time	Desist probability
1st to 2nd	I(R)-I	155	.2377	19.1	I(R)-N	232	.3558	22.6	.4065
	I(C)-I	75	.3164	10.2	I(C)-N	85	.3586	15.3	.3250
	I(O)-I	895	.2861	20.6	I(O)-N	113	.3633	19.7	.3506
	N(R)-I	314	.1527	16.9	N(R)-N	692	.3365	17.7	.5108
	N(C)-I	9	.1451	10.9	N(C)-N	21	.3387	16.5	.5162
	N(O)-I	28	.1783	16.3	N(O)-N	49	.5096	16.3	.5096
2nd to 3rd	I-I(R)-I	49	.4083	9.9	I-I(R)-N	47	.3917	13.9	.2000
	I-I(C)-I	49	.4298	8.2	I-I(C)-N	42	.3684	10.7	.2018
	I-I(O)-I	24	.2824	12.1	I-I(O)-N	40	.4706	11.9	.2470
	N-I(R)-I	34	.2411	13.3	N-I(R)-N	63	.4468	13.2	.3121
	N-I(C)-I	27	.3140	9.6	N-I(C)-N	38	.4419	10.7	.2441
	N-I(O)-I	38	.3065	12.9	N-I(O)-N	37	.2984	11.4	.3951
	I-N(R)-I	76	.2289	10.5	I-N(R)-N	136	.4096	10.5	.3651
	I-N(C)-I	13	.4333	12.0	I-N(C)-N	10	.3333	7.9	.2334
	I-N(O)-I	17	.2500	13.6	I-N(O)-N	20	.2941	9.3	.4559
	N-N(R)-I	116	.1779	8.1	N-N(R)-N	269	.4126	9.1	.4095
	N-N(C)-I	3	.1250	14.1	N-N(C)-N	8	.3333	13.7	.5417
	N-N(O)-I	13	.1512	5.4	N-N(O)-N	43	.5000	11.8	.3488
3rd to 4th[b]	I-I-I(R)-I	16	.5000	10.5	I-I-I(R)-N	12	.3750	7.0	.1250
	I-I-I(C)-I	29	.4328	6.2	I-I-I(C)-N	22	.3284	6.1	.2388
	I-I-I(O)-I	14	.5185	4.9	I-I-I(O)-N	8	.2963	5.9	.1852
	N-I-I(R)-I	6	.1579	13.3	N-I-I(R)-N	22	.5789	9.1	.2632
	N-I-I(C)-I	11	.3056	5.6	N-I-I(C)-N	18	.5000	13.6	.1944
	N-I-I(O)-I	11	.4400	13.4	N-I-I(O)-N	9	.3600	5.9	.2000

[a]I, Index offense; N, Nonindex offense; R, Remedial disposition; C, Court disposition; O, Other disposition.
[b]For this offense sequence, only the offense type combinations with sufficient cell sizes were displayed.

deterrent effect, court dispositions seem to have more value for index offenders in Cohort II than in Cohort I. After the first offense, 47% of the index offenders in Cohort II did not commit a second offense if they had a court penalty, compared to just 32% in Cohort I. After the second offense, 28% of the I-I repeats and 35% of the N-I pattern desist if they had a court penalty, compared to 20% for the former and 24% for the latter in the 1945 cohort. The I-N pattern favors Cohort I, but slightly, where 23% desisted after a court penalty as compared to 20% in Cohort II.

Fourth, of special interest is the fact that the third disposition shown, other, which consists of cases which were formally processed but adjusted without penalty, appears to be as effective (or at least as ineffective) as court penalty. Thus, in many instances, this less severe type of disposition shows desistance probabilities equal to if not greater than those for court penalty. For instance, in Cohort II, the desistance probabilities for "other" disposition and court penalty are nearly equivalent for the I-I and I-N sequence (.44 vs. .47) and the I-I-I and I-I-N sequence (.27 vs. .28), while the adjusted disposition has a greater desistance value compared to court penalty at the N-I, N-N; I-N-I, I-N-N; N-N-I; N-N-N; I-I-I-I, I-I-I-N; and N-I-I-I, N-I-I-N sequences. Thus, when compared to the informal remedial disposition, any court disposition seems to produce a higher, albeit slight, desistance from delinquency.

In Table 12.10 we present data showing the sequence of offenses, court disposition (at least probation), and the probability of this severe disposition. For Cohort I, the probability of receiving a court disposition for the first time varies from a low of .0829 at the fifth offense to a high of .1129 at the fourth offense. The slight variation between the chances of a first court disposition at each offense would seem to suggest that the number of previous police contacts has little to do with the imposition of this disposition type. The data also show a consistent increase in the probabilities of second, third, and fourth court disposition at each offense. For instance, the probability of a first court disposition at the third offense is .1048, whereas the chances of a second or a third court penalty at this offense are .1587 and .3214, respectively. These results clearly point to the fact that once an offender has received a court disposition, he is most likely to receive another court penalty in connection with his next offense. The main diagonal shows that the probability increases sharply from the first through the fifth offense, where a court penalty is given to 60% of the offenders who had four prior court penalties.

The Cohort II results follow these same patterns but are less dramatic. It is clear that a Cohort II offender stands a greater risk of receiving

TABLE 12.10

Probability of Court Dispositions by Offense Number and Cohort

1958 Cohort

Offense number	N	1st disp. probability	N	2nd disp. probability	N	3rd disp. probability	N	4th disp. probability	N	5th disp. probability	N
First	4315	.0936	404								
Second	2511	.1207	303	.1435	58						
Third	1806	.1312	237	.1155	75	.2241	13				
Fourth	1304	.1166	152	.1011	82	.1666	20	.2307	3		
Fifth	982	.1008	99	.0715	63	.0879	16	.2000	6	.6666	2

1945 Cohort

Offense number	N	1st disp. probability	N	2nd disp. probability	N	3rd disp. probability	N	4th disp. probability	N	5th disp. probability	N
First	3475	.0860	299								
Second	1862	.1063	198	.1873	56						
Third	1212	.1048	127	.1587	70	.3214	18				
Fourth	868	.1129	98	.1104	55	.2222	24	.5556	10		
Fifth	627	.0829	52	.0850	46	.1655	23	.2500	6	.6000	6

his first court disposition at each offense number. The chances range between a low of .0936 for a court penalty at the first offense and a high of .1312 for a first court penalty at the third offense. All five of these court disposition probabilities for the first to the fifth offense are higher than their corresponding counterparts in Cohort I. The Cohort II data do not follow the pattern of increasing disposition probabilities for any given offense number. For example, at the third offense an offender with one prior court penalty is not more likely than an offender with no prior court dispositions to receive a court penalty at the third offense (.1155 vs. .1312).

The Cohort II data do repeat the Cohort I finding that a recidivist with a prior penalty has an increasing risk of receiving another court penalty each time he commits another offense. From an initial value of .0936 at the first offense, the chances increase to .1435 at the second, .2241 at the third, .2307 at the fourth, up to .6666 at the fifth offense. The increasing risk of receiving another court disposition is similar to Cohort I, but the increase is less sharp. It would seem, therefore, that a greater variety of dispositions is being used regardless of prior disposition. Alternatively, it may be that the court penalties are more successful in preventing recidivism, and thus, fewer offenders continually commit offenses for which a pattern of repeat court penalties are deemed necessary. The analyses presented in the next section will attempt to address this issue.

Table 12.11 displays for Cohort I the probability of a remedial disposition at each offense, from the first through the fourth. The probabilities of a second, third, or fourth remedial disposition increase at each offense. But, unlike the probabilities of a court disposition, the probability of a first remedial disposition is greatest at the first offense and smallest at the fourth offense. In fact, the probability of a second remedial disposition for the second offense is less than half of the probability for the first offense. These probabilities increase at the third and fourth offenses, but not greatly.

The Cohort II data given in Table 12.11 show similar results. The probability of receiving a first remedial disposition is highest at the first offense (.7082). From the first to the second offense the probability drops considerably to .1219. Thereafter, the chances of a first remedial continue to decline when at the fifth offense only about 1% of the offenders receive their first remedial. The 1958 data show more repeat remedials than in Cohort I. At the second through fifth offenses, the chances are much greater in the later cohort that if the offender was remedialed before, he will be remedialed again. Further, the Cohort II probabilities are not only higher but they show a greater increase as offense number

TABLE 12.11
Probability of Remedial Dispositions by Offense Number and Cohort

1958 Cohort

Offense number	N	1st disp. probability	/ N	2nd disp. probability	/ N	3rd disp. probability	/ N	4th disp. probability	/ N	5th disp. probability	/ N
First	4315	.7082	3056								
Second	2511	.1219	306	.4060	1241						
Third	1806	.0493	89	.1485	315	.5253	652				
Fourth	1304	.0322	42	.0480	91	.1957	177	.5766	376		
Fifth	982	.0102	10	.0270	50	.1198	98	.2384	108	.6702	252

1945 Cohort

Offense number	N	1st disp. probability	/ N	2nd disp. probability	/ N	3rd disp. probability	/ N	4th disp. probability	/ N	5th disp. probability	/ N
First	3475	.7793	2708								
Second	1862	.1359	253	.3663	992						
Third	1212	.0627	76	.1392	274	.4315	428				
Fourth	868	.0276	24	.0491	87	.2458	206	.4346	186		

and number of remedials increases. The Cohort II data range from .40, to .52, to .57, to .67, while the Cohort I scores are .36, .43, and .43 (at the fourth offense).

The previous results for the 1945 cohort indicate that in most instances a court disposition does not reduce recidivism. Data presented in Table 12.12 further support this conclusion. Of the 1,200 first index offenses, 237, or about 20% were given a court disposition. Following these 237 cases through to the fourth offense reveals certain important results.

First, 160, or about 68% of the offenders who received a court disposition for the first offense committed a second offense, and nearly 47% (75/160) of the second offenses were index offenses. Second, about 53% of these 160 second-time index offenders received a court disposition for the second time. Third, approximately 77% (31/40) of those who received a court disposition for the second time violated the law for the third time, and a slight majority of these three-time offenders (51%) committed an index offense. Fourth, just over 81% of the three-time offenders received a court disposition for the third time. Fifth, all of the three-time offenders went on to a fourth offense, with 76% being index offenses. Thus, it seems that two factors—severity of offense and severe disposition—are associated with a substantial proportion of recidivism.

The Cohort II data given in Table 12.12 indicate that court dispositions are slightly more effective than in Cohort I. Of the 1,667 first index offenses, 313, or about 19% (close to the 19.8% in Cohort I), were handled by juvenile court. Of these 313 offenders, 163 committed a second offense, which is a recidivism probability of .52 compared to .67 in Cohort I. Of the 163 second offenses, about 48% were index offenses, and 36 (46%) were given a second court disposition. At the third offense, we see that 23, or about 64% of the offenders, commit a third offense, of which 52% are index offenses (in Cohort I over three-quarters of the two-time offenders committed a third offense). About 58% of the three-time offenders were given a court disposition for the third time. Like Cohort I, all of the three-time court penalty offenders went on to a fourth offense. But, unlike Cohort I, where over 76% of the fourth offenders committed an index offense, the fourth offenders in Cohort II had only a 28% concentration of index offenses.

Although the previous data would seem to indicate that court dispositions are ineffective in *preventing recidivism*, when compared to the data for remedials given in Table 12.13, court penalties are relatively more effective. In Cohort I, 80% of the index first offenders were remedialed. Of these, 61% go on to a second offense, 78% go on to a third, and 79% commit a fourth. Similarly, the percentage of index offenses

TABLE 12.12
Index Offense Transitions following Court Dispositions by Cohort

			1958 Cohort				
			Index offenses		Court disp. for index		
Offense number	N	Index probability	N	Percentage of base	N	Percentage of index	Desist probability
First	4315		1667	38.6	313	18.8	
Second	163	.5207	78	47.9	36	46.2	.4792
Third	23	.6388	12	52.2	7	58.3	.3611
Fourth	7	1.000	2	28.6	0		.0000
			1945 Cohort				
			Index offenses		Court disp. for index		
Offense number	N	Index probability	N	Percentage of base	N	Percentage of index	Desist probability
First	3475		1200	34.5	237	19.8	
Second	160	.6751	75	46.9	40	53.3	.3249
Third	31	.7750	16	51.6	13	81.3	.2250
Fourth	15	1.000	10	76.9	9	90.0	.0000

steadily increases from 34% at the first offense to 41%, 43%, and 70% at the second, third, and fourth offenses, respectively.

The same situation obtains in Cohort II. Here, 62% of the first index offenders commit a second offense, 78% commit a third, and 81% commit a fourth. The steady rise in the percentage of index offenses at each offense number points to the disutility of remedial dispositions. From a starting point of about 38% at the first offense, index offenses constitute 44% of second offenses, 50% of third offenses, and 65% of fourth offenses.

When nonindex offenses are remedialed (see Table 12.14), we observe a pattern of increasing recidivism but a relatively stable share of the offenses consisting of the nonindex variety. In Cohort I, about 97% of the first offenses that are nonindex do not receive a court penalty, while almost 97% avoid a court penalty in Cohort II. About 49% of the Cohort I delinquents and 56% of the Cohort II delinquents commit a second offense. Thereafter, Cohort I recidivism increases to 59% and

TABLE 12.13
Index Offense Transitions following Remedial Dispositions by Cohort

				1958 Cohort			
				Index offenses		Remedial disp. for index	
Offense number	N	Index probability	N	Percentage of base	N	Percentage of index	Desist probability
First	4315		1667	38.6	1354	81.2	
Second	841	.6211	369	43.9	273	73.9	.3789
Third	213	.7802	107	50.2	82	76.6	.2198
Fourth	67	.8170	43	64.2	33	76.7	.1830
				1945 Cohort			
				Index offenses		Remedial disp. for index	
Offense number	N	Index probability	N	Percentage of base	N	Percentage of index	Desist probability
First	3475		1200	34.5	963	80.3	
Second	589	.6116	244	41.4	170	69.7	.3884
Third	134	.7882	58	43.3	34	58.6	.2118
Fourth	27	.7941	19	70.4	9	47.4	.2059

then 64% at the fourth offense, while for Cohort II, recidivism shows a probability of .68 at the third and .71 at the fourth offense.

It is important to note that the percentage of offenses that are non-index at each offense number is somewhat stable, although they increase slightly from first through third offense. In Cohort I the values range from 65% to 68% to 71%, while in Cohort II the percentages are 61%, 62%, and 63%. Movement toward index offenses does not occur until the fourth offense, where for Cohort I, index offenses represent about 35% of the crimes at the fourth offense compared to about 29% at the third; and for Cohort II, index offenses are 42% of the crimes at the fourth offense compared to 37% at the third offense.

Clearly, remedial dispositions for nonindex offenses are expected, and Table 12.14 shows that they are given frequently. It is difficult to tell if this lenient treatment fosters recidivism, but the data certainly show that repeat offending increases as repeat remedial dispositions are given. However, the recidivism does not seem to lead to any offense

TABLE 12.14
Nonindex Offense Transitions following Remedial Dispositions by Cohort

Offense number	N	Nonindex probability	Nonindex offenses		Remedial disp. for nonindex		Desist probability
			N	Percentage of base	N	Percentage of index	
			1958 Cohort				
First	4315		2648	61.4	2557	96.6	
Second	1456	.5694	916	62.9	874	95.4	.4306
Third	595	.6807	378	63.5	355	93.9	.3193
Fourth	255	.7183	148	58.0	138	93.2	.2817
			1945 Cohort				
First	3475		2275	65.5	2213	97.3	
Second	1083	.4893	741	68.4	720	97.2	.5107
Third	427	.5930	304	71.2	294	96.7	.4070
Fourth	190	.6462	123	64.6	114	92.7	.3538

escalation as most offenders increasingly commit nonindex crimes. Not until the fourth offense do we see any evidence of a shift to index violations and, clearly, the shift may not be due to the previous lenient treatment. A variety of other factors may be more important, such as age.

The patterns of results observed in these analyses, especially the court dispositions, lead to two hypotheses which stand apart in their points of reference. As put forth originally with respect to the 1945 cohort, these hypotheses are: (1) the likelihood of a preexisting "hard-core" delinquent group prior to its contact with the juvenile court, and (2) the possibility that the judicial process is a factor which activates and eventually facilitates persistent criminal behavior. The data previously discussed would seem to indicate that both hypotheses are as applicable to the 1958 cohort as they were to the earlier cohort.

The first hypothesis assumes that uniformity in the transition of offense types that receive a severe court penalty, as a consistent mode of disposition from the first offense to the fourth or fifth, is an indication of commitment to future delinquency. If we assume the existence of potentially persistent offenders prior to their first contact with the judicial process, the court's first disposition becomes an adequate screening process. The court has, in effect, selected the potential hard-core or chronic offenders from among the first-time delinquents when the severity of the court's first disposition corresponds to the expected seriousness of future offensive behavior (and especially when this expected seriousness is demonstrated by the probability of the offender's committing subsequent offenses).

On the other hand, the second hypothesis focuses on the judicial experience as its point of reference. Here, it is assumed that the court disposes of first offenders mainly in terms of the immediate severity of the offense that has been committed, and most important, the disposition is not directly related to expected recidivism as in the first hypothesis. The group of first offenders who receive a court penalty is assumed to be, at this stage, the same as the population of first offenders who are remedialed or adjusted. The consequent patterning of the probability of committing a second serious offense and subsequent recidivism is not a prior property (or tendency) of the population disposed by court penalty but, rather, is a result of a process that occurs after the court's disposition. In other words, a severe court penalty such as probation or incarceration fails to curb delinquent recidivism and, in fact, may actually trigger the succession of higher probabilities of committing subsequent serious offenses.

In sum, the first hypothesis assumes the existence of different groups of first offenders who must receive differential dispositions. The subsequently higher recidivism rates for the first offenders handled by the court is not an indication of the failure of the disposition process, but may instead validate the screening process of the court in handling these offenders more severely in the first place. Thus, recidivism merely confirms the initial judgment of the court. The second hypothesis, in contrast, regards first offenders as a homogenous group and thus views the disposition itself as a trigger for future conduct. Specifically, the severe disposition, in contrast to remedial or less severe official action, initiates a process whereby first offenders become persistent and increasingly more serious delinquents by virtue of being handled severely by the court in the first place.

We are unable to conclude from the analysis presented above whether the dispositions afforded juvenile offenders (especially in the early stage of the delinquent career) are serving the purposes for which they were designed. It seems, in both cohorts, that on the one hand, the judicial process has been able to screen out the chronic offenders fairly well. On the other hand, the judicial process and the treatment modes do not seem to function effectively to restrain, discourage, prevent, or cure delinquency. Not only do a greater proportion of those who receive a severe disposition violate the law, but these violations are serious and rapid. The inferences which can be drawn from these analyses are far from conclusive, for other factors which may affect the disposition decision are likely to affect not only the probability of committing a second, third, or any subsequent offense, but also the time between offenses and offense patterns which may themselves influence the probability of recidivism.

The problem of delinquent recidivism is an elusive one. We did not expect to reach either definitive observations or conclusive explanations with just the analyses reported above. However, with these data we are at least in a better starting position to understand the connection between the juvenile justice process and the empirical reality of the repeat offender. The chronic offender exists, and when his career is viewed retrospectively, the extent and severity of his delinquent behavior is fully exposed. These offenders may continue to violate the law in spite of the type of benevolent judicial intervention they receive, or perhaps, even because of their severe treatment in court. At this point we just do not know. Naturally, we plan future analyses of the data, especially concerning the transition of our juvenile offenders in Cohort II to adulthood. For the most part, these analyses will be focused on the issue of prediction. The dispositional experience of the chronic offender, especially in the early stage of his career, will be an important aspect of any models that are developed. Nonetheless, given the results presented above, it will not be altogether surprising to find that available data, including dispositions, are less than perfect predictors of recidivism.

Summary and Implications

Our objective in this study has been to replicate as closely as possible our prior research with the 1945 birth cohort study. Investigation of another birth cohort in Philadelphia has afforded the opportunity to examine the effects on delinquency of growing up in a different time and sociocultural setting. The 1945 cohort was born in the final year of World War II, which sets its years of delinquent involvement in the period from 1955 through 1962. The 1958 cohort was born 13 years later, which frames the period of delinquency from 1968 through 1975. The social milieu of the two cohorts differs and may represent different pushes toward or pulls away from delinquency. For the 1958 cohort, the delinquency years at risk coincide with America's involvement in the Vietnam War, the rise in drug abuse, social protest, and the like. This period of rapid social change and pervasive social unrest is in sharp contrast to the more tranquil period of adolescence experienced by the 1945 cohort.

Although the social environments differ considerably, the criminal justice environments of the two cohorts were very much alike. The policies and procedures for law enforcement, especially in the handling of juvenile offenders, were the same for both cohorts. Likewise, juvenile court policy followed the same statutory provisions for the disposition of delinquents in the 1958 cohort as were in place for the 1945 cohort. Naturally, this consistency in official policy does not preclude the possibility of differences in the informal handling of delinquents in the two cohorts, either by the police or by juvenile court authorities. However, the uniformity of the criminal justice process applied to the two cohorts at least ensures that differences in either the extent or character of delinquency are not an artifact of the system and, more probably, cohort differences are reflective of real differences in behavior.

To ensure that the present study was comparable to its predecessor, the 1958 cohort was defined in the same way and the data collection procedures and sources used were the same as in the 1945 cohort. Thus, the present cohort consisted of those youths born in the target year who had demonstrated continual residence in the city of Philadelphia at least from age 10 through age 17. The residence restriction not only ensures that each cohort member is exposed to the environment at the same time, but also guarantees that the individual will face the same period at risk of delinquency, a span of 8 years.

The data were gathered from three sources: public and private schools, police rap sheets and investigation reports, and the juvenile court. From school records we obtained background data pertaining to the race, sex, date of birth, and residential history of the subject. The last, together with Bureau of Census data, provided the means for determining an environmentally-based social class measure of the cohort members. The school records also yielded data pertaining to school achievement, graduation status, and other school-related measures.

From the records of the Juvenile Aid Division of the Philadelphia Police Department we obtained the delinquency data for the cohort. These data consisted of *all* the police contacts recorded for a juvenile, whether or not the offense resulted in official arrest processing. Thus, delinquency was measured in terms of police contacts for offenses, not just those offenses that resulted in arrests. We supplemented these rap sheets with the police investigation reports, which contain the essential details concerning the offense. These details include information about physical injury, property theft or damage, use of weapons, and any other relevant information about the event, victim, or offender that we deemed important for this or future analyses.

From the records of the Juvenile Court Division of the Court of Common Pleas for Philadelphia we collected data pertaining to how the case was handled by the juvenile court system. This handling ranges from possible diversion by an intake worker to adjustment, discharge, or adjudication by a juvenile court judge.

The 1958 birth cohort is composed of 13,160 male subjects, of which 6,216 (47.2%) are white, and 6,944 (52.8%) are nonwhite. Of the cohort subjects, 6,414 (48.7%) are low SES, while 6,746 (51.3%) are high SES. Compared to the 1945 cohort, the 1958 cohort is noticeably different. The 1958 cohort is larger with almost one-third more members. More important, the racial composition of the 1958 cohort is more even than was the case for the earlier cohort. Whereas the 1945 cohort consisted of 71% white and 29% nonwhite boys, the 1958 cohort has about 47% white and 53% nonwhite.

Further, although both cohorts had slightly more than one-half high-SES subjects (54% in Cohort I and 51% in Cohort II), the racial differences in SES are much less pronounced in the 1958 cohort than in the 1945 cohort. That is, in Cohort I about 70% of the whites compared to just 16% of the nonwhites were high SES. In Cohort II, however, about 79% of the white boys compared to 27% of the nonwhite boys are high SES. In Cohort II, therefore, nonwhites are neither the minority of subjects nor are they as disadvantaged as their counterparts were in the previous cohort.

Summary of Results

Because we have investigated a number of topics surrounding the issue of delinquency, it is desirable to summarize the major findings with respect to the various topic areas of interest. These areas are prevalence, incidence, delinquent subgroups, age, recidivism, and dispositions.

Prevalence

Of the 13,160 males in the 1958 birth cohort, 4,315, or about 33% had at least one police contact before reaching their eighteenth birthday. The proportion of delinquents is thus extraordinarily close in the later cohort to that observed in the first cohort (34.9%). Both cohorts show a relationship between race and delinquency and SES and delinquency, although the relationships are less pronounced in the 1958 cohort. In the present cohort about 42% of the nonwhites were delinquent compared to 23% of whites, for a difference of 19%. In the earlier cohort, delinquency involved 50% of the nonwhite boys compared to 29% of the white boys, for a difference of 21%. Similarly, the SES differential is 18% in Cohort II compared to 19% in Cohort I.

In addition to race and SES, we found several other background variables that were related to delinquency status. Delinquents showed more residential instability than did nondelinquents. Delinquents exhibited much lower scholastic achievement levels than nondelinquents. Perhaps as a consequence, the former completed fewer years of school than did the latter. For all of these variables nondelinquents fare better than delinquents regardless of race, SES, or cohort.

With respect to the levels of delinquency status, we found that the 1958 cohort had a different concentration than did the 1945 cohort. Of the delinquents in Cohort II, about 42% were one-time offenders, 35% were nonchronic recidivists, and 23% were chronic recidivists. Cohort I contained about 4% more one-time delinquents (46%), but a very nearly equal percentage of nonchronic recidivists (35%). Most important, the prevalence of chronic delinquents in the earlier cohort (18%) was 5% less than in Cohort II.

Concerning delinquency prevalence by race, we found that the wide disparity in Cohort I had declined in the second cohort. That is, in the 1945 cohort, white delinquents were much more likely to be one-time offenders than were nonwhite delinquents (55% vs. 35%), and much less likely to be chronic offenders (10% vs. 29%). In Cohort II however, the white versus nonwhite proportions were 52% versus 37% at the one-time offender level and 15% versus 27% at the chronic offender level. In particular, therefore, chronic delinquency increased for whites from 10% to 15%, while it declined among nonwhites from 29% to 27% in the 1958 cohort compared to the 1945 cohort.

We found that the same set of factors that were related to the status of nondelinquent versus delinquent were also related to the level of delinquency. In both cohorts, one-time offenders compared to recidivists moved less often, had higher achievement scores, completed more years of school, and were much less likely to have been disciplinary problems in school.

Incidence

The results pertaining to the character and extent of delinquency in the two cohorts revealed important differences. The 1958 cohort was responsible for 15,248 delinquent acts up to the age of 18, while the 1945 cohort committed 10,214 offenses, which is an increase of nearly 50% (49.2%). Although the volume of delinquent acts is properly a function of the number of delinquents in the cohort, which automatically results in more expected offenses for the larger 1958 cohort, the rates of delinquent behavior confirmed that the later cohort was more offensive per unit of population.

Thus, the Cohort II offense rate (1,159 offenses per 1,000 subjects) was higher than the rate in Cohort I (1,027). This cohort effect is slight compared to the differences that were found for specific offense types, especially serious acts of delinquency. For UCR index offenses, the Cohort II rate (455) was about 1.6 times higher than the Cohort I rate (274). The discrepancy increased to a ratio of over 3:1 when violent index rates were compared. With respect to specific offenses, the data clearly showed the more serious character of delinquency in the 1958 cohort. The Cohort II rate exceeds the Cohort I rate by factors of 3:1 for homicide, 1.7:1 for rape, 5:1 for robbery, and almost 2:1 for aggravated assault and burglary.

When the incidence data were examined by race, we found once again that the predominant race effect in Cohort I diminished in Cohort II. For the earlier cohort, the overall offense rate for nonwhites (1,984) was 3

times higher than that for whites (633). The disproportionate involvement of nonwhites in serious delinquency in Cohort I was 4.6 times
higher for UCR index offenses and 15.2 times higher for violent offenses
compared to the white rates. In the second cohort, the nonwhite to
white comparisons revealed smaller differences for overall offenses for
which the ratio was 2.6:1, and for index offenses for which the ratio was
3.7:1. Most important, the Cohort II violent offense rate for nonwhites
was less than 6 times higher (5.8:1) than the rate for whites. This differential is large but is clearly less startling than the ratio of 15:1 obtained
in Cohort I. When expressed in terms of percentage increases from one
cohort to the other, the data further confirmed the sharper increase for
whites. Violent delinquency increased by about 300% in Cohort II over
Cohort I, but for nonwhites, violent offenses increased by only 86%,
while for whites, violent delinquency increased by almost 500%.

In our research with the two birth cohorts, we have investigated the
severity of the delinquent acts as a quantitative measure as well as on
the basis of the legal categories into which offenses fall. When we analyzed the quantitative seriousness data, the greater severity of delinquency in the 1958 cohort was found once again. Thus, for example, we
observed that while 87% of the Cohort I offenses fell in the lower end of
the severity continuum, 56% of the Cohort II offenses were so rated.
More to the point, less than 1% of the offenses committed by the 1945
cohort fell at the upper ranges of severity compared to 20% of the 1958
delinquent acts.

The severity data further confirm the finding that offense seriousness reflected a smaller race effect in Cohort II than in Cohort I. We
computed offense rates weighted by the severity of the act. In Cohort I,
the nonwhite severity rate was about 4.4 times as great as the white
severity rate. In Cohort II, the nonwhite rate was still higher, but the
ratio declined to a factor of 3:1. When we took offense type into account,
with a particular focus on injury offenses, we observed strong race and
SES effects in both cohorts. In Cohort I, the weighted injury rate for
nonwhites was higher than for whites by a factor of 4 among low-SES
subjects, and by a factor of 5.5 among high-SES subjects. In Cohort II,
the nonwhite rates exceeded the white rates by factors of 3 and 4 at the
low and high levels of SES, respectively. In terms of SES, the low-status
rates exceeded those of the higher status regardless of race. The ratio
was 4:1 in Cohort I and 3:1 in Cohort II.

Injury offenses can involve a range of injury levels, from minor
harm to death. We investigated the distribution of injury levels by
cohort and by race within each cohort. We found that injury offenses
were not only more prevalent in Cohort II than in Cohort I, but they also

involved more serious amounts of harm. The least-serious level of injury, minor harm, accounted for 58% of the injury offenses in the 1958 cohort compared to 71% in the 1945 cohort. Seven percent more treated and discharged cases occurred in Cohort II (28%) than in Cohort I (21%). For the two most severe levels of physical injury, there were twice as many hospitalizations and nearly 3 times as many deaths in the proportions of these events in Cohort II compared to Cohort I.

The injury results by race indicated that nonwhites were more likely to inflict the two most severe levels of physical harm compared to whites. For the 1945 cohort, about 8% of nonwhite injury offenses compared to about 5% of white injury offenses involved death or hospitalization. For the 1958 cohort, the proportions for both races were higher but maintained about the same ratio difference between them. About 14% of the injury offenses by nonwhites and 9% by whites involved either death or hospitalization of the victim.

In addition to offenses involving injury, we analyzed offenses in terms of the two other major components of severity: amount of property theft and/or damage. We found for both cohorts that few offenses involved substantial dollar losses. In Cohort I, 27% of the theft offenses and 13% of the damage offenses involved a monetary loss of $100 or more. In Cohort II, about 19% of the theft offenses and 30% of the damage offenses involved a dollar loss in excess of $100. In the aggregate, the offenses in the 1958 cohort had a greater level of theft and damage than in Cohort I. For theft offenses, the median dollar loss in Cohort II ($40) was over 2 times greater than the median value in Cohort I ($17). Concerning damage offenses, the Cohort II median was also about twice as high as that in Cohort I ($25 vs. $12).

With respect to race differences in the level of property theft or damage, we found distinct cohort effects. For the 1945 cohort, the weighted property theft rate for nonwhites (834.6) was almost 4 times higher than the rate for whites (214.7), and the weighted property damage rate for the former (408.7) was also about 4 times higher than that of the latter (103.6). However, in the 1958 cohort the nonwhite predominance was much smaller among property offenses involving theft and was replaced by a white differential among damage offenses. For theft offenses, the nonwhite weighted offense rate (610) was less than twice as high as the white rate (352), compared to the factor of 4 found in Cohort I. For damage offenses, the white severity rate (523) was higher than that of nonwhites (465), the reverse of the situation observed in Cohort I.

Thus, the incidence and severity results obtained in this research showed distinct differences between the cohorts. The offense rates—

overall and for serious offenses—were appreciably higher in the 1958 cohort than in its predecessor. Serious and violent offenses composed a greater share of delinquency and were of greater severity in Cohort II than in Cohort I. The two cohorts were only alike in the rates and concentration of the relatively minor or trivial acts of delinquency. Further, although both cohorts showed race and SES differences, with non-whites and low-SES subjects appearing to be more delinquent and more involved in serious delinquency, our results clearly indicated that these effects were more pronounced in the earlier cohort than in Cohort II. Of special note was the result that the race differences were much less striking in the later cohort.

Delinquent Subgroups

One of the most important findings of the 1945 cohort study concerned the issue of chronic delinquency. The data that were uncovered demonstrated that a small fraction of the cohort, those delinquents with at least five police contacts, had committed a far greater share of the offenses than their proportionate representation in the cohort would have suggested. While the chronic delinquents constituted just 6% of the cohort members and 18% of the delinquent subset, the chronic offenders were responsible for a total of 5,305 offenses, or 52% of all the delinquent acts. When situated among the recidivists, the chronic offenders composed about one-third of the offenders with at least two contacts but were responsible for over 60% of the offenses attributable to recidivists. When the severity of the delinquency was considered, the role of the chronic offender became even more apparent. The 627 chronic delinquents had committed 63% of the UCR index offenses, while for the most serious delinquencies, the chronics were responsible for 71% of the homicides, 73% of the rapes, 82% of the robberies, and 69% of the aggravated assaults.

These data have been perhaps the most enduring results of the 1945 cohort study. Although it had been long suspected that a small group of habitual, serious offenders had skewed rates of offending, it was not known exactly how small this group actually was or how great a share of offending could be attributed to them. It was with great interest, therefore, that we approached the issue of chronic delinquency in the 1958 cohort. With the data for a second birth cohort, we would be in a position to confirm the existence of the chronic offender as well as the character and extent of his delinquency.

In the 1958 cohort, we found that the chronic offender effect was again quite pronounced. The 1958 cohort contained 982 chronic delinquents. They represent 7.5% of the cohort members and 23% of the delinquents. These chronic delinquents accounted for a total of 9,240 offenses, which amounts to 61% of all the offenses and 69% of the offenses by recidivists. We also found the expected relationship between the chronic offender and serious delinquency. Chronic delinquents were responsible for 68% of the UCR index offenses and were similarly over-represented in the most serious delinquencies—61% of homicides, 75% of rapes, 73% of robberies, 65% of aggravated assaults, and 66% of the offenses which involved injury.

When we examined the chronic offender by race and SES, the 1958 cohort produced results which, when compared to Cohort I, may prove to be the most significant findings of the research. That is, for the 1945 cohort the skewed rates and extreme severity of the chronic delinquent held for nonwhites and low-SES subjects, but not for whites or the high-SES group (who were primarily white). Nonwhite chronics committed 65% of all the offenses by nonwhites and 91% of the offenses by non-white recidivists. On the other hand, white chronics committed a far smaller share of the total delinquency, 35%, and less than half (45%) of the offenses by white recidivists. Similarly, low-SES chronics were responsible for 60% of the total offenses by low-SES offenders, but high-SES chronics were involved in only 35% of the delinquent acts committed by high-SES offenders.

The Cohort II results clearly indicate that the chronic offender was consistently dominant for both races and both levels of SES. Among whites, chronic offenders committed about 50% of the offenses, while for nonwhites the chronics committed 65% of the offenses. By SES the results were almost identical to those by race. High-SES chronics were involved in 51% of the offenses by their SES group, and low-SES chronics were involved in 65% of the delinquent activity of their SES group.

In short, the chronic delinquent was found in the 1958 cohort as he was in the previous cohort. In the present cohort, however, he accounted for slightly larger shares of the pool of delinquents and the offenses they committed. He had a substantial involvement in the most serious and injurious acts of delinquency. Most important, the chronic offender demonstrated these effects regardless of his race or SES level, a situation far different from that in Cohort I.

Recidivism

The starting point of delinquency in the two cohorts was about the same. Over 60% of the first offenses were nonindex, and the most prevalent type of index offense was theft, which accounted for 13% of the first offenses. When we compared the only offenses of one-time offenders with the first offense of recidivists, we found cohort differences. In Cohort I, 72% of one-time offenders committed a nonindex offense compared to 59% of recidivists (at their first offense). In Cohort II, 63% of one-time offenders committed a nonindex offense compared to 60% of the first offenses of recidivists. Further, over one-half of the index first offenders in Cohort I (51%) desisted compared to 43% in Cohort II. Thus, because Cohort I involved a higher proportion of nonindex events at the first offense than did Cohort II, and because the probability of desisting for these nonindex offenders was higher in Cohort I than in Cohort II, more offenders in Cohort II than in Cohort I moved on to at least a second offense.

From the second offense onward, the chance of desistance was greater in Cohort I than in Cohort II. Thirty-five percent of delinquents in the 1945 cohort versus 28% of delinquents in the 1958 cohort desisted after the second offense. For the third offense, the respective chances of desistance were .28 versus .27. Beyond the third offense the likelihood of committing further offenses was higher in Cohort II and ranged between .74 and .83, compared to Cohort I for which the range generally fell between .71 and .79.

With respect to the probabilities of committing the index events of injury, theft, damage, or combination, we found the following. First, the chances of committing an index offense were small when compared to the probability that a nonindex event would be committed at each rank number of offense. Second, the probability of committing an index offense of theft was higher than for any other type. These results were obtained for both cohorts, but the Cohort II probabilities were higher than those in Cohort I.

The recidivism data obtained for the UCR categories of offenses further indicated the cohort effect. Cohort II delinquents were more likely to have engaged in UCR property offenses two, three, four, or more times (.42 to .84 vs. .38 to .65) than were offenders in Cohort I. The two cohorts differed more substantially with respect to violent offenses. The chance that a delinquent had committed a UCR violent offense was 2.5 times higher in Cohort II (.26) than in Cohort I (.10). After the first violent offense, Cohort II probabilities ranged from .35 to .85 at the point of eight or more violent offenses. Cohort I scores were much lower and with one exception (.5) did not exceed .33.

Concerning the severity of offenses across the ranks from the first to the fifteenth offense, we found a slight tendency for severity to increase with offense rank. In Cohort I, the overall offense severity scores increased slightly, nonindex and theft offenses showed almost no severity increase, and damage and combination offenses had moderate severity increments; but for injury offenses, a strong upward trend for the first 10 offense ranks was observed. For the 1958 cohort, the total offense and nonindex offense severity scores were about 1.5 times as high as those of the lower offense ranks. The range of severity scores was less for theft, damage, and combination offenses, but the upward trend was distinct nonetheless, and for injury offenses the severity scores showed great swings up and down across offense ranks.

In addition to recidivism probabilities and severity scores by rank number of offense, our static offense data were concerned with the age-at-offense and time between offenses. Generally, we learned that the offense histories were compressed over a rather short period, regardless of the type of offense. This result pertained to both cohorts. For the 1945 cohort, delinquents averaged about 14 years of age for the first offense and about 16 years of age for the fifteenth offense, for an interval of about 2 years. For the 1958 cohort, first offenses were committed at an average age of just over 14, while the fifteenth offenses were committed at an average age of just under 16, for an interval of just less than 2 years.

As expected, we found that the time between offenses was related to rank number of offense. As the offense rank increased, the time between offenses decreased. The time between the first and second offenses was 18.5 months in Cohort I and 17.6 months in Cohort II. The time between the second and third offenses was about 10.5 months for both cohorts. Beyond this point the interval continued to decline but was never shorter than about 3 months between offenses. Thus, the failure time was different in the early offense ranks, but as more and more offenses were accumulated, failure time was effectively a constant.

Offense Specialization

In the static recidivism analyses, we treated the probability of committing a first, second, third, and so on out to the kth offense as a "static" probability, because in its computation the likelihood of each offense type was considered without regard to the type of prior offense. We unexpectedly found that the probability of committing an offense, even when classified by type, changed very little over offense number. We had assumed that if more serious offenses were more likely to appear among the later offenses in a delinquent career, then the probability distributions of index offenses would have shifted noticeably as the number of offenses increased, thus reflecting a propensity toward the commission of more serious offenses. In short, we expected that the chances of committing an index offense would increase more or less directly with offense number.

Because we found no such increase in the offense probabilities by offense number it can be suggested that the process which generated the offense-specific probability distributions operated in about the same manner at each offense number. If it is true that the chance of committing a particular type of act is independent of the number of offenses that a juvenile has already accumulated, then the search for patterns in delinquent careers must abandon the static mode of analyses, in which the frequency is highlighted, in favor of more dynamic models which link the chances of subsequent activity to both the number and type of prior events.

We focused our later analyses on transition probabilities. Our goal in these analyses was the development of inferential statements about switching from one type of offense to another, or continuing with the same type as offense rank advances. We focused these analyses on several groups of offenders. At first we concentrated on models of offenders regardless of the number of offenses they had committed. Here, the state of desistance was used as a transition state. In later models we eliminated desistance and concentrated on the offense patterns of recidivists. We analyzed separately two groups of recidivists: delinquents who had accumulated at least five offenses, and delinquents who had committed at least nine acts of delinquency. By focusing on different sets of offenders we were able to investigate whether offense patterns were observable generally or whether offense switching and specialization were dependent on a certain career length.

The offense patterns exhibited by the offenders in both cohorts were found to be very much alike. The most likely transition observed was to a nonindex offense regardless of the type of prior offense. For the 1945 cohort, damage offenders were the most likely to move to a nonindex offense, while for the 1958 cohort, nonindex offenders were the most likely to commit a nonindex offense on their next offense. The next most likely transition was to the state of desistance. In both cohorts, injury offenders were the most likely to move to this state. If offenders did not move to a nonindex event or desist from further delinquency, they were likely to commit an index offense involving property theft.

When we examined the probabilities of like-offense repeats and analyzed the cell residuals to determine the extent of offense specialization, we found that like-offense repeats were evident, but the tendency to specialize was stronger for the 1958 cohort. In Cohort I, theft and combination offenders showed the strongest tendency to specialize. Injury offense repeats were moderately greater than chance. Damage offense repeats did not appear to be more frequent than expected by chance. In Cohort II, the type of subsequent offense was related to prior offense type for all offense types. For any offense type, the offender most likely to have committed it on his next offense was the one who had committed it just prior.

The strongest evidence of offense specialization was found for the recidivism models. The five-time offenders in Cohort I showed a significant tendency to repeat theft, combination, and injury offenses, while damage offense repeats were observed only slightly more often than chance. The Cohort II data presented the unmistakable finding that the five-time chronic offenders tended to specialize and did so for all offense types. Combination offenses showed the greatest repetition, followed closely by injury and theft repeats. Damage offenses were repeated very often, but not with the specialization tendency evident for the other offense types.

When we expanded the delinquent career to include at least nine offenses, specialization was again observed in both cohorts but it was more pronounced in Cohort II. The nine-time offenders in the 1958 cohort had the strongest repeat tendency for theft, followed closely by combination offenses. Injury and damage offense repeats were repeated less substantially, but the specialization tendency was clear nonetheless.

The overall offense patterns did not show significant race effects. Whites and nonwhites in both cohorts were likely to move to a nonindex offense regardless of prior offense type. When an index transition was made, the type of offense usually committed was theft. When an offender desisted, he was most likely in a prior state of injury offense than any other offense type.

When we eliminated desisters and concentrated on the offense patterns of recidivists, we found both race effects and cohort effects that were substantively important.

Five-time white offenders in Cohort I most often repeated theft offenses. The results for the other offense types showed only a slight tendency to specialize. In the 1958 cohort, the white five-time recidivists appeared to specialize in two offenses strongly (combination and theft). Damage offenses showed only slight specialization.

The five-time nonwhite chronics in Cohort I showed evidence of repeating more offense types than their white counterparts in either cohort. These offenders tended to specialize in combination, theft, and injury offenses. For Cohort II nonwhite chronics, a strong relationship was found between prior and subsequent offense type for all offenses. The strongest evidence of specialization occurred for injury offenses, while the tendency to repeat theft, damage, and combination offenses was slightly lower.

As we moved to the very chronic recidivists, those with at least nine offenses, we found that the results for five-time offenders were accentuated for all groups.

The nine-time white offenders in Cohort I specialized in theft, damage, and combination offenses compared to just theft for their five-time counterparts. The Cohort II nine-time offenders specialized in injury, theft, and damage offenses compared to combination and theft repetitions for their five-time offense counterparts.

The nine-time nonwhite offenders in Cohort I showed the same tendencies to specialize as did their five-time recidivist counterparts. They both tended to repeat theft, combination, and injury offenses. The nine-time nonwhite recidivist in Cohort II displayed the strongest evidence of offense specialization. Even when compared to his five-time offense counterpart, the evidence of offense patterning was stronger across all offense types for the nine-time nonwhite recidivist in Cohort II.

In short, we found evidence of offense specialization among recidivists (as opposed to occasional delinquents). The evidence became more pronounced as the number of offenses increased. The results were clear for both cohorts, although different patterns were found by race.

Offense Escalation

We learned from our static analyses that offense severity was not greatly influenced by rank number of offense. Thus, offenses that were committed late in the career were not found to be more serious than those that were committed early in the career. This is one way of looking at the issue of escalation. Because this type of analysis does not consider whether the offense being examined was a repeat or an event being committed for the first time (a high rank number does not ensure that it is a repeat), we decided to investigate the issue of offense escalation from a dynamic point of view. In these analyses we examined whether a repeat offense had a higher severity than its predecessor and whether the number of repeats continued to inflate offense severity.

We found, with only a few exceptions, that when an offense was repeated the severity was greater than that of its predecessor. The exceptions were one nonindex repeat (the seventh in Cohort I and the eighth in Cohort II), two theft repeats (the third and sixth in Cohort I and the fourth and fifth in Cohort II), and one damage repeat (the first in Cohort I). Most important, the injury offenses were repeated in both cohorts with substantial increases in severity. The patterns by race did not depart from these overall patterns in a meaningful fashion.

We employed multiple regression analyses to see if we could identify factors which would explain the greater severity of repeat offenses. We used prior severity, age, time between offenses, and number of intervening offenses as predictors. Our models generally did not explain much variation in offense severity, and none of the predictors seemed to stand out consistently.

We can only conclude that offense escalation was evident in both cohorts and was most substantial for injury offenses, but we were unable to identify possible causes.

Age and Delinquency

Age-at-Onset

The point at which a juvenile begins his delinquent career is, from the point of view of research on recidivism and related issues, significant in one crucial respect. Age-at-onset, given the fact that delinquency is limited to some maximum age by statute (age 17 for our two cohorts), forever establishes the maximum career length that a delinquent can attain as a juvenile. Because the period at risk is thus set, the extent of further delinquent behavior, or even the character and severity of the subsequent offenses, may be influenced by the offender's age-at-onset.

Our data indicate that the 1958 cohort had higher rates of delinquency, especially the most serious offenses. We looked to the age-at-onset data as one possible explanation for the cohort offense differences observed in this research. The results pertaining to age-at-onset did not offer a definitive explanation.

We found that the proportions of delinquents who began their careers at various ages from 7 through 17 were about the same for both cohorts. From age 7 through age 9, 6.6% of the Cohort II delinquents and 5.8% of the Cohort I delinquents had started their careers. From ages 10 through 14, 56.1% of the delinquents in the 1945 cohort and 45.8% of the delinquents in the 1958 cohort had initiated their involvement in delinquency. For the late starters, ages 15, 16, and 17, we found that 47% of delinquents in both cohorts were so classified. These findings were generally repeated when race, SES, and chronic offender status were examined.

The two cohorts were also alike with respect to the finding that age-at-onset was inversely related to mean number of offenses. On average, the earlier an offender started, the more offenses he accumulated. The correlation between age-at-onset and mean number of offenses was strong for both races and SES levels in each cohort. The highest correlation was the same in both cohorts—low-SES nonwhites, with values of $-.97$ in Cohort II and $-.99$ in Cohort I. The weakest correlation obtained was also for the same group in the two cohorts—high-SES nonwhites, with values of $-.64$ in the 1958 cohort and $-.74$ in the 1945 cohort.

The assumption that a delinquency career started early will produce severe delinquency was not confirmed by our data. The mean severity of delinquency was only moderately related to age-at-onset in Cohort I, while for Cohort II the severity scores fluctuated across the age-at-onset categories. Although the measured severity of offenses was not strongly related to age-at-onset, we found that age-at-onset was related to the type of offenses that were committed. That is, the earlier an offender began his career, the more likely he was to engage in index offenses compared to delinquents who began at the tail end of the age continuum.

On the whole, age-at-onset was not strongly related to offense severity. Most important, the cohorts were sufficiently similar with respect to age-at-onset so that the starting points of the delinquent careers in the two cohorts did not explain the greater severity of delinquency in the later cohort.

Age-at-Offense

The age distribution of delinquency was very similar for the two birth cohorts. Generally, the proportion of offenses increased with age to a peak at age 16. Most of the offenses were committed late in the career. At ages 15, 16, and 17, 64% of Cohort II offenses and 60% of Cohort I offenses were committed. The results by race, however, showed a cohort effect. For Cohort I, both whites and nonwhites followed the overall pattern of increasing offenses by age and a peak at age 16. In the 1958 cohort, the nonwhite data followed this trend, but the results for whites did not. White offenses continually increased with age and reached their peak at the final year at risk, age 17.

When we computed age-specific crude offense rates and offense rates weighted for severity, we found evidence of different race effects for the cohorts. The data for Cohort I showed a wide disparity by race. Overall, the nonwhite crude rate was three times higher and the weighted rate over 4 times higher than the white rate. These discrepancies showed distinct age effects, however. For both crude and weighted rates, the discrepancy between races was highest at the early ages and decreased steadily by age. The situation in Cohort II was different. The overall rates were closer by race, with nonwhites having a crude rate 2.6 times higher and a weighted rate 3.3 times higher. Further, unlike Cohort I data, the results by race in Cohort II were closer across the age continuum.

The age distribution for index and nonindex offenses differed for the two cohorts. In Cohort I, the proportion of both index and nonindex offenses increased from age 10 to a peak at age 16. Nonindex offenses predominated at all ages but especially so late in the juvenile career. In Cohort II, the proportion of serious and trivial offenses increased as delinquents aged. But in the 1958 cohort, nonindex offenses were not the dominant type of offense. This type of offense showed the higher percentage at ages 10 and under and 13 to 15. Index offenses were the higher percentage at ages 11 and 12 and late in the career (16 and 17), when a higher percentage of the delinquents were active.

The two cohorts were quite similar in the severity of index offenses by age. For this type of delinquency, we found that average severity increased with age regardless of race. The cohorts were dissimilar in nonindex delinquency. The 1945 cohort showed no trend for either race in the mean seriousness of nonindex events by age. For Cohort II, the white severity scores were higher and showed sharp increases late in the career. Nonwhite scores followed the index pattern of increasing severity with age.

We grouped index offenses into four categories—violence, robbery, property, and other—and these data showed a clear cohort effect. In Cohort I, crimes of violence increased steadily from age 10 and under to age 16, robbery events showed a sharp increase from age 12 to age 13 but then fluctuated to age 17, and property offenses generally increased from age 10 to age 15. Thus, although the index offenses of violence, robbery, and property were more likely to occur late in the career, only violent offenses showed a clear and direct relationship with age.

In Cohort II, a clear age effect was evident for all the serious index offenses. Crimes of violence showed a steady increase from age 11 to age 17. Both robbery and property offenses increased up to age 16. The fact that Cohort II offenses were committed later in the career is clearly evident when we see how concentrated the offenses were at ages 15 to 17. The two cohorts were close in violent offenses, for which 67% of the Cohort I offenses and 70% of the Cohort II offenses were committed in the last 3 years of delinquency. For both robbery and property offenses, however, the Cohort II data predominate, with 75% of the Cohort II robberies compared to only 45% of the Cohort I robberies, and 66% of the former's property offenses compared to just 51% of the latter's, being committed at ages 15, 16, or 17.

Taken together, age-at-onset and age-at-offense data for the two cohorts leave unresolved the greater delinquency of the 1958 cohort. Delinquents in both cohorts began their careers almost evenly across the age continuum. The age-at-offense data for Cohort II, however, generally indicate that delinquents were still active beyond the ages when Cohort I offenders reached their peak. This continuance of the career later in the juvenile years is one possible explanation for the greater and more severe delinquency in the later cohort.

Disposition

Our final analyses concerned the handling of the delinquents by the police and juvenile court authorities. Our analyses were concerned with two principal issues. First, we tried to determine whether the various dispositions were related to such factors as race, SES, offender status, type of offense, or offense severity. Second, we investigated whether the type and frequency of dispositions, especially court penalties, had an association with recidivism, or the lack thereof. In other words, we examined whether severe dispositions worked to reduce recidivism. We found cohort differences for each of the two issues.

The initial disposition point in the handling of our delinquents was the police decision to remedial or to arrest the offender. If the police officer decides to remedial the offender, the delinquent is handled informally and released to his parents. If, on the other hand, the police officer decides to arrest the offender, the delinquent is handled officially and may be exposed to a court hearing and a severe penalty. In both cohorts we found that the police were more likely to expose certain offenders to arrest and further processing in the juvenile justice system than was the case for other offenders. However, we also found that the extent of the difference between offenders was greater in Cohort I than in Cohort II.

The 1945 cohort showed race and SES effects in the decision to arrest offenders. Of nonwhite delinquents, 44% were officially arrested compared to 23% of white offenders. For SES, the difference was only slightly less, as 39% of low-SES delinquents were arrested compared to 24% of high-SES offenders. When race and SES were considered together, the discrepancy persisted. The difference was less at the lower level of SES, for which 44% of nonwhites compared to 28% of whites were arrested. The difference at the higher level of SES was 21%, as 41% of the nonwhites compared to 20% of whites were arrested.

For the 1958 cohort, these race and SES differences were diminished. The difference by race was reduced from 19% to 9%, as 60% of nonwhites versus 51% of whites were arrested. The SES discrepancy was reduced from 15% to 4%, 60% of low-SES delinquents were arrested versus 53% of high-SES delinquents. The joint race-and-SES relationship with arrest was similarly lower in Cohort II than in Cohort I. At the lower level of SES, nonwhites were arrested more than whites, with a difference of 8% (61% vs. 53%) in Cohort II compared to 16% in Cohort I. At the higher level of SES, the race difference of nonwhites to whites was 56% versus 51%, or just 5 percentage points compared to 21 percentage points in Cohort I.

Because these differences, especially the large disparities in Cohort I, might be due not to race itself, but rather, the greater likelihood of arrests for recidivists, index offenders, and offenders who commit offenses with high severity (categories which involved nonwhites disproportionately), we examined the race effects controlling for these other factors. The results did not explain the race difference in arrest status.

Whether the offender was a one-time offender or a recidivist, he was more likely to be arrested if he was nonwhite than white. The Cohort I differences disfavoring nonwhites were 17 percentage points (30% vs. 13%) for one-time offenders and 18 percentage points (45% vs. 27%) for recidivists. The Cohort II differences disfavoring nonwhites were smaller and amounted to 10 points (46% vs. 36%) for one-time offenders and 6 points (61% vs. 55%) for recidivists.

By type of offense, the Cohort I results were most pronounced. Nonwhites were about twice as likely to be arrested for nonindex offenses than were whites (21% vs. 10%), while for index offenses the difference was 20% for nonwhites (68% vs. 48%). In Cohort II, we found that there was no race effect for nonindex offenses; nonwhites (35%) and whites (37%) were arrested in almost the same proportion with the slight difference disfavoring whites instead of nonwhites. For index offenses, a race difference was observed, but the difference was 11 percentage points disfavoring nonwhites compared to 20 points disfavoring nonwhites in Cohort I.

Thus, we found that in the 1945 cohort study, nonwhites and lower-SES subjects were treated more severely at the initial disposition of remedial versus arrest. The discrepancies in the 1958 cohort were not as reflective of processing differentials by either race or SES. We also found that offender status and character of the offense—appropriate legal criteria—also influenced the arrest decision in both cohorts.

In addition to differences in the distributions of dispositions, we also investigated the relationship between disposition type and subsequent delinquency. Our findings indicated that severe dispositions, like court penalties involving at least probation, did not appear to reduce recidivism substantially. It was evident, however, that court penalties were more effective in the 1958 cohort than in its predecessor.

In Cohort I, we found that the probability of committing a subsequent offense increased steadily from the first through fourth offense and, most important, the more severe the disposition the higher was the probability of recidivism. Thus, when an offender did not receive a court penalty for his first index offense, the probability of any second offense was .61 and the probability of a second index offense was .25. On the other hand, when an offender received a court penalty at his first index offense, the probabilities were higher. The probability of any type of additional offense was .68 and the probability of index recidivism was .31.

The Cohort II data revealed that court penalties were more effective than in Cohort I. Offenders who were given a court penalty showed a .52 probability of committing another offense compared to a .62 probability for delinquents who were handled more leniently. For index recidivism, the probabilities were closer, as 24% of the court penalty cases committed another index offense compared to 27% of the remedialed offenders.

When we followed the court penalty cases from the first through the fourth offense, the difference between the cohorts was further evident. Of the first-time index offenders in Cohort I, 20% were given a court penalty. Of these offenders, 68% committed a second offense, and of these, 47% were index offenses. About 53% of the two-time offenders received another court disposition and of them, 77% violated the law a third time, with 51% of these third offenses being index. After the third offense, 81% of the offenders received a court penalty and of them, all went on to a fourth offense, with 76% committing an index offense.

When we followed the Cohort II court penalty cases, we found that the proportion of desisters was greater, and if the offender did not desist, the chances that his next offense was of the index variety were lower than in Cohort I. Of the 1,667 first index offenses, about 19% were given at least probation. Of these, 52% committed a next offense compared to 68% in Cohort I. Of the second offenses, 48% (vs. 53% in Cohort I) were index offenses. At the third offense, we found 64% of the offenders, with 52% having committed index offenses (vs. 78% and 52% in Cohort I). Like Cohort I, all of the three-time recidivists in Cohort II went on to a fourth offense but, unlike the former for which 76% of the fourth offenses were index, only 28% of the fourth offenses in Cohort II which followed a court penalty were index offenses.

It is clear that the use of court penalties made some difference in Cohort II. What is equally important is the fact that repeat court penalties for serious offenses were not used frequently. In Cohort II, a court penalty was given in 18% of first index offenses, 29% of second index offenses, 31% of third index offenses, and 54% of fourth index offenses.

Thus, 46% of the recidivists who had accumulated up to four index crimes had not received at least a penalty as severe as probation for one or more of their index offenses. The Cohort I data showed similarly low prevalence of court dispositions.

Implications

We have investigated the phenomenon of delinquency in two birth cohorts. The cohorts contained just over 23,000 male subjects. We identified 7,790 as delinquent. Over the course of their juvenile careers, these delinquents were responsible for a total of 25,462 official acts of delinquent behavior. We have amassed a considerable array of data. We have described these data and have analyzed the relationships among them. We have been particularly concerned with the possible differences exhibited between the cohorts. But we have also investigated the cohort similarities and the continuity over time exhibited with respect to crucial aspects of delinquency, and it is these cohort consistencies that time and again commanded our attention.

Our purpose in this research was to analyze and describe, not to prescribe. Yet, the body of findings we had originally uncovered in the 1945 cohort and have now replicated with the new cohort is such that offering a few recommendations is unavoidable. Our concluding task, therefore, is to draw on the results in order to identify the more salient and more policy-relevant implications of this research.

Our data do not support etiological observations, and thus we cannot properly speak of causes. The measurement aspects of this research focused on delinquency-related variables rather than the personal characteristics of the subjects, and thus, the lack of background variables precludes theoretical speculations. But some of our findings are suggestive of significant relationships that should not be ignored.

Delinquency was more prevalent among nonwhites and subjects of lower SES than among whites and boys of higher SES. Delinquency was also associated with residential instability, poor school achievement, and failure to graduate from high school. These factors were also related to the extent of delinquency as well. Taken together, these factors portray a disadvantageous position which may encourage delinquency, be correlative with it and some other factor, or in some instances, be a consequence of delinquency rather than a cause.

In criminological terms, these factors indicate the failure of customary control mechanisms to inhibit delinquent acts, and suggest the presence of social structural strain that disfavors certain segments of the society. These concepts are not new and, in fact, form the core of two of the more important contemporary criminological theories. What is important, therefore, is not that we found evidence of strain or a breakdown of controls, but rather, that these factors operated for two different cohorts of youth. The cohorts differed with regard to the strength of the relationship to delinquency of the various factors but, essentially, notable differences were observed.

The implication for criminological research seems clear. Future research should be less concerned with whether the differences we observed, especially with respect to race and SES, are real or an artifact of society's response to delinquency. More attention, and more focused attention, must be centered on delinquency where it is located most often, and on the conditions which foster the differences that we have found. Criminology can ill afford to continue a research agenda that so refuses to acknowledge sociodemographic differences in the prevalence, incidence, and severity of delinquency that it is unable to explain them.

Although our data did not permit us to focus on the antecedents or causes of delinquency, they did focus extensively on the phenomenon itself. In this regard, the findings suggest several policy-relevant issues.

Cohort II, born 13 years after Cohort I, was larger and had more youths and more delinquent youths, but significantly, the proportion of delinquents was the same. Further, the offenders in Cohort II, growing up in the late 1960s and early 1970s, committed more crimes and much more serious crimes. A pervasive question is thus whether Cohort II, with a very violent criminal population, a small number of nasty, brutal offenders, is a demographic aberration. Laub (1983) has shown that, over the period between 1965 and 1983, youth crime rates were surprisingly stable. Thus, will the delinquents in Cohort III, born, for example, in 1970 or 1980, be as violent over their juvenile careers as Cohort II, or will they regress to the trend found by Laub? We do not know, but we suspect several things.

The rate of violent crime by "dangerous" offenders will decrease nationally because of the reduction of the 15-24 age group in the population. We also suspect that, because fertility rates of nonwhites will continue to be higher than white rates, violent crime among nonwhites will probably not be abated until the end of this century. Thus, ordinary crimes of violence should, in the aggregate, decline. But a smaller adolescent/young adult population may still have an increase in violent crime. Furthermore, and especially worthy of attention, is the fact that the chronic juvenile offender will be a continuing problem no matter how large or small the demographic base from which he is drawn. Even if juvenile crime declines, or perhaps just stabilizes owing to the reduction of the juvenile population (see, for example, Cook and Laub, 1986), the chronic delinquent will still exist and will continue to be responsible for a far disproportionate share of delinquency. This share is important and must be responded to, regardless of the total volume of delinquency of which it is a part.

Cohort II may be just an aberrant display of illegal behavior, particularly violent juvenile crime. Cohort III may be less offensive overall and less violent in particular. We need to consider the future seriously. If Cohort II had a social response that was more retributive, perhaps the effect would be reflected in lower rates of violence among the offenders in Cohort III. The social policy of today can affect the behavior of the juveniles of tomorrow. We need not, however, direct our policy to what the offense rate might be 10 years from now. We should have a policy for the present cohorts. The Cohort II juveniles were violent, more violent than their predecessors. Society must react to the present corpus of violence whatever may be the diminished or increased exhibition of criminal violence in the cohorts of the next generation.

Cohort II was an escalation of violent criminality, a fearful phenomenon for the public and a surplus of cases for prosecutors, judges, and other agents of the criminal justice system. But, Cohort II was not unusual in the small cadre of serious, chronic, violent offenders. They were simply more delinquent and more violent than their Cohort I counterparts. Our social reaction to such criminality should be related to our knowledge that chronic offenders started their violent harm early in life and will apparently continue if allowed to do so.

There are many possible ways in which to respond to the problem of the chronic juvenile offender. There are historical precedents that guide present juvenile justice policies, and likewise, there are theoretical and philosophical underpinnings that shape our response to juvenile as opposed to adult criminals. Boland and Wilson (1978) have argued that one of the prime reasons for the currently ineffective handling of the serious juvenile offender is the historically based two-track system of justice.

In their view, the procedure of handling juvenile and adult offenders in separate and different justice systems, without the benefit of coordinated criminal history record keeping, is ineffective and can lead to undesirable sentencing practices. First, the manifestly rehabilitative and preventive philosophy of juvenile courts allows lenient (or at least less punitive) sentencing practices. Consequently, severe sentencing and punishment for the serious and habitual offender must wait until he progresses to adult criminality. Second, however, because a juvenile's record is unavailable (sometimes by statute) to adult authorities, he in effect starts over in adult court and may be treated as a first offender, in spite of a possibly long juvenile career. This process of starting over in terms of one's criminal history can greatly delay more appropriate punitive actions by the courts that the chronic offender seems to warrant.

Reflective of this, Zimring has noted that recent attempts to reform sentencing practices in juvenile courts are "efforts to lead sanctioning models away from the jurisprudence of treatment and towards concepts of making the punishment fit the crime" (1981: 884). It does seem that juvenile justice sanctions are increasingly based on just-desserts principles and less on the notions of rehabilitation and prevention. It also seems clear that public attitudes toward violent and chronic delinquents have shifted toward a philosophy of retribution rather than one of reform.

Whatever direction the policy developments may take, it is crucially necessary that change within the juvenile justice system be guided by accurate data concerning the extent, character, and complexity of juvenile crime and the particular role of the chronic offender. Thus, the few specific proposals we offer here, given the state of our knowledge as reflected in results such as we have reported above, are the minimum response we can expect of the juvenile and/or criminal justice systems.

Juvenile courts should more often consider the adoption of close probation supervision for perhaps first-time and certainly for second-time index offenders. When these offenses, although serious, occur early in the life of delinquents (as they do for chronic offenders), there is a temptation to be lenient and give the delinquent the benefit of the doubt. What is hoped for is that some process of spontaneous remission will occur, whereby the delinquent will desist from subsequent offenses on his own without the possible damaging effects of labeling that may be brought about by adjudication. Yet, we know that the chronic offender is detached from the schools and other community-based socialization and control agents. Failure to impose sanctions at all, or failure to impose necessary controls early on, can encourage further delinquency. This is apparently what happened in Cohort II. Initial index offenses were not singled out for severe dispositions early enough to have a deterrent effect.

When less severe sanctions, like probation, are tried but fail to curb recidivism, intensive intervention is warranted. Incapacitation in a secure facility after the third index offense should become the rule rather than the exception. This sanction is already available to juvenile courts of course, but scarce resources have limited the number of spaces that are available. Often, judges are unable to order incapacitation for some offenders due to space constraints, and must rely instead on the continued use of probation. We believe that this is not a sufficiently severe penalty for a three-time index offender, who, with his accumulation of nonindex and index offenses, has quite probably committed five, six, or seven total offenses.

Thus, either the available spaces in secure facilities should be reserved for the chronic offender or more space should be created. Certainly, the preferred alternative would be to discontinue sending inappropriate cases to treatment facilities and thereby make room available for those delinquents, who by their continued commission of serious acts of delinquency require such commitment. Most important, the voluntary avoidance of incapacitative dispositions must be remedied. Clearly, therefore, a homogenous juvenile justice policy that resists making necessary distinctions among delinquents, and fails to respond differentially on the basis of these distinctions, must be replaced with a policy that acknowledges the problem of the chronic delinquent and the appropriateness of more severe dispositions in his case.

An example of such a policy, which is designed to eliminate sanctioning inconsistencies and system failures in the processing of chronic delinquents, is the initiatives that are increasingly being used now to help the juvenile justice system to identify, prosecute, and punish/rehabilitate the chronic offender. Known variously as habitual offender programs, operation hard-core, and the like, these programs apply many of the procedures followed in adult career criminal programs to the juvenile justice process. These initiatives are too new for us to know if they work (see, AIR, 1988). We believe, however, that they have the potential to have a very beneficial effect on the juvenile justice process, its clients, and therefore, on the volume of repeat juvenile crime.

We believe that the improved handling of offenders *within* the juvenile justice system is, at least for now, preferable to the increasing tendency to remove juveniles from the juvenile justice process by "certifying" or "waiving" them for adult prosecution. This process is fostered by the legislative belief that the juvenile system has failed to curb recidivism and that adult courts hold a better promise of severe sanctions. Removing juveniles from the province of juvenile court may not only be premature but may be faulty in major respects.

First, the rationale for waiver is based on the assumption that more severe penalties are not just available in adult court, but will in fact be applied to the transfer case. The available evidence on this issue does not show that juveniles who have been referred for adult prosecution, with the exception of juvenile murderers, generally receive more severe sentences. In many instances, these offenders received more lenient sanctions than comparable offenders in juvenile court.

Second, the waiver procedure assumes a degree of efficiency in predicting dangerousness (usually expressed as the likelihood of an additional serious offense) that is not supported by available evidence. Most waiver statutes specify that an offender's age in combination with current offense and prior record are legally permissible factors that predict future misconduct, and thus, may be used as waiver criteria. We know of no body of research that indicates that these specific criteria, or any other set of criteria that might be used, are useful predictors of recidivism generally or violent recidivism in particular. Most studies with which we are familiar show a considerable percentage of "false positives," which refer to cases that were predicted to be recidivist but actually were not. In addition, there is a considerable number of "false negatives," which are actual recidivists who were nonetheless predicted by the criteria to be desisters and not in need of special attention.

Thus, waiver processes that rely on such faulty prediction criteria will mislabel many offenders with great consequences. Some will be misidentified as "dangerous" and will be waived to adult court. They will face adult criminal justice procedures and, if convicted, can face harsh sentences and possible incarceration with adult felons. Some offenders, who will be recidivists, will be misidentified as potential desisters and will be exposed to the more benign dispositions of the juvenile court.

Thus, juvenile waiver is a faulty policy, but even if this were not true, a waiver policy is premature. Juveniles can and should receive severe penalties in juvenile court when their instant offense and prior record warrant such action. Although the juvenile justice system is based on the notion of judicious nonintervention, we can revise our thinking and expectations according to the severity of the offender. The chronic juvenile offender is special and warrants special handling. We need not waive such offenders to adult court before we have tried to improve their handling in the juvenile system. Waiver is not only no substitute for sound juvenile justice policy, but may even provide an excuse for not developing such a policy.

Juvenile justice must be flexible so that it can adjust its reaction to different cohorts. It should react strongly to that small cadre of violent people and react softly to nonserious offenders. Cohort III could be less violent if we had a more rigorous and informed reaction to Cohort II. Or Cohort III may, *sui generis*, be less violent.

Each birth cohort, however large, is but a life history, a single case study in the demography of time. Although these biographies march through time together biologically, at least generally so, they do not all cross the threshold from legally conforming to legally violating behaviors. And among those who do have different paces, some start earlier than others and never stop, while most turn back over the threshold and are not seen officially again. Now, the application of social control, of social intervention to reduce future crime, can make use of that knowledge by recognizing differential life paths and paces, by taking into account delinquent/criminal transition probabilities. A juvenile justice and criminal justice policy that focuses on the few at the most propitious time has the greatest likelihood of effecting change. Social intervention applied to those few need not be merely restrictive and depriving of liberty; it can also be healthful for and helpful to those who are under control.

No scheme for the control of criminal violence can have immediate and universal effect. If at all successful, it will have systemic effects rippling through a successive chain of cohorts. Thus, when and how 15-year-old violent offenders are handled in one decade can have an effect on how 15-year-olds behave in a later decade. By observing several birth cohorts we can hope to measure the socially vertical effects over time.

We are still sufficiently close to the juvenile years of Cohort II to design policy based on what we have learned in analyzing delinquent and violent careers. Preparing now for a program aimed at reducing future violence (of one, two, or three decades) is proper and desirable. A Cohort III might be less violent without a concerted policy of social control now, but inaction could be a dangerous and costly social experiment. Planning social interaction now may or may not produce a less dangerous Cohort III. If Cohort III were to be less violent, we might not know whether it was due to a past policy or to a kind of generational spontaneous remission. But developing policy now, based on what we have observed, is at worst most likely to be benign and at best to be benevolent.

References

AIR. (1988). *Evaluation of the habitual serious and violent juvenile offender program, executive summary.* Washington, DC: United States Government Printing Office.

Ball, J. C., Ross, A., & Simpson, A. (1964). Incidence and estimated prevalence of recorded delinquency in a metropolitan area. *American Sociological Review, 29,* 90-93.

Baltes, P. B. (1968). Longitudinal and cross-sectional sequences in the study of age and generation effects. *Human Development, 11,* 145-171.

Barnett, A., Blumstein, A., & Farrington, D. P. (1987). Probabilistic models of youthful criminal careers. *Criminology, 25,* 83-107.

Bishop, Y. M., Fienberg, S. E., & Holland, P. W. (1975). *Discrete multivariate analysis.* Cambridge, MA: MIT Press.

Blumstein, A., Cohen, J., Roth, J. A., & Visher, C. A. (Eds.). (1986). *Criminal careers and career criminals, Vol. I, II.* Washington, DC: National Academy Press.

Blumstein, A., Cohen, J., & Farrington, D. P. (1988a). Criminal career research: Its value for criminology. *Criminology, 26,* 1-35.

Blumstein, A., Cohen, J., & Farrington, D. P. (1988b). Longitudinal and criminal career research: Further clarifications. *Criminology, 26,* 57-74.

Boland, B., & Wilson, J. Q. (1978). Age, crime, and punishment. *The Public Interest, 51,* 22-34.

British Home Office. (1960). *Report of the conference on research into the causes of delinquency.* London: Home Office.

Bursik, R. J. (1980). The dynamics of specialization in juvenile offenses. *Social Forces, 58,* 851-864.

Christiansen, K. O. (1961). Kriminalitetstruede generationer. *Nordik Tidss, Kriminalvidenskab, 49,* 268-274.

Christiansen, K. O. (1964). Delinquent generations in Denmark. *British Journal of Criminology, 4,* 259-264.

Christiansen, K. O. (1974). Seriousness of criminality and concordance among Danish twins. In R. Hood (Ed.), *Crime, criminology, and public policy.* London: Heinemann.

Christie, N. (1960). *Unge norske lovovertredere.* Oslo: Universitetsforlaget.

Cohen J. (1986). Research on criminal careers: Individual frequency rates and offense seriousness. In A. Blumstein, J. Cohen, J. A. Roth, & C. A. Visher (Eds.), *Criminal careers and career criminals, Vol. I.* Washington, DC: National Academy Press.

Collins, J. J. (1977). *Deterrence by restraint: Two models to estimate its effect in a cohort of offenders.* Ph.D. dissertation, University of Pennsylvania.

Conger, J. J., & Miller, W. C. (1966). *Personality, social class, and delinquency.* New York: John Wiley and Sons.

Cook, P. J., & Laub, J. H. (1986). The surprising stability of youth crime rates. *Journal of Quantitative Criminology, 2,* 265-277.

Dalgard, O. S., & Kringlen, E. (1976). A Norwegian twin study of criminality. *British Journal of Criminology, 16,* 213-232.

Denno, D. (1982). *Sex differences in cognition and crime: Early developmental, biological, and, sociological correlates.* Ph.D. dissertation, University of Pennsylvania.

Douglass, J. W. B., Ross, J. M., Hammond, W. A., & Mulligan, D. G. (1966). Delinquency and social class. *British Journal of Criminology, 6,* 294-302.

Elliott, D. S., & Ageton, S. S. (1980). Reconciling race and class differences in self-reported and official estimates of delinquency. *American Sociological Review, 45,* 95-110.

Elliott, D. S., Huizinga, D., & Ageton, S. S. (1985). *Explaining delinquency and drug use.* Beverly Hills, CA: Sage Publications.

Facella, C. S. (1983). *Female delinquency in a birth cohort.* Ph.D. dissertation, University of Pennsylvania.

Farrington, D. P. (1973). Self-reports of deviant behavior: Predictive and stable? *Journal of Criminal Law and Criminology, 64,* 99-110.

Farrington, D. P. (1979). Longitudinal research on crime and delinquency. In N. Morris & M. Tonry (Eds.), *Crime and justice.* Chicago: University of Chicago Press.

Farrington, D. P. (1981). Longitudinal analyses of criminal violence. In M. E. Wolfgang & N. A. Weiner (Eds.), *Proceedings of a workshop on interdisciplinary approaches to the study of criminal violence.* Beverly Hills, CA: Sage Publications.

Farrington, D. P., Ohlin, L. E., & Wilson, J. Q. (1986). *Understanding and controlling crime: Toward a new research strategy.* New York: Springer-Verlag.

Farrington, D. P., Snyder, H. N., & Finnegan, T. A. (1988). Specialization in juvenile court careers. *Criminology, 26,* 461-485.

Ferguson, T. (1952). *The young delinquent in his social setting.* London: Oxford University Press.

Ferguson, T., & Cunnison, J. (1956). *In their early twenties.* London: Oxford University Press.

Figlio, R. M. (1981). Delinquency careers as a simple markov process. In J. A. Fox (Ed.), *Models in quantitative criminology.* New York: Academic Press.

Fox, J. A., & Tracy, P. E. (1988). A measure of skewness in offense distributions. *Journal of Quantitative Criminology, 4,* 259-274.

Glueck, S., & Glueck, E. T. (1930). *Five hundred criminal careers.* New York: Knopf.

Glueck, S., & Glueck, E. T. (1937). *Later criminal careers.* New York: Commonwealth Fund.

Glueck, S., & Glueck, E. T. (1943). *Criminal careers in retrospect.* New York: Commonwealth Fund.

Glueck, S., & Glueck, E. T. (1968). *Delinquents and nondelinquents in perspective.* Cambridge, MA: Harvard University Press.

Gordon, R. A. (1976). Prevalence: The rare datum in delinquency measurement and its implications for the theory of delinquency. In M. W. Klein (Ed.), *The juvenile justice system.* Beverly Hills, CA: Sage Publications.

Gottfredson, M., & Hirschi, T. (1986). The true value of lambda would appear to be zero: An essay on career criminals, criminal careers, selective incapacitation, cohort studies, and related topics. *Criminology, 24,* 213-233.

Gottfredson, M., & Hirschi, T. (1987). The methodological adequacy of longitudinal research on crime. *Criminology, 25,* 581-614.

Gottfredson, M., & Hirschi, T. (1988). Science, public policy, and the career paradigm. *Criminology, 26,* 37-55.

Haberman, S. J. (1973). The analysis of residuals in crossclassified tables. *Biometrics, 29,* 205-220.

Haberman, S. J. (1978). *Analysis of qualitative data.* New York: Academic Press.

Hagan, J., & Palloni, A. (1988). Crimes as social events in the life course: Reconceiving a criminological controversy. *Criminology, 26,* 87-100.

Hamparian, D. M., Schuster, R. S., Dinitz, S., & Conrad, J. P. (1978). *The violent few: A study of dangerous juvenile offenders.* Lexington, MA: D.C. Heath.

Hathaway, S. R., & Monachesi, E. D. (1963). *Adolescent personality and behavior: MMPI patterns of normal, delinquent, dropout, and other outcomes.* Minneapolis: University of Minnesota Press.

Havighurst, R. J., Bowman, P. H., Liddle, G. P., Matthews, C. V., & Pierce, J. V. (1966). *Growing up in river city.* New York: John Wiley and Sons.

Hindelang, M. J., Hirschi, T., & Weiss, J. G. (1979). Correlates of delinquency: The illusion of discrepancy between self-report and official measures. *American Sociological Review, 44,* 995-1014.

Hirschi, T., & Selvin, H. (1967). *Delinquency research: An appraisal of analytic methods.* New York: The Free Press.

Hirschi, T., & Gottfredson, M. (1983). Age and the explanation of crime. *American Journal of Sociology, 89,* 552-584.

Hutchings, B., & Mednick, S. A. (1974a). Biological adoptive fathers of male criminal adoptees. In *Major issues in juvenile delinquency.* Copenhagen: World Health Organization.

Hutchings, B., & Mednick, S. A. (1974b). Registered criminality in the adoptive and biological parents of registered male criminal adoptives. In R. R. Fieve, D. Rosenthal, & H. Brill (Eds.), *Genetic research in psychiatry.* Baltimore, MD: John Hopkins Press.

INSLAW. (1977). *Curbing the repeat offender: A strategy for prosecutors.* Washington, DC: Institute for Law and Social Research.

INSLAW. (1979). *The scope and prediction of recidivism.* Washington, DC: Institute for Law and Social Research.

Jasinski, J. (1966). Delinquent generations in Poland. *British Journal of Criminology, 6,* 170-182.

Kimberly, J. (1976). Issues in the design of longitudinal organizational research. *Social Methods and Research, 4,* 321-347.

Kobner, O. (1893). Die methode einer wissenschaftlichen ruckfallsstatistik als grundlage einer reform der kriminalstatistik. *Zeitschrift gesamter strafrechtswissenschaft, 13,* 670-689.

Laub, J. H. (1983). Trends in serious juvenile crime. *Criminal Justice and Behavior, 10,* 485-506.

Laurer, C. A. (1981). Statement before the subcommittee on juvenile justice of the United States Senate Committee on the Judiciary, hearings on violent juvenile crime.

Lefkowitz, M. M., Eron, L. D., Walder, L. O., & Huesman, L. R. (1977). *Growing up to be violent: A longitudinal study of the development of aggression.* Elmsford, NY: Pergamon Press.

McCord, W., McCord, J., & Zola, I. K. (1959). *Origins of crime.* New York: Columbia University Press.

McCord, J. (1978). A thirty-year follow-up of treatment effects. *American Psychologist, 33,* 284-289.

McCord, J. (1979). Some child rearing antecedents of criminal behavior in adult men. *Journal of Personality and Social Psychology, 37,* 1477-1486.

Mednick, S. A., & Hutchings, B. (1978). Genetic and psychophysiological factors in asocial behavior. In R. D. Hare & D. Schalling (Eds.), *Psychopathic behavior: Approaches to research.* Chichester: Wiley.

Monahan, T. P. (1960). On the incidence of delinquency. *Social Forces, 39,* 66-72.

Monahan, T. P. (1962). On the trend in delinquency. *Social Forces, 46,* 158-167.

Monahan, T. P. (1970). Police dispositions of juvenile offenders: The problem of measurement and a study of Philadelphia data. *Phylon, 31,* 129-141.

Moore, M. H., Estrich, S., & McGillis, D. (1983). *Dealing with dangerous offenders.* Final report submitted to the National Institute of Justice.

Mulligan, G., Douglass, J. W. B., Hammond, W. A., & Tizard, J. (1963). Delinquency and symptoms of maladjustment: The findings of a longitudinal study. *Proceedings of the Royal Society of Medicine, 56,* 1083-1086.

Nevares, D., Wolfgang, M. E., & Tracy, P. E. (1990). *Delinquency in Puerto Rico: The 1970 birth cohort study.* Westport, CT: Greenwood Publishing Group.

Otten, L. (1985). *A comparison of male and female criminality in a birth cohort.* Ph.D. dissertation, University of Pennsylvania.

Patterson, G. R., Loeber, R., & Reid, J. B. (1983). Understanding and prediction of delinquent child behavior. Research proposal submitted to the National Institute of Mental Health.

Petersilia, J., Greenwood, P., & Lavin, M. (1977). *Criminal careers of habitual felons.* Santa Monica, CA: The Rand Corporation.

Petersilia, J. (1980). Criminal career research: A review of recent evidence. In N. Morris & M. Tonry (Eds.), *Crime and justice, Vol 2.* Chicago: University of Chicago Press.

Peterson, M., Braiker, H., & Polich, S. (1980). *Doing crime: A survey of California inmates.* Santa Monica, CA: The Rand Corporation.

Piper, E. (1983). *Patterns of violent recidivism.* Ph.D. dissertation, University of Pennsylvania.

Polk, K., & Shafer, W. E. (Eds.). (1972). *Schools and delinquency.* Englewood Cliffs: Prentice Hall.

Polk, K., Frease, D., & Richmond, F. L. (1974). Social class, school experience, and delinquency. *Criminology, 12,* 84-96.

Polk, K., (1975). Schools and the delinquency experience. *Criminal Justice and Behavior, 2,* 315-358.

Rojek, D. G., & Erickson, M. L. (1982). Delinquent careers: A test of the career escalation model. *Criminology, 20,* 5-28.

Sellin, T., & Wolfgang, M. E. (1964). *The measurement of delinquency.* New York: John Wiley and Sons.

Shannon, L. W. (1978). A longitudinal study of delinquency and crime. In C. Wellford (Ed.), *Quantitative studies in criminology.* Beverly Hills, CA: Sage Publications.

Shannon, L. W. (1980). *Assessing the relationship of adult criminal careers to juvenile careers.* Washington, DC: United States Government Printing Office.

Shannon, L. W. (1988). *Criminal career continuity: Its social context.* New York: Human Sciences Press.

Slater, S. W., Darwin, J. H., & Ritchie, W. L. (1966). Delinquent generations in New Zealand. *Journal of Research in Crime and Delinquency, 3,* 140-146.

Smith, D. R., & Smith, W. R. (1984). Patterns of delinquent careers: An assessment of three perspectives. *Social Science Research, 13,* 129-158.

Thornberry, T. P., & Farnworth, M. (1982). Social correlates of criminal involvement: Further evidence on the relationship between social status and criminal behavior. *American Sociological Review, 47,* 505-518.

Tittle, C. R. (1988). Two empirical regularities (maybe) in search of an explanation: Commentary on the age/crime debate. *Criminology, 26,* 75-85.

Tracy, P. E. (1987). Race and class differences in official and self-reported delinquency. In

M. E. Wolfgang, T. P. Thornberry, & R. M. Figlio (Eds.), *From boy to man, from delinquency to crime.* Chicago: University of Chicago Press.

Tracy, P. E., Wolfgang, M. E., & Figlio, R. M. (1985). *Delinquency in two birth cohorts, executive summary.* Washington, DC: United States Government Printing Office.

Tracy, P. E., Wolfgang, M. E., & Figlio, R. M. (1989). *Patterns of delinquency and adult crime in the 1958 Philadelphia birth cohort, executive summary.* Washington, DC: United States Government Printing Office.

Trenaman, J., & Emmet, B. P. (1952). An estimate of the incidence of delinquency in England and Wales. In J. Trenaman (Ed.), *Out of step.* New York: Philosophical Library.

VERA. (1976). *Violent delinquents: A report and recommendations to the Ford foundation.* New York: The Vera Institute of Justice.

Visher, C. A. (1986). The Rand inmate surveys: A reanalysis. In A. Blumstein, J. Cohen, J. A. Roth, & C. A. Visher, (Eds.), *Criminal careers and career criminals, Vol II.* Washington, DC: National Academy Press.

von Mayr, G. (1917). *Statistik und gesellschaftslehre, Vol. 3: moralstatistik mit einschluss der kriminalstatistik.* Tubingen: Mohr.

von Scheel, H. (1890). Zur einfuhrung in die kriminalstatistik, insbesondere diegenige des deutschen reichs. *Allgemeines Statistisches Archiv, 1,* 183-194.

West, D. J. (1969). *Present conduct and future delinquency.* London: Heinmann.

West, D. J., & Farrington, D. P. (1973). *Who becomes delinquent?* London: Heinmann.

West, D. J., & Farrington, D. P. (1977). *The delinquent way of life.* London: Heinmann.

Wilkins, L. T. (1960). *Delinquent generations.* London: H.M. Stationary Office.

Witkin, H. A. (1976). Criminality in XYY and XXY men. *Science, 193,* 547-555.

Wolfgang, M. E., Figlio, R. M., & Sellin, T. (1972). *Delinquency in a birth cohort.* Chicago: University of Chicago Press.

Wolfgang, M. E., Figlio, R. M., Tracy, P. E., & Singer, S. I. (1985). *The national survey of crime severity.* Washington, DC: United States Government Printing Office.

Wolfgang, M. E., Thornberry, T. P., & Figlio, R. M. (Eds.). (1987). *From boy to man, from delinquency to crime.* Chicago: University of Chicago Press.

Zimring, F. E. (1981). Kids, groups, and crime: Some implications of a well known secret. *Journal of Criminal Law and Criminology, 72,* 867-885.

Index

Achievement level
  and delinquency, 49–51
Age-at-offense
  and offense rates, 216–220
  and offense types, 220–243
  and race, 213–216
  summary of, 282, 287, 289
Age-at-onset
  definition of, 175
  and mean number of offenses, 187–188
  and offense severity, 189, 192–196
  and offense types, 196, 200–210
  and race, 176–177, 181
  and SES, 181, 183–184
  summary of, 286, 287, 289
Ageton, S., 30, 300
AIR, 296, 299

Ball, J. C., 37, 299
Baltes, P. B., 299
Barnett, A., 16, 17, 299
Birth cohort
  introduced, 1–4
  in longitudinal research, 13–20
  need for, 5–7
  previous studies of, 7–11
  1958, 21–28
Bishop, Y. M., 128, 299
Blumstein, A., 13–14, 18–19, 176, 299, 303
Boland, B., 294, 299
Bowman, P. H., 301
Braiker, H., 302
Brill, H., 301
British Home Office, 6, 299
Bureau of the Census, 25
Bursik, R. J., 114–116, 127, 299

Census tracts
  and SES, 34

Christiansen, K. O., 8, 10, 299
Christie, N., 7, 299
Chronic delinquency
  and background variables, 51–53
  and frequency of offenses, 82–83, 87, 90
  and offense transitions, 131–132, 134, 137–138, 140
  and offense transitions by race, 153, 156, 159
  prevalence of, 38–46
  previous research of, 15–17
  and severity of delinquency, 92–93, 95–97
  summary of, 276, 279–280, 284, 294–295
Cohen, J., 114–115, 160, 299, 303
Collins, J. J., 9, 299
Conger, J. J., 8, 299
Conrad, J. P., 301
Cook, P. J., 115, 294, 299
Court dispositions
  distribution of, 246–252
  and offense contingencies, 254, 259–260, 263
  probability of, 265, 267–269
  summary of, 270, 292
Court referral, 246
Cross-sectional research, 18–19
Crude delinquency rates
  by age, 216–217
  by offense type and age, 226–228, 230
Cunnison, J., 7, 300

Dalgard, O. S., 10, 300
Darwin, J. H., 302
Delinquency status categories
  by background variables, 46–56
  by race and SES, 38–46
Delinquent recidivism
  static probabilities of, 103, 105, 107

Delinquent recidivism (cont.)
    static probabilities by offense type, 107–
        112
    summary of, 271–272
Denno, D., 9, 300
Dinitz, S., 301
Douglass, J. W. B., 7, 37, 300, 302

Elliott, D. S., 14, 30, 300
Emmet, B. P., 6, 303
Erickson, M. L., 115, 127, 160, 302
Eron, L. D., 301
Estrich, S., 302

Facella, C. S., 4, 300
Farnworth, M., 34, 302
Farrington, D. P., 7, 9–10, 16, 18, 30, 81,
    114, 116, 160, 299–300, 303
Ferguson, T., 7, 300
Fienberg, S. E., 299
Fieve, R. R., 301
Figlio, R. M., 1, 8, 14, 21, 115, 117, 300,
    303
Finnegan, T. A., 300
Fox, J. A., 92, 300
Frease, D., 302

Glueck, E. T., 14, 300
Glueck, S., 14, 300
Gordon, R. A., 37, 300
Gottfredson, M., 14, 17–19, 176, 300, 301
Greenwood, P., 302

Haberman, S. J., 128, 300
Hagan, J., 14, 18, 301
Hammond, W. A., 300, 302
Hamparian, D. M., 10, 15, 81, 301
Hare, R. D., 301
Hathaway, S. R., 38, 301
Havighurst, R. J., 8, 38, 301
Hindelang, M. J., 30, 301
Hirschi, T., 6, 7, 14, 17–19, 30, 176, 300,
    301
Holland, P. W., 299
Huesman, L. R., 301
Huizinga, D., 300
Hutchings, B., 10, 301

Incidence
    by chronic offenders, 82–83, 87, 90

Incidence (cont.)
    definition of, 57
    by offense type, 58–59
    by offense type and race, 59, 61–65
    by offense type and SES, 69–70
    summary of, 276–278, 293, 299
INSLAW, 81, 301
Investigation reports
    and delinquency data, 28

Jasinski, J., 301
Juvenile Aid Division
    records of, 24, 28–29, 245–246

Kimberly, J., 301
Kobner, O., 5, 301
Kringlen, E., 10, 300

Laub, J. H., 293–294, 299, 301
Laurer, C. A., 23, 301
Lavin, M., 302
Lefkowitz, M. M., 10, 301
Liddle, G. P., 301
Loeber, R., 302
Longitudinal research
    issues in, 13–14
    replication of, 3–5
    value of, 17–18

Markov models
    and offense transitions, 116–117, 127
Master delinquency file, 246; see also Juve-
    nile Aid Division
Matthews, C. V., 301
McCord, J., 14, 301
McCord, W., 14, 301
McGillis, D., 302
Mednick, S. A., 10, 301
Miller, W. C., 8, 299
Monachesi, E. D., 38, 301
Monahan, T. P., 37, 301, 302
Moore, M. H., 81, 302
Morris, N., 300, 302
Mulligan, D. G., 7, 300, 302

Nevares, D., 302

Offense probabilities
    of first delinquent act, 100–103
    of first fifteen delinquent acts, 105, 107

Offense probabilities (*cont.*)
  by offense type, 111–112
  and transition matrices, 125–126, 140–152
  summary of, 260, 283
Offense specialization
  by all delinquents, 114–118, 121–131
  by race, 140, 142, 147, 148–150, 152, 156, 159
  by recidivists, 131–132, 134, 137–138
  summary of, 167, 172–175, 282–285
Offense transitions, *see* Offense specialization
Ohlin, L. E., 300
Otten, L., 4, 302

Palloni, A., 14, 18, 301
Patterson, G. R., 11, 302
Petersilia, J., 15, 302
Peterson, M., 15, 302
Philadelphia
  school records of, 25–26, 35
Pierce, J. V., 301
Piper, E., 4, 302
Polich, S., 302
Polk, K., 10, 302
Prevalence
  by age-at-onset, 176–177, 181, 183, 184, 187
  and background variables, 46–53
  and chronic offenders, 83, 87, 90, 92
  multivariate analyses, 53–56
  and offender rates, 44–46
  percentages of by race and SES, 38–44
  summary of, 275–276, 292–293, 299
Public school records, 25–26, 35, 46

Reid, J. B., 302
Richmond, F. L., 302
Ritchie, W. L., 302
Rojek, D. G., 115, 127, 160, 302
Rosenthal, D., 301
Ross, A., 299, 300
Ross, J. M., 300
Roth, J. A., 299, 303

Schuster, R. S., 301
Sellin, T., 1, 6, 8–9, 14, 21, 29–30, 63–64, 70, 90, 105, 107, 115, 117, 196, 210, 302–303

Selvin, H., 6, 7, 301
Seriousness of offenses
  by age-at-offense, 216–217, 220–223, 225–226, 228
  by age-at-onset, 189, 192–194, 196, 200, 202, 208
  and chronic offenders, 92–93, 95–97
  escalation of, 159–163, 167
  incidence and, 70, 72–74, 79
  measurement of, 30–33
  and recidivists, 100–101, 105, 107
  summary of results, 271, 277, 288, 299
Shafer, W. E., 302
Shannon, L. W., 11, 15, 38, 81, 302
Simpson, A., 299
Singer, S. I., 303
Slater, S. W., 8, 302
Smith, D. R., 115–116, 302
Smith, W. R., 115–116, 302
Snyder, H. N., 300
Socioeconomic status
  measurement of, 33–35

Thornberry, T. P., 34, 302–303
Time between offenses
  and court dispositions, 260
  first to fifteenth offense, 107
  and severity escalation, 163
  summary of, 282, 286
Tittle, C. R., 14, 18, 302
Tizard, J., 302
Tonry, M., 300, 302
Tracy, P. E., 4, 30, 92, 300, 302–303
Trenaman, J., 6, 303

Uniform Crime Reports (UCR)
  and offense severity, 31
  and offense type incidence, 59, 61–64
  and probabilities of offenses, 107–113
  and age-at-onset, 208, 210
  and age-at-offense, 237
  summary of, 276–277, 279–281

VERA, 11, 303
Violent offenses
  and age-at-offense, 233, 235, 239, 242
  and chronic offenders, 90
  incidence of, 62
  probabilities of, 110–112
  summary of, 277, 279, 281, 288

Visher, C. A., 15, 299, 303
von Mayr, G., 5, 303
von Scheel, H., 5, 303

Walder, L. O., 301
Weighted offense rates, 70, 72, 73, 75
  and age-at-offense, 217, 220, 227–228,
    230, 243
  summary of, 287
Weiss, J. G., 30, 301

West, D. J., 10, 303
Wilkins, L. T., 8, 303
Wilson, J. Q., 294, 299–300
Witkin, H. A., 10, 303
Wolfgang, M. E., 1, 6, 8–9, 13–16, 21–22,
  29–30, 63–64, 70, 90, 105, 107, 115–
  117, 196, 210, 300, 302, 303

Zimring, F. E., 295, 303
Zola, I. K., 301